The Seven Inconvenient Truths of Business Strategy

To Lyn and children Simon, Elissa and Rhys.

The Seven Inconvenient Truths of Business Strategy

PAUL HUNTER

Routledge
Taylor & Francis Group
LONDON AND NEW YORK

First published 2014 by Gower Publishing

Published 2016 by Routledge
2 Park Square, Milton Park, Abingdon, Oxfordshire OX14 4RN
711 Third Avenue, New York, NY 10017, USA

First issued in paperback 2016

Routledge is an imprint of the Taylor & Francis Group, an informa business

British Library Cataloguing in Publication Data
A catalogue record for this book is available from the British Library.

Library of Congress Cataloging-in-Publication Data
Hunter, Paul Wilson, 1954–
 The seven inconvenient truths of business strategy / by Paul Hunter.
  pages cm
 Includes bibliographical references and index.
 ISBN 978-1-4724-1247-8 (hardback) – ISBN 978-1-4724-1248-5 (ebook) – ISBN 978-1-4724-1249-2 (epub)
 1. Business planning. 2. Strategic planning. I. Title.

 HD30.28.H86824 2014
 658.4'012–dc23
                                                                    2014016368

ISBN 13: 978-0-415-78841-0 (pbk)
ISBN 13: 978-1-4724-1247-8 (hbk)

Contents

List of Figures

List of Tables

About the Author

Paul Hunter is a highly experienced management educator, consultant and business executive. He is founder and Chief Executive of the Strategic Management Institute (SMI), having previously been managing director of an independent management consulting firm. Before establishing that entity with his colleagues, Paul was a partner with the global management consulting firm PwC. Prior to consulting, he worked in industry in a finance and accounting capacity. He commenced the consulting stage of his career in Indonesia, where he was based for approximately two years.

A key aspect of the SMI is the Certified Strategy Practitioner (CSP) accreditation programme, of which Paul is leader, program designer and teacher. Paul developed content for the practitioner component ('Strategy as Practice') of this course over a 15-year period, and is now focusing on the development and roll-out of this award on an international basis. Another fundamental component of the course is the content developed as part of the thesis that contributed to Paul's award of Doctor of Business Administration and the content of this book. Paul is also a past office-bearer and current paper reviewer for the international Strategic Management Society.

Paul has worked with numerous global corporations in both consulting and leadership development roles. In addition to this book, he has co-authored professional practice papers and given presentations in numerous seminars, briefings and conferences addressing a diverse range of audiences.

Paul's more recent publications include co-authoring with M. Rademakers the chapter 'Mars University: Raising the Bar' in *Corporate Universities: Drivers of the Learning Organization* (2014), and with T. O'Shannassy 'Contemporary Strategic Management Practices in Australia: "Back to the Future" in the 2000s', *Singapore Management Review*, 29(2) (2007). He has also been quoted in *Business Review Weekly*, contributed blogs to the *LeadingCompany* online magazine, and conducted surveys on strategic management practice in Australian organisations. His public speaking engagements have included strategy workshops in Tehran as the guest of the Iranian Strategy Academy, presenting the paper 'The Conduct of Business Strategy in Australia' at the Australian and New Zealand Academy of Management (ANZAM) Conferences, contributing to Strategic Management Society Conferences in Vienna, as well as giving presentations at a number of Certified Practising Accountants Australia (CPA) conferences, including the CPA Congresses in 2010 and 2013.

About the Strategic Management Institute

Grounded in research and practical in application, the SMI is a member-based learning and networking organisation. Its objective is to augment the effectiveness of the practice of strategic management and to contribute to knowledge in the field. Formed in 2005, the fundamental principles of the SMI are to:

- facilitate the personal development of the strategy professional;

- capture, align and assimilate the combined knowledge of strategy professionals, and to facilitate the dissemination of that knowledge to make a positive contribution to the standard of strategic management practice in general;

- enhance the strength of practitioners and the organisations with whom they work by sharing strategically oriented performance-enhancing knowledge.

The SMI Certified Strategy Practitioner accreditation programme is designed to provide individuals with demonstrable proficiencies and competencies in strategy at the level of a profession, and a medium through which they can grow their skills through continual learning. Strategy as Practice and Strategy as a Profession coursework uses this book as it central tenet. For updates and discussion on this book and debate on topics of strategy in general on our blog, please go to our web site: www.smiknowledge.com.

ACCREDITATION PATHWAY

Certified Strategy Practitioner programmes start with the Member level, an annual subscription-based networking facility. From there, accreditation pathways follow four levels of certification: Affiliate, Associate, Senior Associate and Fellow. For more details, visit our website: www.smiknowledge.com. To contact Paul, email smi@smiknowledge.com, or join us on LinkedIn: www.linkedin.com/groups/Strategic-Management-Institute-3762509.

We look forward to hearing from you.

Reviews of *The Seven Inconvenient Truths of Business Strategy*

We know a lot about effective strategies, but little about effective strategizing. This is where Paul Hunter's hands-on approach to the art of making strategy is a great leap forward. Finally a book that helps practitioners 'reinvent strategic planning' to make it work in the twenty-first century.

Ron Meyer, Tilburg University, The Netherlands and Managing Director, Center for Strategy & Leadership, The Netherlands

Having had many roles in and around strategy execution for many clients, as well as the reality of leading strategy development for our own organisation, I can attest to the shortcomings as described in Paul's book. His very useful advice for how to make the process far more effective, including tackling dominant logic and traditional thinking, will be hugely valuable to anyone involved in the creation of strategy, which in today's world, is most people.

Sammy Kumar, Executive Board Member and Managing Partner, Enterprise and Strategy & Transformation PwC, Australia

Acknowledgements

No book is written without the help, input and advice of others. Some of those who provided initial inspiration and an evaluation of the proof of concept with regard to the concepts discussed in this book include Gaye Mason, Matthew Donato, John Coates, Greg Baker, David Thompson and Denis Bourke. Formation and launching of the proof of concept in the form of strategy master classes was assisted by those mentioned previously, as well as Andrew Brown, Fernando Schiavone, Steve Perera, Dianne Kelleher, Duncan Webster and Tim O'Shannassy. Ongoing advice and general support were provided by John Toohey, Veronique Ambrosini, Laurence Gartner, Peter Halcomb and Noordin Shehabuddeen. Technology support was provided by Simon Hunter, while design work (including the cover of the book) and presentation advice were provided by Elissa and Rhett Luciani.

My thesis supervisor also had a substantial role to play, although neither of us knew it at the time; his name is Bobby Banerjee. Additional and ongoing support in the form of proofreading of this book and advice came from Martijn Rademakers and my wife Lyn, who was also my financial backer, researcher and spiritual inspiration. Early formatting advice was given generously by Tracey Palser, while subsequent advice from early adopters has also been invaluable. These include Andrew Downard, Philip Lange, Vito Cincinnato, Anthony Claridge, Fred Davis, Jim Egan, Bob Boesten, Alexie Seller, and last but not least, Simone Tierney. To all of those I have omitted, and I am sure there are many, I apologise.

I would like to acknowledge more broad-based contributors: the authors who have influenced this work as a result of their own publications in their fields of expertise. In particular I would like to acknowledge Deborah Cadbury, who, as author of *Chocolate Wars: From Cadbury to Kraft – 200 Years of Sweet Success and Bitter Rivalry* (2010), provided a whole-life perspective of the history Cadbury company. Deborah Cadbury's insights informed my knowledge of the management of the company, which in turn provided a basis for illustrating ways in which aspects of strategy practices explored in this book could be applied to the Cadbury case.

Similarly, I would like to acknowledge the work of Peter Senge and Robert Flood. Senge in particular provided me with insight into the notion of systems thinking which enabled me to validate an additional perspective on the construct of a Strategic Management Framework as a system, not just a process. As the foundation of the notion of learning organisations, Senge's *The Fifth Discipline* (1990) provided insights into the causes of the various problematic aspects of strategy that are explored in this book and ways to resolve them. In addition to systems thinking, they included the implications associated with the impact of an individual's mental models and the associated aspect of personal mastery. From a team perspective, they included a team's shared vision and ultimately team learning. Senge's views on systems thinking were explored further by Robert Flood, who in turn provided me with insight into ways in which the notion of strategy evaluation could be applied to strategy as practice. Following on from Peter Senge is Ron Meyer and Martijn Rademakers who have provided insight into the fundamentals of strategy perspectives and also the formal construct of a learning organisation in the form of Corporate Universities.

There are also many other strategy scholars to whom I and my fellow strategy practitioners are deeply indebted. Without the depth and rigour of their research there would be no strategy theory, and by definition, a far less functional basis upon which I could build a practical Strategic Management Framework. Too numerous to name, their work can be found in specialist strategy and management journals and their individual publications. More formally, they can be found in conferences held by the Strategic Management Society, of which I am a member and from which my work and management of our own Strategic Management Institute takes guidance and direction.

Finally I would like to acknowledge the hard work of the Gower Publishing team whose professionalism has proved to me the value of the publishing industry as well as the enormity of the task that they undertake. Without them, this book would not be at the standard of presentation of which I am sure you will enjoy and appreciate.

Introduction:
From Corporate Planners to
Professional Strategy Practitioners

A question I am often asked when discussing the topic of strategic management with business professionals is: 'What is your definition of strategy?' Although it comes across as a test of my knowledge, the question is usually motivated mainly by pure curiosity. Nearly everyone in business has their own interpretation of the meaning of the word. Their understanding, though, is mostly informed by, and dependent on what strategy text books they have read, what business school they attended, the terminology adopted by the company they work for, or the preferences of their consulting firm.

There are in fact numerous definitions of 'strategy' in the context of the business environment. In light of this, I propose that we stop worrying about the wording of a definition per se, and instead re-focus our attention on finding an appropriate reason for its existence – in other words, its *purpose*. The more relevant questions to ask, then, would be: 'Why do we do strategy?', 'How can we optimise our investment in strategy?' and 'What do we want to achieve from development of a strategy and a strategic plan?' With an emphasis on purpose, attention is automatically oriented towards the 'why' rather than the 'what'.

The use of the term 'we' is also important, as it points to the question of *who* does strategy. Although skills in strategy are held by individuals, strategy formation and its subsequent implementation are nearly always undertaken in groups or teams. Any discussion around the *doing* of strategy therefore must be considered within the context of a group activity. In this case, a book about strategy (especially one with a focus on practice) must be cognisant of the need to appropriately impart knowledge to *individuals* while at the same time considering the need to express an appreciation of the elements of *leadership* and the way in which individuals work in *teams* to develop meaningful and powerful strategic content and outcomes.

Strategy as Practice

The history of language and practices that explore the discipline of strategy as a support mechanism to business managers is explored in more detail in Appendix 1. That history can be traced as far back as Ancient Greece, where an army general was referred to as a *strategos* (plural *strategoi*). In their role as generals, *strategoi* were held responsible for deciding in which parts of the world wars should be started and at what times. The individual *strategos*, on the other hand, was responsible for drawing up the battle plans and the effective implementation of those plans in the theatre of battle. As illustrated in Figure A1.1 in Appendix 1, the more modern application of the *strategos* terminology emerged in the late-1940s postwar period with the practice of long-range planning, and before that, linear programming. One of the first known applications of this planning tool can be attributed to Henri Fayol, a French mining senior executive who in a 1949 publication reported that the use of ten-year forecasts (revised every five years) was a valid management tool for future-focused managers. The general purpose in developing linear programming and long-range planning was to attempt to predict the future. Both techniques were eventually discarded, though, as they were bound to be. The reality is that the future quite literally doesn't exist. Any attempts to predict or even forecast it (especially using quantitative techniques that represent an extrapolation of the past, as linear programming does) are futile.

The popular successor to long-range planning is the well-known process of corporate or strategic planning. The creation of this methodology is largely attributable to Igor Ansoff, a highly regarded academic from North America who is informally acknowledged as being the 'father of strategy'. Ansoff was the first author to describe a way to develop a deliberate strategic plan in his aptly titled book *Corporate Strategy* (Ansoff, 1965).

Ansoff's corporate strategy methodology was widely adopted by business managers and is still used by up to 80 per cent of organisations (Whittington and Cailluet, 2008) today, mainly because it provides them with a set process and suite of instructions to follow. However, it is logical to suppose that prior to the development of this business tool, effective strategy and strategic thinking would have relied solely on an individual's capacity for intuition. In this book I illustrate the reliance on intuition as a method of strategic thinking by exploring the Cadbury confectionery business from its origins that date back as far as 1824. It is broadly demonstrated by the founder of Cadbury, John Cadbury, who confirms that an absence of intuitive strategic thinking at that time would have made it very difficult for corporations to survive, at least for as long as many of them did.

Examples of organisations that exhibit a degree of tenure, and by implication a capacity for intuitive strategic thinking, include Sotheby's (whose auction rooms were founded in London in 1744), Sveriges Riksbank (a Swedish bank founded in 1668) and Fiskars (a Finnish kitchen accoutrements company founded in 1649). North American examples are The King Arthur Flour Company (founded in Boston, Massachusetts in 1790) and Weitz (a construction company that commenced operations in Des Moines, Iowa in 1855).

It is therefore prudent for us to recognise that instinct and intuition, and even invention, play a large part in constructive strategic thinking from the origins of business in the early years of industrialisation right through to today. The irony, however, is that it is exactly that kind of thinking that gave rise to much of the strategy theory and the strategy tools we now use. This is because of the nature of the scientific method that is deployed to conduct the research. It is in fact the physical strategy practices of a few practitioners that give rise to theory, rather than the other way around. Specifically, broad-based strategy theory is deduced from the experiences and apparent practices of those managers known to have benefited from successful outcomes. The source of new knowledge is the feedback obtained from the strategy practitioners who have either implemented known theory successfully or more simply acted on intuition and instinct alone.

One of the earliest examples of this research method can be found in another book published on strategy in the early 1960s titled *Strategy and Structure: Chapters in the History of the Industrial Enterprise* (Chandler, 1962). Chandler was researching the strategic implications of business diversification when he drew his conclusions that were based on an analysis of the way in which the world's top 25 multinational (now more broadly referred to as 'global') corporations structured and managed their overseas strategic business units (divisions) up until the time of his study. He was surprised that each corporation he reviewed had followed similar methods of diversification, even though there was no prior research on the topic other than his own. Organisations that were included in Chandler's research all demonstrated a form of divisionalisation as a means of international diversification. The subjects of his research were all major and international North American corporations, including DuPont, General Motors, Sears and Standard Oil.

A more recent example of strategy theory to have emerged from this research method is 'blue ocean strategy' (Kim and Mauborgne, 2006), which was born out of research into value-added/market positioning strategies adopted by well-known corporations, including Southwest Airlines, Cirque du Soleil and Casella Wines (Yellow Tail brand).

For individuals seeking to assume the role of strategy practitioner, therefore, there is a need to accept the component of intuition in decision making, as well as a need to ensure we can learn from experience – the subject of most theories, and indeed future research. Strategy is ultimately a trade-off between learned methodologies and pure intuition. This makes for a rather complex activity and a difficult challenge for those who choose to participate at a professional level.

Bridging the Gap: From Strategy Theory to Strategy as Practice

Another element of strategy theory that needs to be understood is the limitation of the nature of research and the research method itself. Strategy is not conducted in laboratories, rather it is derived from surveys and interviews undertaken with individuals and teams and based on observations from those who are directly engaged in business activities. As access to corporations and the right people in those corporations is quite often difficult (for numerous reasons) for external parties, the scope of the research is limited to the quality of audience that *can* be physically reached, as opposed to the audience the researcher would perhaps *prefer* to reach. As a result, the translation of theory into practice can also be disjointed and require additional research to be undertaken if it is to be sufficiently robust. The outcome from such rigour is therefore often judged to be 'interesting' rather than conclusive. Another limitation is the fact that the topics/subjects selected are usually determined by even less scientific means. They tend to be the subject of an individual's personal agenda or specific area of interest. As a result, the overall strategy research programme can be, and often is unaligned and unrelated to what actually happens in practice.

In order to reduce the level of confusion surrounding the prevalence of opposing but equally compelling perspectives of strategy theory that have arisen in the literature, De Wit and Meyer capitalise on the value of this disparity, and in fact celebrate it. In their text *Strategy: Process Content and Context – an International Perspective* (De Wit and Meyer, 2010), the authors use the diversity of content in the discipline of strategy theory to advantage. Rather than attempting to lump the numerous topics of strategy into a variety of subjects, De Wit and Meyer choose to structure their book around a representation of the value the different extreme views in strategy bring. Treating these extremes as a paradox, the authors capitalise on the fact that although the many theories of strategy adopt opposing viewpoints, none of them are either right or wrong in their own right. An example is the two opposing views of the speed of strategic change, which can be viewed as being either evolutionary or revolutionary in nature. The authors propose that readers of their book explore the tensions that exist between the prevailing polarities of each extreme, rather than criticise them or treat them as a number of unrelated or independent methodologies.

Another example of a dichotomy in strategy theory is that of an emergent versus a deliberate strategy process. A key proponent of emerging strategy is Henry Mintzberg (1994), whose view of strategy embraces the notion that it is freewheeling – it emerges as the world evolves. In his view, this is like 'a potter who crafts clay' (Mintzberg, 1987). An opposite but equally correct view of strategy process is provided by Ansoff (1965), who, as described above, suggests that a deliberate and structured approach to strategy development should prevail, and that this capacity be developed through the formation of an annual formal strategic plan.

It is on this point in particular that this book commences a significant point of departure from contemporary strategy literature. The debate between the issue of emergent and deliberate strategy is one of the most hotly contested topics within the strategy scholastic community. It is my view however, that even though strategic planning has a place, the need to consider emergent strategy as a viable aspect of strategising is just as important or at the least, demanding of a balance between the two. In support of this view I argue in this book that an over reliance on strategic planning as a single strategy tool is commonplace, and that this reliance is fraught with danger. I have in response devised a fully integrated Strategic Management Framework (discussed below and illustrated in Figure 1.1) as a mechanism that accommodates both planning and emergent strategy, and a basis upon which strategy is managed in practice. It is in effect a reinvention of the way that strategy is done; and provokes an appreciation of best-of-both world alternatives between deliberate and emergent strategy.

This book is therefore sympathetic to an emerging trend in the academic world which is also seeking to address the dilemma associated with the deficiency in focus of strategy research in the past. Research has historically focused almost entirely on elements of strategy that reflect what we *have*, the physical tools and econometrically based models *used* by strategists to strategise, there is now an emphasis on the physical *doing* of strategy. This is the practice of strategy itself; the *praxis* (Vaara and Whittington, 2012). The emerging emphasis of strategy research today is focused very much on gaining an understanding of aspects of strategising *activities*, literally, strategy *in* practice.

Meyer (2007), proposes that the act of doing strategy (strategising) is made up of three elements determined and designed by a driving organisational purpose as the 'why' of strategy:

1.   **process** – the *how*, *who* and *when* of strategy – the flow of activities (praxis) through which strategy is practised;

2.   **content** – the *what* of strategy, the product of a strategy process and a result of strategising activities – its output;

3.   **context** – the *where* of strategy and the set of circumstances under which both the strategy process and strategy content are determined.

As a part of the movement leading a transformation towards strategy in practice, the Strategic Management Society (SMS), a global strategy-focused research organisation is exploring the idea of making strategy a profession. The Strategic Management Institute (SMI), with which I am closely involved, already offers courses and accreditation for professional strategy practitioners. I therefore propose that when you read this book, you treat its content as a foundation for the practice of strategy as a profession.

Support for Strategy as a Profession

My objective with this book is to help you to transform your intuitive appreciation of strategy as well as your understanding of prevailing strategy theory and transform these into a useable, powerful and structured application of *strategy in practice*. I am also seeking to help you to conduct your strategically focused activities within a standard of practice that can be correctly considered to be at the level of a *profession*. This is why I propose that in this book we explore together the deployment of a boundaryless, professionally recognised framework for strategy that is explained through 'The Seven Inconvenient Truths of Business Strategy' (see Table I.1). This is a description of strategy practice which can be construed as a system (more than a process) and defined within the construct of a fully integrated Strategic Management Framework (see Figure 1.1 and Appendix 2 for a full overview). The content of this structure informs the majority of the content presented in this book.

Table I.1   The Seven Inconvenient Truths of Business Strategy

The Seven Inconvenient Truths	Consequences
1. The content of a strategic 'plan' lacks relevance. The entrenched 1960s 'planning' regime is no longer as relevant as it was at the time of its inception – a period of certainty, predictability and continuity.	In a complex, dynamic and ambiguous world, the content of a strategic plan is bound to become increasingly obsolete the closer it gets to the expiry date of the typical three-to five-year planning period.
2. Strategy is an undefined and dynamic system rather than a closed-loop process. Unlike the rigidity of accounting and law, strategy is an open-loop system that flourishes within a world of contradiction and conflict – a taunt of the unknown, and a challenge of what could be.	Viewed only as a part of a process or independent methodology, value realised from the quantum of strategy tools becomes suboptimal and their application overly reliant on simplistic, 'flavour of the month' methods. This leads to the development of the right answers, but to the wrong problems.
3. Measures of strategy effectiveness are misplaced and ill defined. The primary focus of strategy evaluation activities is mostly assessed on incorrect measures – an assessment of specific outcomes rather than the 'causal' factors arising from inevitable assumptions/guesstimates that contribute to its formulation and renewal (shaping) and its implementation (reviewing).	In the absence of an appropriate strategy evaluation capability, unforeseen outcomes and unintended consequences arise, including: • incomplete, inappropriate strategy content; • continued investment in invalid strategies; • poor responses to unforeseen change.
4. Individual subconscious preferences exert an invisible, adverse influence on decision making. Strategy is dominated by individual subconscious preferences and an often destructive dominant logic that prevails in groups/teams.	A dominant logic leads to hubris and myopia, which contribute to tensions within teams. This leads to discontent, conflict, organisational discord, and inevitably, suboptimal strategic outcomes.
5. Implementation is notoriously unsuccessful. Terminology such as 'a relentless focus on execution' emphasises redundancy and discontinuity compared to the more positive 'programme of continual strategy renewal'.	A focus on execution alone evokes notions of the cessation of strategy as opposed to a combination of short-term outcomes and a dynamic programme of continual, strategically aligned renewal.
6. An organisation's strategy content is often disjointed and disconnected from the external environment as well as many internal components of the organisation. Alignment is often missing between the firm and environment (fit), its mission/vision and realised outcomes, as well as its internal structure across, up and down the organisation, such as innovation and learning.	A lack of fit with the external environment results in poor strategic outcomes. Lack of internal alignment devalues belief in the benefits of the strategic activities and increases levels of risk. It also has a negative impact on a leader's ability to align employees around a common sense of purpose and direction.

Table I.1   The Seven Inconvenient Truths of Business Strategy
concluded

The Seven Inconvenient Truths	Consequences
7. Strategy practices lack an appropriate perspective of professionalism. Strategy is not a natural science, but a socially constructed convention that exists between peers. There is no 'absolute' such as the absolute zero of -273° C. It is a learned capability and a lived experience that professionals *do*, as opposed to systems, processes and capabilities that we *have*.	Over-reliance on science-based academic approaches to strategy practice results in poor outcomes, wrong strategies and sometimes bad strategy. In the absence of a comprehensive method of strategy practice, our understanding is vague, its integration difficult, its application problematic and its implementation all too often sub-standard.

The human/behavioural (people) aspects of strategy are also considered in our transformation agenda: they provide the foundation for strategy as a profession and the successful conceptualisation and management of the 'doing' of strategy in practice. These components of strategy are incorporated into the methodology through the consideration of individual and team behaviours and their contribution to *business* transformation, renewal and growth.

When viewed as an open-loop system the Strategic Management Framework facilitates the people factor (those who engage in the activity of strategising) of strategy formation. The framework provides a structure to strategy and the strategic conversations that will be enhanced and enabled in some considerable way through the application of the attributes associated with those of a learning organisation. In proposing the adoption of the philosophies of a learning organisation, my approach is informed by the work of Senge (1990), who makes the observations that organisational learning is important because 'The rate at which organizations learn may become the only sustainable source of competitive advantage,' and that a learning organisation is a place where 'people continually expand their capacity to create the results they truly desire, where new and expansive patterns of thinking are nurtured, where collective aspirations are set free, and where people are continually learning how to learn together' (Senge, 1990).

Professional Strategy Practice: Systemic Strategising Conducted within the Context of a Learning Organisation

The fully integrated Strategic Management Framework is in itself an *enabler* of a strategy praxis – a method of aligning and structuring each of the various elements of strategy to form an integrated *system*. I apply the attributes of a learning organisation therefore, to provide insight into the appropriate behaviours and activities that strategy practitioners will apply in order to bring the framework to life – the *enactment* of strategy in practice. Content contained in each element of the framework that makes up the system is grounded in empirical research. Examples include elements of competitive strategy, strategic change, strategy evaluation, transforming activities (dynamic capabilities), resource leveraging (a resource-based view of the firm) and increasingly (as well as being another primary theme that contributes to the overall message contained in this book) the concept of continual strategy and (subsequently) organisational *renewal*.

Specific tools and techniques incorporated into the framework include environmental scanning, scenario analysis and portfolio analysis. While each of these theoretically grounded tools is recognised as adding value in its own right, the Strategic Management Framework provides additional value to the professional strategist as it provides a structure to strategising that would not otherwise exist. In effect, I am suggesting that the framework allows strategy professionals to locate the many and various strategy tools and techniques within a natural but deliberate construct. Through the deployment of this framework, strategy in practice is optimised. However, the extent and method of optimisation will vary in accordance with the differences in the circumstances, size, industry and environment within which the business operates.

Support for the Reinvention of Strategic Planning

Just as there is a clear link between *theory* and *practice*, there is also a distinct difference between *process* and *system*. The divide in both perspectives has for too long been captured in an unchallenged method of doing strategy. The dominance of the orientation towards *process* adopted by strategy practitioners when strategising has in my view placed far too much weight on the deliberation of a mechanistic, end-to-end annual corporate or strategic plan (sometimes known simply as a 'plan') over that of a system of strategy renewal and a framework that accommodates both *deliberate* and *emergent* strategy. I have identified three issues that inhibit effective strategy practice as a result of practitioners' over-reliance on the otherwise useful device, the ubiquitous strategic plan.

Firstly, as a written document, a strategic plan can best be identified as being something we *have*, not something we *do*. We have a new software system, for example; it is a tangible asset. There is nothing tangible about a strategic plan other than the fact that it is a physical document. All too often, that document is filed away on hard drives in electronic formats or in bookshelves and top drawers when in printed form. Rarely does it see the light of day after presentation and board approval. Secondly, the strategic plan is generally something that is developed in the absence of critical interaction and contributions from the people who are most likely to have the greatest insight into its makeup. Regrettably, little communication is then afforded to those who will be subjected to the greatest impact from the decisions that are a part of its output. Thirdly, while strategic plans assume an external environment that is treated as something that is static over time, the business environments in which such plans are formulated are becoming increasingly dynamic, complex and chaotic.

What I am seeking to do in this book, therefore, is to present an approach to the management of strategy in a format that is based on a reinvention of strategic planning – the way the plan is developed, used and implemented. I propose to do this by transforming/reinventing its function, by turning it into a document (or better still, interactive system) promoting and leading (as opposed to inhibiting) organisational transformation and renewal, and a construct that captures dynamism, innovation and complexity. The transformation will be physically achieved by redirecting our focus from that of a static extrapolation of the past to one of an envisioned future and an expression of a dynamic programme of continual strategy renewal – within the boundaries of a creatively inspired *system*, not a process.

The charge of irrelevance levelled at the unassuming strategic plan appears as the first of The Seven Inconvenient Truths of Business Strategy described in Table I.1. The full range of inconvenient truths highlights, and through this book addresses, the consequences of the apparent over-emphasis on strategic planning as a *deliberate process* and under-emphasis on an *emergent, systems* perspective, as well as the people factors (including learning) that are so critical to successful outcomes.

The Mechanics of Strategy as a Profession

Rather than presenting another attempt to define what the many elements of strategy are, this book seeks to share a method of *doing* purposeful strategy at a professional standard – that of a Certified Strategy Practitioner (CSP). Current practices of the SMI recognise that professional strategy practitioners are individuals who possess appropriate levels and standards of skills and experience in strategy. The formal approach to strategy practice that allows the SMI to recognise strategy as a profession is similar to that applied by accountants who rely on a set of standards that are officially described as generally accepted accounting principles (GAAP) which provide the basis for the recording, summarising and preparation of the financial statements of a business entity. These are quite simply the doctrines, policies, tools and techniques that must be mastered if professional accountants are to comply with their professional body's standards. Examples include the doctrine of double-entry bookkeeping and methods of accrual used to facilitate the 'timing principle' which requires accountants to match income with expenses over consistent periods.

A strategy professional has access to numerous strategic analytical tools, but there have been no guidelines as to what, how and when they should be used, together – until now, through the medium of this book. Although I am not proposing a definitive suite of 'generally accepted strategising principles' nor a comprehensive application of tools here, I am aiming to establish a foundation for further development. To date, little has been published on the practical aspects of strategy practice, but again, that is the objective of this book. As we will see, its purpose is to provide you with a structure to strategy, an indicator of appropriate strategy tool use, and insight into co-operative ways of doing strategy; including formation, evaluation, alignment and implementation. Topics covered also include aspects of governance, which is a critical element of a profession, as is communication, leadership, teamwork, strategic and organisational transformation and the treatment of the issue of strategic risk.

The Strategy Professional's Influence on Organisational Renewal

A primary benefit of making strategy a profession is the potential for the Office of Strategy, led by the Chief Strategy Officer (CSO), to act in a professional capacity in the initiation and leadership of programmes and reviews of a strategic nature and, of course, the articulation of strategy content (in a role that provides support to the undisputed owners of strategy: the business unit leaders, the Chief Executive Officer (CEO), and ultimately the board of directors). Another important aspect of the role will be its influence on the instigation and leadership of organisational transformation and renewal. As will be shown in the content of this book, desired change in individual and organisational behaviour is driven largely by a capacity to learn from experience, a process of attaining relevant knowledge and developing wisdom. The formal capture of that organisational learning, experience and knowledge has never been strong in business, although numerous attempts to make it so have been attempted.

The rise of formal education through the mechanism of real or virtual corporate-owned universities (also known as academy) is increasingly being seen as the means to ensure that organisational learning makes an impact. The establishment of corporate universities/academies is an emerging phenomenon in business. Growing in stature, such entities are being seen to add significant value to their parent organisations through their contribution to the realisation of the businesses' strategic goals and objectives. A corporate university can be used to empower its employees through dissemination of knowledge in a format that meets the specific needs of that organisation and its strategy. While this knowledge will result in better implementation and renewal of strategy, more mature corporate universities will inevitably be in a position to complete the cycle by feeding knowledge back to their sponsors, thereby acting as a driving force in the continual renewal of strategy, and as a result the organisations themselves.

Examples of corporations that currently operate their own university or academy include Mars Inc. (Mars University), Ikea (The College) and Canon (Canon Academy Europe). There is also evidence that their use is increasing in not-for-profit and municipal councils in North America and Europe (Rademakers, 2014).

How to Use this Book

In order to fully capture the evolutionary nature of the concept of strategy and its emergence as a profession in this book, I use the history of Cadbury as a supplement to the story of The Seven Inconvenient Truths of Business Strategy. I chose Cadbury specifically because of the intriguing circumstances surrounding that company's longevity, the fascination of its spiritual and entrepreneurial roots, the strength of its culture and the appeal of the evolutionary changes in the market dynamics in which it operates. The Cadbury story is one of passionate human endeavour and an illustration of sometimes sharp, but sometimes flat strategic thinking. It is also a story of relentless ambition passed through generations of family members until the company was floated on the stock market in the mid-1960s – at about the same time when formal strategy theory was born.

The book is structured into seven chapters, each of which can be read independently in accordance with the flow of The Seven Inconvenient Truths of Business Strategy presented in Table I.1. Each inconvenient truth is associated with an element of the Strategic Management Framework when it is process- or system-related. Chapter 4 is concerned with the people issues of leadership and teams. Chapter 7 expands on the people component to extend strategy practice to promote strategy as a profession. It therefore addresses a number of other human/behavioural aspects of strategy in practice.

The story of Cadbury commences with an introduction to the business that emerged as a result of the commitment to humanity of Richard Cadbury and his son John, as well as John Cadbury's dedication to the business which would eventually pass through the hands of four generations. The independent entity that was Cadbury lasted for 186 years. It ended on the 19 January 2010, following the announcement by the US-based food industry giant Kraft Foods that it had agreed to purchase all of Cadbury's shares for US$18.9 billion. By following the Cadbury story, we will be able to relate the content discussed in each chapter to the circumstances facing the company during the various periods of its life. My objective in doing this is to provide a means of illustrating their value and application to you as someone who is no doubt actively engaged in some form of business endeavour.

I hope you enjoy the content of this book and find value in the application of the framework in its use. The construct that I present is robust, and it is grounded in practical experience I obtained as a partner of an international management consulting firm. It is also grounded in a depth of research that includes a doctoral thesis followed by subsequent research conducted over a 10-year period.

Chapter 1

Relevance Lost:
Strategic Planning and a Lack
of Certainty – a Loss of Value

> **INCONVENIENT TRUTH NO. 1: THE CONTENT OF A STRATEGIC 'PLAN' LACKS RELEVANCE.**
>
> The entrenched 1960s 'planning' regime is no longer as relevant as it was at the time of its inception – a period of certainty, predictability and continuity.

One of the greatest strategic challenges faced by business leaders today is the imperative to address the tension that exists between the direction in which business leaders would *like* to take their organisation as opposed to the direction *imposed* on them by external environmental forces. This is a challenge that is faced by many companies, as shown by our survey, which found that a substantial 82 per cent of participants agreed that their firm's strategy content 'is influenced mostly by industry forces and emerging trends'.[1]

The depth of this strategic challenge is compounded by the fact that both the internal and external environments that leaders must deal with are becoming increasingly unpredictable and difficult to align; in many instances, each are moving in a *different* and sometimes *opposite* direction. Further tension is added by the fact that just as business leaders struggle to meet demands for the delivery of year-on-year *growth*, key elements of the external environment are fundamentally moving in a unilateral state of *decline*. Worse still, the nature of that decline is one of an erratic and irrational 'random walk'. Business leaders must therefore possess a capacity for agility and responsiveness in their

---

1   The Strategic Management Institute survey on strategic management practices conducted in conjunction with Swinburne University in 2013 has not been published, but copies are available on request by emailing the SMI at smi@smiknowledge.com.

strategising capabilities if they are to overcome the significant uncertainty and complexity that have become part of everyday business management.

Based on my own research and experience as a management consultant and executive development professional, I have noticed that the necessary level of robustness required to deliver such a strong leadership is not the norm. Rather, the overarching method of doing strategy (strategy as practice) is on the whole anything but agile and responsive. In particular, I have found that the predominant method of *making* strategy – the production of a static three- to five-year strategic plan – is actually a hindrance to good strategy content and can in fact have a negative impact on the strength of a firm's leadership. In support of my observations I refer you to just one example (out of many) of survey results that express the extent of dissatisfaction with the process of conventional strategic planning. The results report that of 156 executives in major corporations worldwide, only 11 per cent believed strongly that strategic planning is worth the effort (Mankins and Steele, 2006).

The First Inconvenient Truth of Strategy

> *The entrenched 1960s 'planning' regime is no longer as relevant as it was at the time of its inception – a period of certainty, predictability and continuity. The consequence of this is that in a complex, dynamic and ambiguous world, the content of a strategic plan is bound to become increasingly obsolete the closer it gets to the expiry date of the typical three- to five-year planning period.*

The purpose of this book is to provide you with insight into the detail, implications and methods of resolution to the full suite of Inconvenient Truths of Business Strategy that, when combined, act as a major hindrance and blocker to the effective management of strategy in business. In addressing the apparent lack of faith in strategic planning, and all the other issues that are articulated in The Seven Inconvenient Truths of Business Strategy, I propose the application of a fully integrated Strategic Management Framework (Figure 1.1) as a solution – in particular to the system and process components of strategy.

People issues are also addressed within the context of The Seven Inconvenient Truths of Business Strategy, they include individual behaviours and capabilities and the management and effectiveness of those individuals as leaders and members of teams. Ultimately, the people issues related to strategy as practice are assessed in a context of strategy as a profession.

Each chapter in this book addresses The Seven Inconvenient Truths of Business Strategy sequentially. I have also sought to provide a conceptualisation of the content, context and implications that are integral components of the suite of Inconvenient Truths, presented in a story format and viewed through the lens of a tale of the history of the world-famous confectionery company Cadbury. The story unfolds in chronological order, it commences at the time of the company's foundation in 1824 by entrepreneur John Cadbury who as a man of strict religion, sought to provide his customers and community with a solution to the socially irresponsible habit of excessive alcohol consumption.

Birth of the Cadbury Chocolate Company of Birmingham: A Tale of Values-driven Entrepreneurship

We commence the story of Cadbury at the time of the birth of the business which took place in the same year that Charles Dickens, renowned author and storyteller (*A Tale of Two Cities, David Copperfield, Great Expectations*), then aged 12, was removed from school following the unexpected imprisonment of his father, who had been found guilty of not paying his debts. Passed into the care of a family friend, Dickens was sent to work in a shoe polish factory ('the blacking-warehouse'), allowing him to earn enough money to pay for his keep. Conditions in the factory were dire, and are described in John Forster's book *The Life of Charles Dickens* (Forster, [1874] 2011): 'The blacking-warehouse wainscoted room had rotten floors and staircase, old grey rats swarmed in the cellars, the sound of their squeaking and scuffling coming up the stairs at all times.'

Thanks to this vivid description of Dickens's unfortunate circumstances, we can readily summon images of the 22-year-old John Cadbury who in the same year as Charles Dickens's father's imprisonment established a spice, herb and condiment shop in the city of Birmingham in the English West Midlands. John Cadbury had a natural entrepreneurial bent, and his first endeavour saw him specialise in the supply of tea, coffee, hops, mustard and similar products to the local townsfolk. Struggling to survive as an independent proprietor in a period long before the business application of the word 'strategy' was even dreamed of, John Cadbury intuitively found a way to differentiate his shop and service delivery from many prevailing and potential competitors. He found considerable success with this first business venture; it was achieved through the use of unique and differentiated market-oriented activities.

John Cadbury's mostly unconscious and decidedly informal strategy focused on dominating the marketplace on two primary fronts. One was the use of alternative forms of in-store presentation that included the discreet placement of Asian ornaments and artefacts as well as the oriental-style clothing worn by the shop assistants. The combination served to promote a distinct air of mystique to his customers. Secondly, John Cadbury was able to attract people from far away, as many of his customers travelled to Birmingham just to view the shop front window, which was unusual at that time. It was designed in the format of small squares of mahogany-framed plate glass. This represented an attractive alternative to the larger single panes of glass used by everyone else. Overall, the appeal of John Cadbury's shop was based on an atmosphere of sensuality and intrigue on the inside and a unique look and feel to the premises from the outside.

In addition to the market-oriented strategy that focused on attracting customers through a range of distinctive features, John Cadbury's product range was also unusual. In order to maintain and renew his competencies in this unique market space, John Cadbury also focused on the conduct of activities that would ensure their continual renewal. In particular, John Cadbury invested in skills and equipment that would allow him to reinvigorate his product range as well as continue the refinement of other new products and service offerings. To this end, John Cadbury focused largely on the processing of a rare, and for its time unusual, product made from the mystical cacao bean (or nib) sourced from the far-off tropics in the form of a chocolate-flavoured drink widely known as cocoa.

John Cadbury's commitment to his belief in the future of cocoa and perhaps chocolate as a commercially viable endeavour led him to establish a separate manufacturing facility in 1832. Located near his shop in Crooked Lane, Birmingham, he devoted the majority of his time to the development and manufacture of cocoa-based drinking chocolate from freshly ground cacao nibs. Such was his commitment to the promise of prosperity the future of chocolate held that in 1849 he chose to give up his involvement in his retail shop altogether, effectively reinventing himself and his business model. He literally transformed his business from a market-focused retailer – a business that benefited from differentiating activities from competitors in the manner described above – to that of a pioneer in the research, development and manufacture of the emerging consumer product cocoa. As you will see later, these business models represent a transformation from an outside-in (market-driven) strategic orientation to that of an inside-out (resource-based) strategic orientation.

The primary motive in exerting his entrepreneurial skills in cocoa manufacture and business in general was the principle espoused by the puritanical religion to which John Cadbury and his family subscribed, one that is still in existence today and is known as the Religious Society of Friends, or more generally the Quakers. Formed in the seventeenth century, the Quaker movement (created by a breakaway group from the Church of England) set out to convert others to what they believed were the proper practices of the early Church. As a Quaker, John Cadbury held a deep commitment to an envisioned future that was based on the hope that the cocoa drink could provide a hearty, healthy alternative to the common alcoholic drink that was being used and abused by many at that time: gin. Representing an extreme social problem, alcohol was seen by the Cadbury family as being 'a curse on the modern day family and a source of ruination'.

In reality, John Cadbury's target market was quite ill defined, and although he hadn't realised it, was fundamentally out of reach, because the customers who chose to visit his shop were usually quite prosperous, and regrettably represented only the privileged few who were able to afford his products. They were not the impoverished drunks upon whom the Cadbury family had chosen to focus their altruistic concerns. Had the Cadbury family had an appreciation of even the fundamentals of strategy, they might have noticed the discrepancy between their vision and their obvious lack of capability to realise their proposed long-term purpose. Instead, John Cadbury, supported by his family, carried on doing exactly the same thing, and although successful to an extent, didn't live long enough to enjoy the rewards of success which the business eventually delivered to his heirs.

John Cadbury had hoped to contribute to society as well as to build a viable business out of the obscure and bitter-tasting cacao nib that formed the foundation ingredient of the solid chocolate bar we relish today. At the time of John Cadbury's entrepreneurial endeavour, cacao nibs had to be ground by hand and turned into a powder to be mixed with milk or water as the basis for the cocoa drink. In the early 1800s and for some time later, the product was barely edible. The enormity of the problem John Cadbury faced as a manufacturer learning to tame the science of food processing was similar to the challenge faced by many manufacturers in the early years of the Industrial Revolution: the fact that scientists understood little about *why* things worked, they just knew that they did.

Examples of challenges similar to those forced on John Cadbury are all scientifically based, and include paper manufacturers who had to fight to find the best way to transform wood pulp into paper, the glass industry whose participants sought to turn sand into glass through the application of intense temperatures, and the steel industry whose challenge was to use extreme levels of heat to turn iron ore into steel. John Cadbury had no notion of how to improve the relatively inefficient and, worse still, elusive science that allowed cacao nibs to be efficiently turned into an edible product. Even so, in the absence of sufficient knowledge of the science of cacao production, John Cadbury resolved to persevere, in total ignorance of any potential advances in chocolate processing technology that might emerge in the future – and the number of years it would eventually take to finally produce a quality chocolate product. For most of his life, John Cadbury clung to his belief that a viable product would become more than a dream. He hoped that such a development would allow him and his team to benefit from the intuitively certain but realistically unknown potential of chocolate. In language that we only understand today, John Cadbury's business in effect had minimal core competencies in the processing of cacao nibs and the effective manufacture of chocolate drinks, and later chocolate confectionery.

Making Strategy Relevant

As illustrated in the introduction to Cadbury, the over-riding factor of success for industry in the lead-up to the peak of the nineteenth century's Industrial Revolution was an acquired capability to benefit from economies of scale through mass production of commoditised goods that readily lent themselves to standardisation of product, supported by evidence of international distribution opportunities. In a sense, that was the substance of strategy at that time. It was a period of minimal resources, but a great deal of resourcefulness. The markets of the day exhibited a strength of certainty in the future, and from a market growth perspective, minimal complexity coupled with an absence of ambiguity. For John Cadbury, the actual production of quality chocolate in the form of the cocoa drink would continue as the primary challenge for a long time; he understood (or at least, he thought he understood) what his long term strategy was, he didn't need a short term strategic plan.

The challenge for a strategy practitioner such as yourself therefore begins with the task of reassessing the relevance of the annual strategic plan to you, in the form that you use it today. To be honest, I doubt that you would be even reading this book if you didn't share my doubt as to its real value. In writing this book, therefore, my objective is to help you reach your own conclusions as to the value of strategy and relevance of the strategic plan. Overall, my objective is to help you seek resolution of the issues raised that are associated with each of the Inconvenient Truths discussed herein, and to explore how they may help you to improve your strategising capability and the quality of outcomes from your strategy. As illustrated in the Introduction, the issues I have identified as The Seven Inconvenient Truths of Business Strategy are the outcome of considerable research, experience and soul-searching on the topic.

Making Sense of Strategy: Systems Thinking and a Matter of Purpose

If you are involved in any way in a business entity, you will be aware of the extent to which business leaders are driven to identify robust solutions to multifaceted problems. These problems typically relate to a wide variety of issues, which could include topics of marketing, customer service, service delivery, manufacturing, logistics, procurement and all forms of business management. To help you develop solutions to these complex and sometimes 'wicked' strategically oriented issues (along with the many challenges laid out in our exploration of The Seven Inconvenient of Truths of Business Strategy), I propose the fully integrated Strategic Management Framework (Figure 1.1) is a tried and tested way to structure strategy that can serve as an aid to help you think about solving your most challenging strategic problems. 'Wicked' problems are defined by Rittel (1972) as 'those problems that are difficult or impossible to solve'. They have also been characterised as possessing incomplete, contradictory and changing attributes that are difficult to explain (Australian Public Service Commission, 2007).

Logically, a good place to start making sense of strategy is the theory, by determining how you can use it to your greatest advantage. Although comprehensive definitions of strategy theory are widely available from the literature, there is regrettably no single universally accepted definition. The reason for this is that, as explained in Appendix 1, strategy is a relatively new discipline in the context of business. As a result, the prevailing approach to understanding the topic is still complex, its research disjointed, and a method of practice that has not yet reached the realms and standard that would otherwise be required at the level of a profession. Since its inception there has also been a lack of integration in strategy practices. In laying a foundation for its recognition at the level of a profession, I propose in this book that strategy, strategic planning, strategy evaluation, strategic renewal, alignment and implementation be treated as a multi-looped and open system – evaluated and realised through a mindset of *systems thinking*.

In his book *The Fifth Discipline*, Senge (1990) defines systems thinking as 'the intangible and unconscious ability to combine unknown, unseen phenomenon into a whole'. To illustrate the application of this principle in practice, I have adapted an example used by Senge. It refers to an unconscious or 'taken-for-granted' appreciation of the knowledge that dark clouds in the sky means rain. From a systems thinking perspective, we naturally associate rain with dangerous roads as well as higher dam levels. In the first context, the systemic view of dark clouds and rain implies danger on the roads, which in turn provokes the need for awareness of safety when driving. In the second context, a systemic view of dark clouds and rain invokes a suggestion of water replenishment for farmers and landowners. This in turn leads to an expectation of high crop yields and a reduced risk of forest fires. From there we can extrapolate expectations of crop prices, reduction in the need for fire prevention equipment and so on.

The format for the system I am proposing in linking systems thinking to strategy is explored as a journey of continual strategy renewal – and as an outcome continual organisational renewal supported by a constant alignment and realignment of the fit between the firm and the continually evolving external environment within which it coexists. Renewal, regeneration and sometimes reinvention of that system and the business is informed through a formal programme of organisational learning.

An example of the application of systems thinking to Cadbury is grounded in the values the Cadbury family held as justification for their initial investment in the industry, and the reason for their unreserved commitment to its success. That reason was the discovery of the nutritious but bitter-tasting cacao nib that, in the form of a chocolate drink, could provide a solution to alcoholism as well as a source of satisfaction to consumers and a basis for the sharing of wealth between the Cadbury family and its stakeholders. As observed previously, the apparent disconnect between any form of systemic alignment with the primary objective of chocolate drink being a remedy for alcoholism and the actual market they reached was not noticed by the Cadbury clan. For as long as those values and aspirations prevailed internally, the reality of the market was such that consumers were slow to respond to their product offering; it initially delivered not much more than a product of poor quality (albeit with the best possible ingredients) and a high price (as a result of the use of pure ingredients and because of the imposition of a tax on chocolate). It was also highly uncompetitive in the marketplace because of the predominance of cheaper, albeit lower-quality competitors.

As the external environmental forces shifted over time, however, the system the Cadbury family envisaged did eventually come into being, but more as a result of luck than design (often a factor of strategy that is underestimated by business leaders in general). Changes in the external environment worked considerably to Cadbury's advantage. These included the elimination of taxes on chocolate and the passing of the UK's Adulteration of Food Acts of 1860 and 1872 that ensured the prohibition of the use of unhealthy 'illicit' substances that had hitherto been the ingredient of choice among many of Cadbury's competitors. Well known for the promise of 'absolutely pure, therefore the best', Cadbury was gifted an immediate competitive advantage over other less scrupulous industry participants. Internally, product quality improved as a result of the Cadbury brothers' dogged persistence with activities that would ultimately transform their core competencies from a level of novices (driven by trial and error) to those of connoisseurs – producing higher quality chocolate products both efficiently and effectively. As we will see later, such activities are theoretically referred to as *dynamic capabilities* (Ambrosini and Bowman, 2009), but I prefer to call them *transforming activities* because this is a more relevant and broad-based interpretation of the theory of dynamic capabilities. Transforming activities are those activities that the firm does to either improve or renew its resource base and as a result, maintain or develop a new form of sustainable/renewable competitive advantage.

Therefore, when seeking an understanding of the definition of strategy, a systems approach provides a holistic view of ways in which strategy can be most relevant and add value for the practitioner. In terms of seeking a conclusive definition of what strategy is, however, my advice to you is not to bother. Rather, I recommend that you re-focus your attention towards an appreciation of the following five specific objectives of strategy that will provide you with a *purpose* for its use – and then the basis for its maturation into a profession:

1.   Provide an articulation of the way in which the vision of an individual or group of individuals for a business's future will be translated into the long-term imperatives that combine to form the content of its strategy. This is initiated through a clear and open narrative of the stakeholders' values and an articulation of what the entity *must do* (strategic imperatives) in the long term to realise the ambition articulated in its vision whilst remaining cognisant of the organising principles described in its mission. An appreciation of long term is determined by the often unseen

'rules of the game' of an industry. As we will see later, Toyota has held the same fundamental strategy for 50 years or so.

2.   Fundamental to an articulation of a long-term strategy is an understanding and agreement among relevant stakeholders of the preferences, aspirations, purpose, goals and desired outcomes that will be reflected in decisions to include, or exclude content. In this context, strategy can be seen to be an aspirational expression of a future that is encapsulated in the firm's vision and mission which is imagined, expressed and articulated under the influence and at the behest of the entities leaders.

3.   Develop a plan that describes how long term strategy will be implemented and renewed in the short term– its strategic plan and associated programme of continual strategy renewal. The strategic plan is an expression of the immediate strategic goals and objectives that must be realised if the long-term strategic imperatives are to be met, and the subsequent elements of that plan that must be continually evaluated if the strategy and strategic plan are to remain relevant now and into the future.

4.   Provide the basis for leadership by describing the emotive and inspirational reasons why networks, teams and individuals should collaborate to realise a shared vision as well as generally agreed strategically aligned imperatives, goals and objectives.

5.   Provide the basis for strategic responsiveness to changes that may materialise from time-to-time in order to inform decision making and business policy. Responsiveness can occur in the three formats of reactive, proactive and designed. A reactive response is required to deal with unforeseen events whereas a proactive response is required to manage anticipated events. A designed response is an outcome from strategy which seeks to influence and/ or change the entity's strategic posture as a result of a deliberate desire to do so. In each case, responsiveness and agility is required to enable the continual renewal and potentially reinvention of the business and to explain the method of transformation required as the organisation adapts to or helps to create changes in its internal operations or external environment that are vital to its survival or more importantly, success.

6.   Provide support to the resolution of 'wicked' strategic *problems*: a process that is both an input to and outcome from strategising activities that address and seek resolutions to problems that are complex (sometimes extremely so) and difficult to solve. Each are aligned to (long-term) strategy (strategic imperatives) whilst also providing relief to the immediacy of those short-term strategic objectives expressed in the strategic plan.

In assessing the value of strategy, especially at the level of a profession, it is necessary to address the fundamental flaw we have identified with the method of strategic planning as The First Inconvenient Truth of Strategy and its role in providing a key purpose in doing strategy, especially as a single approach to the conduct of strategising per se. An explanation of the flaw in the planning approach begins with the fundamentals of long-standing doctrines in strategy that insist that:

- minimal changes in the business environment will impact the business whose strategic plan is based on the predetermined time lapse and linkages for 'planning' which are one year for a budget, three to five years for a plan and five to ten years for a vision;

- the annual strategic plan is the primary symbol and instrument of strategy creation through to implementation (never mind that the existence of an overarching long-term strategy is very often ignored in practice or simply not recognised, beyond the generally vague utterings of a vision and mission statement).

Given these fundamental beliefs, it is no wonder that strategy practice and the enunciations of strategy practitioners are regularly misunderstood. The underlying issue and greatest cause of a lack of relevance in strategic planning activities can be summed up in the following observation:

Strategy is about the future, but the future doesn't exist, so plans that are made are based on assumptions, guesstimates, faith and hope. As a result, the validity of a three- to five-year strategic plan is bound to depreciate in value at least as fast as the assumptions and guesstimates decline in relevance over time. When treated as a steadfast road map to the future, therefore, it is not the people or map that are wrong; rather, it is the timeliness of the content. Relevance is bound to decline as soon as the reality of the actual (physical) road is being built and the future gradually unfolds.

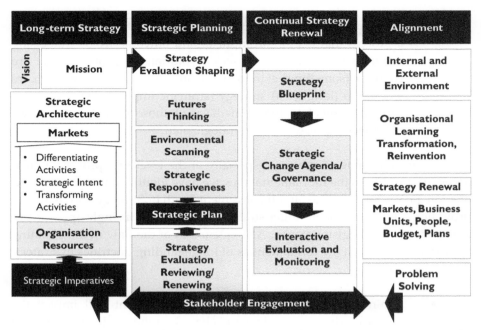

Figure 1.1   Summary: fully integrated Strategic Management Framework

The dilemma associated with the prevailing design of a static strategic plan is therefore the assumption that its application in practice is no more than that of a snapshot of proposed activities that *will* (must?) be delivered over a relatively short period – board approval given, decision made! I suggest that a more useful way to structure strategy in order to address its apparent shortcomings is to position the strategic plan in particular within the system that I refer to as the fully integrated Strategic Management Framework; and managed on a continual basis within the component of the strategic management framework that I refer to as the Program of Continual Strategy Renewal. A detailed illustration of a fully integrated Strategic Management Framework and the renewal element appears in Figure 1.1 and in detail in Appendix 2 and is explained more fully next.

Overview of the Components of the Fully Integrated Strategic Management Framework

The Strategic Management Framework is made up of four primary elements which combine to form an integrated system:

1.   strategy – vision, mission and a strategic architecture;

2.   strategic planning – strategy evaluation, shaping and reviewing;

3.   a programme of continual strategy renewal;

4.   alignment.

ELEMENT 1: STRATEGY: VISION, MISSION AND A STRATEGIC ARCHITECTURE

The first component of the Strategic Management Framework is concerned with the underlying purpose of the long-term *strategy*. Firm-specific strategy is grounded in a *vision* for the business which is mostly derived from the leaders' (or leadership teams') aggregated determination of an *envisioned future*. From our discussion of Cadbury, you may almost be able to feel John Cadbury's perceptions of relevance to an envisioned future: a chocolate empire that would contribute to the resolution of the ills of society, bringing pleasure to all whilst at the same time generating a viable value proposition for himself, his family and his employees.

The firm's *mission* defines the values, purpose, direction and the fundamental attributes of the business's proposed market position, its renewable activities and resource requirements and its constraints. It also reflects the different perspectives that the majority of stakeholders and shareholders will have towards the business as those that contribute to an understanding of its purpose. John Cadbury's mission was to exercise an altruistic commitment to prosperity, wealth creation and the founding of an environment of good health and welfare for all.

Strategy is the basis upon which individual motivation is captured, anticipated outcomes articulated, aspirations expressed and a desired future identified. An articulation of *long-term strategy* is provided by the *strategic imperatives* that must be realised if the firm is to succeed in realising its vision; they also combine to form the makeup and structure of the *strategic architecture*, as illustrated in Figure 1.1. Examples of strategic imperatives of relevance to Cadbury during the period discussed in this chapter could be to:

•   build a competency in the manufacture of cocoa;

•   ensure employees have access to a healthy working environment;

- make products that only contain healthy ingredients;

- target those customers who are the most vulnerable.

Strategic architecture

The terminology applied to a strategic architecture was first coined by Hamel and Prahalad (1994), who defined it as 'a road map of the future that identifies which core competencies to build'. I have broadened their definition of the phrase to depict a strategic architecture as a formal and substantial structure of strategy made up of the following elements:

- **Stakeholder outcomes** – These are an articulation of the desired outcomes from strategy that may be financial or non-financial in nature, quantitative or qualitative in content, but predominantly long-term (10 years plus) in focus. In more recent times, the need to address social responsibility issues have become just as important as outcomes addressing economically based objectives.

  - *Cadbury Stakeholder Outcomes* – The Cadbury family and their Quaker colleagues each held similar views regarding social responsibility in business, each set financial and social objectives as outcomes from their commercial activities at very early stages of their development. Financial viability was important to John Cadbury, it was seen as an enabler of the greater social objectives such as employee welfare that he, his father and later his sons would hold dear.

- **Renewable market position** – Porter (1985) identifies a unique market position as the basis of a sustainable competitive advantage. A market-oriented approach to strategy, as we observed above, is referred to as an outside-in strategy. This stands in contrast to the resource-based perspective of strategy, which we refer to as an inside-out strategy. In view of the dynamics that result from an increasingly rapid change in the external environment that we are experiencing today (as exemplified by increasing changes in customer expectations and behaviours) I refer to a market positioning strategy as one offering a *renewable* competitive advantage. This is an enhancement to Porter's definition of a sustainable competitive advantage and a more recent perspective proposed by McGrath (2013) as that of a transient competitive advantage.

-   *Renewable market position at Cadbury* – Cadbury suffered badly in its attempts to attain even a *sustainable* competitive advantage from its market positioning in its early years although it can be seen to have pursued a *renewable* competitive advantage throughout its life; with mixed results. Quality was its primary defining advantage early on, and for the first part of its history, product purity served as its primary point of differentiation in the marketplace. As a result of the inherent cost of the product's purity though, Cadbury found it very hard to compete on price; it was in fact a decidedly competitive disadvantage. A sustainable competitive advantage would finally arrive in the form of its unique taste and high quality dairy milk chocolate product; regrettably long after John Cadbury had died.

-   **Differentiating activities** – These are the market-oriented activities a firm will conduct in order to differentiate itself from its competitors in the marketplace. Differentiating activities are also the *doing* component of a renewable market position, they complement the way a firms resources are *leveraged* into those differentiated/renewable market positions; the construct of an outside in strategy. In highly competitive markets, differentiating activities are known to provide a first mover advantage, and if easily copied, the basis of a defensible market position to be harvested before competitors can catch up. In this context in particular, knowledge obtained from an organisational learning capability will be a primary contributor to a firm's capacity to stay ahead of competitors (Rademakers, 2014). Arguably, an organisational learning capability is critical to a firm seeking to maintain a renewable competitive advantage.

    -   *Differentiating activities at Cadbury* – Trust, business integrity and reliability were key differentiators for Cadbury in the initial period of its life – to the extent that in the late 1800s Cadbury was appointed as an official supplier to Her Majesty the Queen of England. However, ultimately these differentiating activities will lose their value as a competitive advantage, since competitors will be able to eventually copy them, or simply catch up. We will discuss later an example of such an advantage at Cadbury. It occurs in the early 1960s, when the Cadbury value proposition was considerably eroded as a result of the entry of supermarkets into the grocery industry. Following this event, supermarkets literally obliterated Cadbury's traditional customer base of greengrocers and corner stores and caused it to rethink ways to rebuild its competitive advantage that had previously been secured through its offer of high service, low cost pricing (as a result of considerable economies of scale in its supply chain) and strong relationships with the corner store owners and greengrocers who were traditional purveyors of its products.

- **Strategic intent** – This is another term used by Hamel and Prahalad (1994), it can be loosely defined as 'a readily understood and expressed articulation of the direction that the leaders of a business will take their company in the future'. I have adapted their interpretation of the concept to propose it as a description of the driving force for renewal which in general is an articulation of the purpose of the strategy; it is also a basis for transformation, innovation and growth that the strategy and associated strategic plan are seeking to describe.

  - *Strategic intent at Cadbury* – Cadbury's initial strategic intent evolved as a natural outcome from its vision and mission, and could be identified, especially in its early years, as 'to provide a wholesome beverage as a viable replacement for alcohol'.

- **Transforming activities** – These are the *doing* components of a resource based strategy. They are the physical activities that contribute to the continual renewal of the resource base (and associated competencies of the firm), as well as the transformation/ continual improvement of the transforming activities themselves; the construct of an inside out strategy. In differentiating between organisational resources and transformational activities, I apply the concept of dynamic capabilities (Ambrosini and Bowman, 2009) which is a concept not widely recognised by practitioners as it is still a relatively new topic of research. In an organisational learning context, knowledge dissemination can be seen to be an example of a transforming activity as a continuous improvement program. Both transformational and differentiating activities represent things an organisation can *do* to differentiate itself, compared to market positioning and resources as something an organisation needs to *have* (examples of each are market share, unique manufacturing skills) if it is to compete.

– *Transforming activities at Cadbury* – An example of the transforming activities that were vital to the success of Cadbury, especially during the period discussed in this chapter, is the relentless pursuit of perfection in the refinement of its core competency that would eventually result in a prowess in the production of chocolate, to the extent that Cadbury became one of the world's highest-quality mass producers of milk chocolate products.

• **Organisational resources** – Underpinning the entire structure of strategy and serving as the basis of the strategic architecture are the organisational resources that are both the tangible and intangible attributes and assets of the business. Organisational resources are either built, maintained or acquired over time, and are essential components of a firm's level of competitiveness. In this sense they actually contribute to a source of competitive advantage; they are most effective when they are at a level where they are incapable of being copied by competitors. In contrast to the outside-in marketing-oriented strategy described above, a resource-based strategy is said to have an inside-out orientation. In addition to the usual resources of plant, equipment and buildings, resources required to support strategy were identified by Hamel and Prahalad (1994) as including the *core competencies* of the firm; Amit and Schoemaker (1993) refer to these more broadly as the firm's *strategic assets*.

– *Organisational resources at Cadbury* – Once Cadbury became a full manufacturer of chocolate products, its organisational resources would become its manufacturing prowess and physical assets as well as its strong brand and a highly dextrous workforce that was wholeheartedly committed and dedicated to the success of the business. Although difficult to find in the earlier part of its history, Cadbury's defining competitive advantage would be the recipe that it finally developed to produce a defining taste in chocolate. Cadbury turned this advantage into a marketing phenomenon also; that was the 'glass and a half of full cream dairy milk in every 200g of chocolate'.

As we will observe in more detail in Chapter 2, the strategic architecture is in itself a micro system and is illustrative of the synthesis within which the dual perspectives of outside-in (market positioning-focused strategy) and inside-out (resource/core competency-focused strategy) strategic postures are connected and interact. Toyota is an example of a corporation that operates an essentially inside-out strategy which is captured in a strategic intent and complemented by the formality of transforming activities that are embedded within its management doctrine that is referred to as the Toyota Way.

Toyota is also an example of an organisation that has usefully expressed a sentiment that supports the longevity and existence of structure to long term strategy (consistent with the design of the Strategic Architecture) supported by a short term strategic plan. Replacing the word strategy with more contemporary terminology of the day ('policy', refer to Appendix 1), Toyota rose to the position of world leader in the automotive industry through consistent adherence to its long-term policy, which as I observed previously has remained unchanged for around 50 years.

Toyota's success in global markets can be attributed to a suite of strategic imperatives that are quite simple; to quote from its official history (as published on its website):

> Toyota resolved to further strengthen the full-participation TQC [Total Quality Control] promotion system and to ensure employee awareness and compliance by collating and clarifying the company management policies in writing. The Toyota Corporate Policy was released in January 1963 and included a basic policy, a long-term policy, and an annual policy. The basic policy expressed the company's fundamental view toward management, and was comprised of the following three items:
>
> 1. To develop Toyota into a world leader by gathering resources from within and outside the company.
> 2. To develop Toyota's reputation as a quality leader through an uncompromising focus on 'Good Thinking, Good Products'.
> 3. To contribute to the development of Japan's economy by achieving a mass production system and low prices.[2]

ELEMENT 2: STRATEGIC PLANNING: STRATEGY EVALUATION, SHAPING AND REVIEWING

The strategic architecture is concerned with long term strategy at a level of market positioning and competition in an *industry*, addressing for example the question 'Which business should we participate in?'

---

2   See www.toyota-global.com/company/history_of_toyota/75years/text/entering_the_automotive_
business/chapter1/section1/item6.html (accessed 6 May 2014).

The *strategic plan* is the outcome from the next component of the fully integrated Strategic Management Framework (Figure 1.1) *strategic planning*. The strategic plan is an independent but integral element of the overall *system* that aligns the firm's long-term strategy with the short term plan's method of implementation (or ideally ongoing renewal). At the level of a plan, the strategically oriented marketing question is more concerned with markets and customers. It assumes the questions of which business in which industry are already resolved.

It is important to understand the difference between a strategy and the strategic plan. In the absence of a full appreciation of a long-term vision and associated articulation of strategy, a reliance on the implementation of a strategic plan alone cuts a long-term perspective of strategy short and creates a disjointed approach to the firm's growth. Apple Inc., for example, lost considerable market share in the mid-1980s. Assuming Apple, like most other companies at that time, was sticking to the normal five-year planning regime we have discussed here, we can appreciate that it would have been a mistake to continue its focus on its commitment to an increasingly outdated product which was Apples version of the personal computer, or PC. Had the founder of Apple, Steve Jobs, not been brought back to lead the company, the more typical response to a decline in market share would no doubt have been enacted: to develop another five-year strategic plan which, in view of the rapid rate of change in the PC market, would again become obsolete well before its implementation could have been successfully completed. The industry was simply moving too fast for Apple and its strategic plan to keep pace. Faced with the reality of what *was* happening instead of a blind belief in what *should* have been happening, Apple's strategic direction seemingly lurched from one strategic plan to another with little real appreciation of what it should have been doing – until the return of Steve Jobs, that is. Building on a re-energised vision of the future for Apple, Job's disregarded the direction of his predecessor's strategic plan. Jobs sought instead to re-focus a long term strategy on the renewal of the business through the application of new forms of technology and new forms of technology delivery (the iPod and later iTunes, for example). I suggest that in general, a short-term perspective of strategy that arises from a strategic plan's horizon alone is bound to result in a *reactive* response to change. On the other hand, a short-term perspective that is continually evaluated within a context of a long-term vision and strategy will in most cases enable a more *proactive* response to change. The delightful thing about the Apple story overall of course is that it is a prime example of an organisation benefitting from the *design* of a deliberate, intended change.

The Apple example points to the value of the notions of *strategy evaluation shaping* (see Chapter 2) and *strategy evaluation reviewing* (see Chapter 3 and 7) as the two components of the strategic planning element I refer to above.

Strategy evaluation shaping

Strategy evaluation shaping is concerned with the way that strategy is formed; within the context of the previously described issues of uncertainty, ambiguity and complexity that are a natural component of strategy formation. As a discipline, strategy is firmly focused on the future, but because the future is unknown, many assumptions, guesstimates and other fundamentals of strategic decision making are applied to provide a depiction of an aspirational future which then becomes the primary content of a strategy or strategic plan.

Strategy evaluation reviewing

Strategy evaluation *reviewing* is made up of two components. The first focuses on the more difficult aspect of outcomes that are the result of those guesstimates and assumptions that are a necessary component of aforementioned strategy evaluation *shaping*. Although it happens rarely in practice, this content must be monitored for re-evaluation on an ongoing basis. Emerging trends must be assessed, warning signs noticed, the unimaginable imagined and the unthinkable thought through if the short-term strategic plan is not to become too irrelevant too soon. To take the necessity to be constantly aware of the unplanned and unexpected to an extreme, it is hard to imagine that any business leader would plan to enter bankruptcy for example, yet according to the UK government's Insolvency Service there were a total of 15,279 bankruptcies recorded in the UK over the twelve-month period ending September 2013. Content contained in this aspect of strategy evaluation is treated as an issue of strategic governance and is addressed further in Chapter 7.

The second component of strategy evaluation reviewing focuses on the way that strategy implementation is being managed, in particular, the efficiency and effectiveness of the strategic plans implementation (hence the emergence of the program of continual strategy renewal, discussed in the next element of the Strategic Management Framework below). It can also legitimately focus on an evaluation of the outcome from the strategy per se – that is, an assessment of whether the desired outcomes were actually achieved (for example, 'increased market share', or 'introduced a new manufacturing system').

ELEMENT 3: A PROGRAMME OF CONTINUAL STRATEGY RENEWAL

Although the Strategic Management Framework is an integrated system overall, this programme represents a refocusing of the managerial discipline; from that of the professional strategy practitioner, whose role is characterised by practically oriented, but otherwise unstructured, free-flowing creative thought and the preparation of the firm for a wealth creating future. This contrasts with the role of the operational performance practitioner who is more concerned with understanding why things happened in the past as well as the here and now, in the form of immediate responses to performance reports describing short term outcomes and results. In many organisations, the responsibility for operational performance falls within the domain of the chief financial officer (CFO). Increasingly though, it is the CFO who is looking for, and accepting the mantle of, the development of content contributing to an informed strategic management capability that encompasses both elements of strategy development and implementation.

The programme of continual strategy renewal ensures the maintenance of the ongoing relevance of the strategy and strategic plan and provides a home for the application of the more familiar strategy tools and templates that are static in nature and workshop-oriented in practice. I propose that the strategic plan is a fundamental component of the programme of continual strategy renewal. This purpose provides a stark contrast to the often misinterpreted purpose of a strategic plan; that of the sole vehicle of strategy implementation or worse, a list of 'top' priorities, some of which may not be strategic in nature at all.

A discussion introducing the content of the programme of continual strategy renewal follows. Aspects of each topic are introduced here and explored further in Chapters 3 and 5 and illustrated in Figure 3.1 and Figure 5.1.

Strategy blueprint

The strategy blueprint adopts the same essential structure as a strategic architecture; it includes the elements of inside-out (resource/competence-oriented strategy) and outside-in (market-focused problem solving strategy) strategy in a linked structure, but is grounded in and derived from the specific content (specifically, strategic objectives) contained within the formal strategic plan. The strategic objectives that are contained in the strategic plan and articulated in the strategy blueprint provide the basis for the focus of the strategic plan's and by definition the strategy blueprint's *implementation*.

Each project identified as a part of implementation is subject to a strategy evaluation reviewing (above) criterion that is a normal component of programme and project management. These include the identification and quantification of relevant performance measures, time frames for results, assignment of responsibilities, and the identification of resources required to deliver the desired outcomes. The purpose of the *strategy blueprint* is not to provide a template for strategy, but rather to provide a structure within which the short-term strategic plan that has been developed from the long-term strategy can be validated, aligned and acted upon as critical elements of implementation.

As illustrated in Figure 1.1, the strategy blueprint provides content for the *strategic change agenda*, each is overseen by the *strategy evaluation reviewing and monitoring mechanism* (the primary contributor to the physical management of strategy renewal) and a foundation for the communication of strategy. It provides visibility to strategy content overall and is a primary focus for *stakeholder engagement*.

I use the term 'strategy blueprint' because it evokes a more action-oriented, proactive and exciting representation of what *could be* than most other terminology. A strategy blueprint creates a focus on and aura about the continuity of strategy as well as a flirtation with uncertainty that is a natural but often uncomfortable aspect of *future*-oriented (blue ocean?) decision making. The opposite view is a prescriptive, typecast outcome from a *static* three- to five-year strategic plan.

Toyota developed its own system of strategic planning which it refers to as Hoshin Kanri. This is a formal process of annual planning and renewal conducted within the highly structured management philosophy that we referred to previously as the 'Toyota Way'. This discipline is in turn defined by Toyota as the set of principles and behaviours that contribute to the philosophies that make up Toyota Motor Corporation's culture. It includes the principles of 'Continuous Improvement' and 'Respect for People'. The full suite of managerial philosophies describes the principles and behaviours that are grounded in Toyota's culture and underlie its entire approach to management, problem solving and decision making over time. These methodologies are in turn used to cascade strategic goals and objectives and thereby inform decision making in a similar format as those that I have referred to as the strategy blueprint, and associated strategic change agenda.

Strategic change agenda

Designed as a dynamic, continual management control mechanism, the term *strategic change agenda* is used in two ways. The first is similar to the strategic intent described above, a short sharp description of the underlying purpose of the strategic plan as articulated within the construct of the strategy blueprint. Designed in the form of a message a generic example could be 'enabling international expansion'. A more specific example drawn from the health industry where a hospital may express a strategic change agenda of service transformation as: 'managing wellness not sickness'. This form of strategic change agenda sits in the middle of the strategy blueprint as a reminder of the strategic plans purpose.

The second application of a *strategic change agenda* is an extension of the first, in the form of a process; the formalisation of the way in which the content contained within the strategy blueprint will literally be implemented. It is a priority-focused and structured approach to programme and project management.

Strategy evaluation reviewing and monitoring mechanism

The *strategy evaluation reviewing and monitoring mechanism* is the physical instrument that is used to monitor the implementation of the projects that are identified in the strategic planning process and articulated in the strategic plan itself – through the strategy blueprint and then into the process I referred to above as the *strategic change agenda*. A second application is the monitoring and articulation of any changes in the assumptions, estimates and guesstimates that were included in the makeup of the strategy and the strategic plan's background and content (through the activity of *strategy renewal monitoring*). A third application is an evaluation of the impact that either may have on the strategy implementation programme that may already be under way. In this capacity, it can also be used to deal with any aspects of strategic governance as and when such issues arise (see Chapter 7).

Common examples of appropriate performance measures and target outcomes for those implementation projects include: 'market share increase – a target performance criteria being 2 per cent increase every year' or 'a reduction in costs of 10 per cent by the end of the year'. In the case of project and programmes that have already started, the *strategy evaluation reviewing and monitoring mechanism* is relied upon to ensure they remain relevant. If they are, they will continue until completion. Alternatively, and much more dramatically, those projects deemed no longer relevant may be stopped/redirected if that action is thought to be more appropriate.

This latter outcome has been known to occur when assumptions that were made to set the initial strategic plan turn out to be no longer relevant. One example of this is a multi-billion-dollar water purification plant that was being built on the southern coast of Victoria, Australia. Funded by the State Government and approved on the assumption that the 10-year drought would continue for some time to come, an incoming government mothballed it as soon as it came into office as, coincidentally, the drought had broken.

ELEMENT 4: ALIGNMENT

Discussed further in Chapter 6, alignment can also be included as an element of the strategy evaluation reviewing and monitoring mechanism, through the evaluation of measures of *fit*, which at the highest level addresses alignment between the operations of the firm and the external environment. Measures of fit are also used as an assurance that the strategic imperatives and short-term goals and objectives are aligned across the organisation. When aligned with organisational learning capabilities in particular, the effectiveness of both individuals and teams is affected by the firm's position within the cycle of organisational transformation and renewal. Details of the cycle of organisational transformation and renewal will be discussed further in Chapter 3 (Figure 3.2).

Stakeholder engagement

Stakeholder engagement is an all-inclusive element of the strategic change agenda and Strategic Management Framework in general. Although it is represented as the smallest component of the framework shown in Figure 1.1, it is the largest factor in the success of its operation. The concept of *strategy practice* reflects the reality that success is highly dependent on people and what they do, individually, in teams and in collaboration with other stakeholders and parties (each of these issues will be discussed in more depth in Chapter 4). Stakeholder engagement is therefore relevant to all factors of strategic management.

Without adequate engagement of the right people, a framework would just be a framework and strategy would not be realised. Without an adequate learning programme, it is difficult to expect stakeholders to know how to respond to current issues on the one hand (business as usual) and futures thinking on the other (strategically). High-level stakeholder engagement priorities are established as an integral component of strategic management. Their content is also included in the strategy evaluation reviewing and monitoring mechanism referred to previously.

Application of the Fully Integrated Strategic Management Framework: An Assessment of the Value of Strategy

The fully integrated Strategic Management Framework provides a structure for strategy; it operates as a system. Accordingly, it provides insights into the ways different strategy tools and techniques can work together and an appreciation of how to navigate the often confusing and difficult passages that make up a strategy footprint.

In assessing the value of strategy as a management tool, it is difficult to be critical of any individual's capabilities or apparent lack of know-how and even interest in strategy. As I alluded to previously, in the grand order of things, strategy is a relatively new discipline, and as a result is ill structured, and as a profession, in its infancy. Although there are many, many parts, no one has yet developed an appropriate structure and associated suite of guidelines that can claim to be a comprehensive representation of strategy; hence my proposal in this book to deploy the construct I refer to as the fully integrated Strategic Management Framework. To illustrate the depth of the lack of value obtained from strategy that is representative of the current and apparent over-reliance on strategic planning as a strategy system, SMI research found that although an impressive '83 per cent of participants agree that strategy in their organisation is a dynamic system that is constantly revised by the senior leaders', only '21 per cent thought strategy and strategic thinking is one of their main strengths'.

The terminology of strategy and strategic planning was not well recognised in the regular management lexicon until the launch of a few strategy focused books as recently as the mid-1960s. Prior to this, and as illustrated in Appendix 1, long-range planning had been the future-oriented leader's primary tool of choice. Prior to the development of the notion of futures thinking, strategy was considered to be more a matter of *policy*. Long-range planning was even more structured than strategic planning is today, and was certainly more quantitative in format. Its predecessor was a mathematical modelling mechanism known as linear programming. This specific tool was deployed to forecast estimates of quantitative values of linear functions (for example, sales volumes, market share, volume growth) which were extrapolated into the future, subject to given constraints (for example, advertising expenditure, number of sales representatives and the launch of new products). To develop a long range plan forecasts were used to rather optimistically (and often overly so) predict a view of what *will be* in the future. This idea is, of course, nonsense.

Since the concept of strategy has become accepted as a valuable management tool, many significant developments in its theory and practice have emerged. Some of the more commercial applications for strategy tools and techniques have afforded their creators guru status in the popular press – but isn't that the problem? A lack of agreement about which guru is right, or more broadly, a common acceptance of one true meaning of strategy over another has resulted in its use and abuse in application in many forms and formats; characterised by a predominance of ad hoc solutions over professional practice. Some of these solutions are much more complex than others and are all too often expressed in a way that is hard to understand. Overall, the enormity of the variety of definitions results in confusion and ineffectiveness.

Consequences of an Over-reliance on Planning as the Only Tool for Strategy

The consequences of an over-reliance on planning as the only tool for strategy can be devastating. Consider the fortunes of retailers as a result of the occurrence of the 2008 Great Recession. For example, David Jones, an Australian department store chain, suffered a considerable blow to its credibility through its overly strict adherence to a strategic planning regime. In 2008 its senior management team had established what its board had thought was a rigorous four-year strategic plan. Confident in its content at that time, the board authorised the release of the plan to investors and analysts. With an expectation that it would remain relevant until late 2012, the validity of key elements (the financial services component in particular) appeared to be increasingly doubtful some twelve months before the full plan was set to expire. By March 2012 the board was forced to issue a press release (amid rumours that the CEO was being asked to stand down) announcing that a request to suspend trading in its shares had been made to the Australian Stock Exchange. This, it observed, was a potential outcome attributed in large part to the fact that the economic downturn was having a particularly negative impact on financial performance, but also a recognition of the need for the board to 'consider the company's strategic plan'.

As with many retailers at that time, David Jones was seemingly unprepared for the more broad-based but very significant changes that had, and would continue to, adversely impact its operating environment. David Jones faced a number of issues in addition to the onset of the Great Recession. The first was the continual decline in the attractiveness of department stores, whose value proposition was now being seriously ignored by twenty-first-century consumers. The second was the Great Recession's impact on price competitiveness (a factor also influenced by another externality, the rapid increase in online shopping). The third was an issue associated with the Great Recession in the form of the onset of a 'buyers strike' as credit-driven impulse buying gave way to a return to a traditional value of saving instead of spending.

David Jones's prevailing 2008 strategic plan had literally become irrelevant; a new one was called for and was hastily rolled out before any further strategic decisions or trading in its shares could be made. However, the dilemma for the company was not just the reliance on an outdated plan per se, but its sole reliance on a single management tool whose content had clearly become less relevant in the fast-moving, significantly complex and global environment of modern retailing which saw a transformation in its supply chain that included a rapid swing to online shopping rather than in-store buying.

It doesn't stop there, though. In addition to the use of an outdated mode of managing for the future, company leaders in general continue to rely on outdated and sometimes underwhelming strategy tools and techniques that are still broadly used in businesses around the world today. This is a result of an over-reliance on an assumption that they will provide sufficient insight, information and knowledge for the development of the strategic plan itself.

Loss of Relevance, Loss of Value

Relevance is defined by Hjørland and Christensen (2002) as 'something that serves as a tool; applied as a contribution to the realisation of a goal'. As we saw with David Jones in particular, its ultimate strategic goals and objectives were expressed convincingly in its plan, along with a well-articulated and hoped-for outcome. The company's real future, though, was unfolding independently of any of the senior managers' expectations (plans). The external environment was literally being steered in a different direction to that which the company leaders thought could possibly be the case. Purely from an observer's perspective, what appears to have happened is typical of the problems that arise from an over-reliance on a static planning methodology alone:

- a lack of appreciation of an aspirational outcome from strategy (vision);

- a lack of articulation of company purpose, complicated by a lack of appreciation of what the problem was that the company set out to resolve (and an explanation of its associated value proposition, defined as being the reason why customers buy from one company over another);

- an imprecise explanation of how the firm expected to compete and renew in the long term (its strategy);

- a failure to address the prevailing wicked problems arising from the emergence of online retailing and the impact of the Great Recession and other contemporary strategic issues;

- an over-reliance on a single view of the future that can be attributed to an over-reliance on process (form-filling) and over-strategising (responding, renewing and monitoring).

Ultimately, David Jones had effectively entered into a strategic drift (Johnson et al., 2011) – a situation that arises when a company responds far too slowly to changes in the external environment and continues (for too long) to pursue the strategy that once served it very well. This is despite the presence of obvious signs that the company is becoming increasingly out of touch with external trends (lack of alignment). This is an unfortunate phenomenon that we will explore further in Chapter 6.

The fundamental premise of our discussion in this book is the resolution of deficiencies in strategy that are driven in large part by an over-reliance on the sole use of strategic planning, its loss of relevance and, in fact, an over-reliance on strategy systems and process all together. A fully integrated Strategic Management Framework is proposed as a tool that complements an essential appreciation of the cognitive elements of strategy (stakeholder engagement). That includes the thoughtful analysis of strategy content, the inclusion of individual and group contributions to strategic thinking, and a consciousness of continual change in the external environment as well as internal capabilities. In relation to grounded strategy theory, the inclusion of cognition can be described as a breaking down of formalised processes that are proposed as *deliberate* corporate planning rather than emerging strategy – a system of strategic thinking that, as we saw previously, is strategy that literally evolves over time.

Survey Data in the Use and Application of Strategy Tools and Techniques Today

Evidence of the haphazard use of strategic planning and associated tools abounds. In addition to research conducted by the SMI, other research organisations have also contributed to an appreciation of what happens in practice. The physical use of strategic planning as a primary management tool, for example, has been found by Jarzabkowski et al. (2009) to be used by up to 85 per cent of organisations globally; however, this and other similar tools are generally recognised as being very high-level in analysis, but at the same time inconsistent in the way they are used. In a broader sense, we continue to experience a prevalence in the use of independent strategy tools across the board, each attributable to any number of strategy gurus who each trumpet their proclaimed method to be *the* best way, or in some instances *the* theory of strategy. Shapiro (1989), for example, includes in the title of a published paper that his approach to game theory is *the* theory of strategy. In reality, there is always more than one best way to *do* strategy.

In order to clarify the place and position of strategy today – that is, why strategic planning is so dominant, how other components of strategy were formed, and basically, why strategy is what it is – Appendix 1 offers a brief review of the history of strategy theory.

Is Strategy Worthwhile?

Some businesses have no use for advanced strategy practices and methodologies. If you are lucky enough to run a business that operates in an environment of certainty and high predictability, the use of forecasts (as proposed by proponents of traditional 'planning' regimes) can be made with a high degree of confidence and a focus on plans legitimised accordingly. The obvious challenge, though, is the scarcity of such an environment. Feelings of instability, ambiguity and uncertainty have prevailed in economies and in business for ever. What is different today is the level of complexity and the extent of uncertainty that is increasing over time, compared to the availability, quality and depth of strategy research as well as operational 'business intelligence' made available through advanced, technologically enabled business systems. A lot of this research represents an illumination and thereby an extension of what is known. Much of the research agenda's content is new, and sometimes groundbreaking. In an ideal world competent practitioners would cooperate much more deeply with researchers (and the other way around of course, that is researchers cooperating with practitioners) to optimise the power offered by this research, to align with the researchers and to apply their findings in practice, both taking up an opportunity to capture the value offered by the potency of solid and structured strategic thinking.

However, there are many unseen consequences for business entities that don't have a depth of understanding of strategy. In one of the few companies with which I have worked that didn't have a strategy or strategic plan, its absence was noticeable. As a business whose fundamental service was the facilitation of gambling, the company attracted significant disapproval from some quarters of society. Apart from a lack of direction, an absence of strategy meant that that company found it difficult to engage the community in the way it was responsibly managing the social implications of its business model. The employees were similarly disempowered, which meant they could not easily defend their employer when called upon to do so, even in social environments.

Just as importantly, when going about their everyday work, I observed a lack of strategy could seriously impair the firm's decision making capability. If the firm couldn't articulate what its strategic imperatives were and in which direction the business was going, how could the managers and employees make informed decisions about values, investments, behaviours and areas where the business could improve their strategic position or even operating performance in any serious way?

In the next few chapters we will explore a more comprehensive form of the fully integrated Strategic Management Framework in order to extend its understanding and appreciation by consultants, managers and leaders undertaking strategising activities and as a means to help leaders improve their efficiency and effectiveness in decision making. The content of the fully integrated Strategic Management Framework provides relief for a substantial component of process-focused and people issues associated with the topic of this book: The Seven Inconvenient Truths of Business Strategy.

Chapter 2

Relevance Regained; Reinventing Strategic Planning: A Programme of Continual Strategy Renewal

> **INCONVENIENT TRUTH NO. 2: STRATEGY IS AN UNDEFINED AND DYNAMIC SYSTEM RATHER THAN A CLOSED-LOOP PROCESS.**
>
> Unlike the rigidity of accounting and law, strategy is an open-loop system that flourishes within a world of contradiction and conflict – a taunt of the unknown, and a challenge of what could be.

A key benefit of a common appreciation of a business's strategy is that its content contributes to the reinforcement of a sense of organisational purpose, individual aspirations and thereby the basis for strong leadership. Conventional wisdom supposes that the *tangible* outcome from strategising, the method deployed to develop good strategy, is a formal strategic plan. As suggested in Chapter 1, though, I seriously challenge the wisdom of that assumption. A strategic plan does make a useful contribution to decision making; however, I suggest that a greater contribution would be its application as a basis for decisions made in a context of *continual strategy renewal* and as an outcome from that, a foundation for organisational renewal and sometimes reinvention. Organisational renewal is essential to the survival of modern-day business, and appears to me to be one of the most widely ignored strategic imperatives of all.

There are numerous examples of organisations that have failed to renew, literally continuing to do the same thing in the same way until eventually there is just no more demand for their products or services. One is Finland-based Nokia, which procrastinated on the development of its version of a smartphone, to the extent that the company, once estimated to be valued at almost USD $300 billion, saw its market value fall 77 percent to $25.6 billion since the introduction of the Apple iPhone in 2007 (Kharif et al, 2011). In Australia, Telstra's Yellow and White Pages Directory business (Sensis) literally died a gradual death as demand for advertising in its printed telephone books diminished over a number of years. The impact was similar to Nokia, in 2005 Sensis was estimated to be valued at close to AUD $12bn. When it was sold in 2014 its value had reduced to a mere AUD $649m.

The challenge we face as strategy practitioners is to overcome the danger that the strategising system that we are responsible for fails to deliver much more than the staid content that is all too often seen in static strategic plans. In this chapter I return to the construct of a fully integrated Strategic Management Framework (see Figure 1.1) as a mechanism that facilitates and enables renewal and a considerably more meaningful way of structuring strategy in a format that represents the reinvention of the traditional notion of strategic planning itself. This is one of the many benefits available from the application of the Strategic Management Framework, it will also provide us with:

- a means to express the aspirations of leaders and motivational elements of an envisioned future and the way in which those *soft* desires will be transformed into *hard* results over time;

- insight into the *structure* of strategy (identifying gaps and possible exclusions in content as well as provoking innovative inclusions), and as a result a construct facilitating implementation and the continual renewal of strategy; the means by which strategic alignment can be achieved;

- a basis for the development of a common language (*our* strategy), and thereby the means to engage colleagues in structured and strategically aligned dialogue;

- a way to facilitate the application of specific learning regimes in our own organisation and, by definition, the means to capture and expand knowledge which as an outcome;

  - provides a basis for organisational renewal and quite possibly reinvention, and;
  - contributes to personal learning through its application to our own, company specific formal education programme(s).

It is through the Strategic Management Framework, therefore, that we have addressed the as yet unstructured approach to strategising which also provides a foundation for the development, implementation and communication of strategy in a professional manner, and in a format that can be recognised as *generally accepted strategising principles* (GASP).

The Second Inconvenient Truth of Strategy

In proposing The Second Inconvenient Truth of Strategy, I suggest that you, the strategy practitioner, explore the application of the fully integrated Strategic Management Framework as a succinct construct and method of addressing the conundrum that is identified in this chapter:

> *Strategy is an undefined and dynamic system rather than a closed-loop process. Unlike the rigidity of accounting and law, strategy is an open-loop system that flourishes within a world of contradiction and conflict – a taunt of the unknown, and a challenge of what could be. The consequence of this inconvenient truth is that when strategy is viewed only as a part of a process or independent methodology, the value realised from the quantum of strategy tools becomes suboptimal and their application overly reliant on simplistic, 'flavour of the month' methods. This leads to the development of right answers, but to the wrong problems.*

The Strategic Management Framework captures the dynamics of an open open-loop system and is a basis upon which continual strategy renewal can be enacted. In this chapter I focus on the first element of the Strategic Management Framework as a tool that in its entirety captures the many components of strategy and corrals them into a structured system. That system, and therefore this chapter, commences with an explanation of the *vision* and *mission* and the operations of a *strategic architecture* in detail, and its alignment with the next element of the framework, *strategy evaluation*.

In Chapter 3 we expand on the elements of strategy evaluation, especially that of *shaping*; the search for information contributing to the strategic plan, strategic decision making, and subsequently the primary target for the activity of strategy evaluation *reviewing*. This follows in Chapter 5 with a review of the next element of the Strategic Management Framework; concerned specifically with a *program of continual strategy renewal*. In Chapter 6 we address the final element of the framework, strategic alignment.

We commence this chapter with an update on Cadbury, and a continuation of a story where an empathetic management style grounded in the Cadbury family's values as Quakers is evident, commercial aspirations and ambitions are high, but systematised and informed strategic conversations decidedly sparse. In Chapter 1 we observed that when John Cadbury opened his shop in the Northern England city of Birmingham in 1824, he did not have a formal business strategy or strategic plan, nor did he have access to any form of strategy tools and techniques. Now this absence of strategising capability has carried over to the late nineteenth century, which is the setting of the Cadbury story in this chapter.

Significant changes have taken place in the city of Birmingham where Cadbury is based. The world in general is now more crowded, competitive and busy than in the early years. Fortunately it is still not overly complex or unpredictable – at least from our perspective of complexity today.

From Cadbury Chocolate to Cadbury Brothers of Birmingham: A Time of Passing, a Time of Questionable Inheritance

Although Cadbury founder John Cadbury had great faith in the concept of the chocolate drink known as cocoa as a saleable product, there was no science from which complexity could emerge to deliver the dream of the rich and creamy dairy milk chocolate product that it was to become. John Cadbury was effectively ignorant of the full potential of the cacao nib as the key ingredient in chocolate and the way in which it would be produced on mass, never mind its level of acceptance in the marketplace. Acting primarily on intuition (and a lot of hope), John Cadbury's aspirations, as with most entrepreneurs then and now, were based purely on an inside-out (resource/competence-leveraging) philosophy which saw the family members toil for years to perfect the chocolate texture and taste (transforming activities) that consumers would eventually learn to savour.

John Cadbury's dedication to puritanical religious beliefs drove his vision and market orientation by default. Based on an entrenched values-based philosophy – and ultimately the marketing slogan 'absolutely pure, therefore the best' – the Cadbury family tradition was grounded in a competency that would serendipitously ensure that the brand carried a reputation of quality and trust for all time. Emerging in an era when less scrupulous competitors were known to be adding arsenic and red brick dust as fillers on top of flavour enhancers to hide the naturally sour taste of the butter fat found in the middle of the cacao seed, Cadbury was gifted an automatic competitive advantage based on multidimensional values of purity that would nonetheless remain as a point of differentiation for the life of the company.

By 1842, the business was doing reasonably well, to the extent that John Cadbury invited his brother to join him in the firm, and later his two sons. Now known as Cadbury Brothers, the business was experiencing modest success, selling 16 lines of drinking chocolate and cocoa in both cake and powder forms (Cadbury, 2010). A further boost to the potential prosperity of the business presented itself to Cadbury Brothers when in 1854 the firm was awarded a Royal Warrant of Appointment to Her Majesty the Queen. With it came permission to display the Royal Coat of Arms on Cadbury packaging. From a competitive perspective, however, the business environment was particularly harsh even in these early years. By the time Cadbury had opened its London sales office in 1853, for instance, one of Cadbury's biggest competitors, Fry's of Bristol, in the English West Country, had already built one of the largest chocolate factories in the world.

During the course of the 1850s Cadbury Brothers fell into serious decline, an outcome attributable in part to the severe economic conditions that were experienced in the UK in the 1840s. However, much of the misfortune can be attributed to John Cadbury's declining health, which became so bad that he chose to dissolve the partnership with his brother in 1861. This caused him to formally hand the business over to his sons Richard and George, both of whom had been working in the business for some time. Each had shared John Cadbury's vision for the business, and his values, they accepted their inheritance with enthusiasm. George's role in the new venture focused on manufacturing and purchasing whilst Richard focused on sales and policy. Both George and Richard remained committed to meeting the demands of their Quaker beliefs, even though it came with inbuilt despair and a crippling financial burden that would last until at least the mid-1860s.

Representing the extremely early years of the Cadbury story, the level of strategic thinking is again limited to an interpretation of intuition and assumptions about the more complex problems that the business faced. Given the circumstances of the era, the thoughts of the Cadbury family and other team members were restricted to the preordained mental models they held in their roles as managers and leaders of the business. Mental models are defined by Senge (1990) as 'deeply ingrained assumptions, generalisations, or even pictures or images that influence how we understand the world and how we take action'. Regrettably for the Cadbury brothers, their mental models of the world were limited to an environment of low technology, insufficient scientific know-how, and most importantly, an absence of an appreciation of the true potential of the modest but complex cacao nib. Hope, belief, shared vision, continual dialogue and above all perseverance were the required characteristics of the day.

Just as science started to deliver explanations for chemical reactions that made up the foundation of many manufactured products, so too did the second stage of the Industrial Revolution take hold. This period is thought to have commenced around the mid-1860s, a time when the integration of inventions that included electrification, mass production and the assembly/production line combined to allow low-cost manufacture – on a very large scale. An example is the Bessemer steel process. As a predecessor to open hearth furnace technology, Bessemer is considered to be one of the earliest methods of producing high-volume, low-cost industrial-quality steel from molten pig iron.

In the case of Cadbury, it wasn't until 1866 that George and Richard Cadbury would experience the beginnings of the Cadbury family dream: the realisation of wealth creation for all stakeholders and the low-cost production of a quality cocoa product that could act as a substitute for alcohol. Ironically, it came as a direct result of George's last-ditch effort to save the company from bankruptcy. George elected at that time to spend the last of his inheritance from his father on a 'big bet move' into automation. George had resolved that he would invest in a European machine (the Van Houghton press) to automate the grinding of cacao nibs. The press was known to run at a very fast pace and produce a product of far higher quality than the Cadbury brothers had previously been able to achieve.

However, John Cadbury's grandson, George Cadbury Junior, a trained chemist, wouldn't be successful in mixing milk with the bitter-tasting cacao butter fat to produce the sweetened milk chocolate product that we now know and enjoy today until 1904. The notion of a journey of discovery that was the driver of John Cadbury's, and later his son's, ambition was all about transforming activities with a concentration on resource and competency development, which in this case was focused on the core competencies of food (ingredient) management, cacao nib processing and chocolate production on a mass scale.

John Cadbury and his descendants were in effect driven by the increasing opportunities that became evident from growth in commercial activity in industry through the late 1800s and early 1900s, at which time the priority for businesspeople in general was focused mostly on inside-out activities, including product design, manufacture and distribution, rather than the more outside-in, market-oriented issues of marketing, market share and differentiation. In this period of the Industrial Revolution, growth was a certainty – you just had to make good products that could benefit from the economies of scale offered by mass production and get them to market in the most efficient way possible.

Relevance Regained: Reinventing Strategic Planning Within the Construct of a Fully Integrated Strategic Management Framework

From the foregoing scenario of Cadbury in the late 1800s, we can identify levels of complexity that would justify the application and use of a formal strategy. Although a few fundamentals representative of a long-term strategy at Cadbury are evident, there was one, overriding strategic imperative that continued to challenge the tenacity of the Cadbury brothers as entrepreneurs; whether or not they would ever be able to produce a viable chocolate product at all. Although John Cadbury was initially driven by his and his father's shared vision of the future of the mysterious cocoa nib, the realisation of that vision continued to evade him all his life. Would his sons suffer the same fate they wondered?

As we saw in Figure 1.1 the framework commences with an appreciation of a *vision* as well as a *mission*, each driven by *organisational purpose* and the definition of the *strategic imperatives* that provide the grounding for long-term strategy. These preliminary foundation elements contribute to the firm's strategic purpose and should not be treated too lightly. As we saw with Cadbury, they capture the imagination and aspirations of leaders and incorporate the external industry influences as well as their preferred approach to competing in national and international markets. They are also an expression of the internal essentials of management style and organisational culture. Just as designers need inspirational features as anchors for their designs, so does strategy need a focal *purpose* from which a strategic plan and programme of continual strategy renewal can evolve.

Not only do vision and mission provide the nucleus for the design of strategy, they also describe the long-term and future direction upon which a firm's leadership can be enacted. These articulations of desired futures also contribute to the resolution of strategic issues related to organisational purpose and the environment within which the firm operates. Mission statements are often the subject of derision as their contents are often vague, overly descriptive or used only as a public relations exercise for surfers of corporate websites. When used appropriately, however, they provide a sense of purpose and are used to clarify as much as inspire. I use the word 'clarify' as an open statement that is complimentary to the mission statement's other purpose, which is to articulate (briefly) a description of policy, which in turn provides the operating guidelines upon which strategic boundaries can be clarified and defined. Organisational *values* form an integral component of a mission statement, providing the basis for all management decision making and the backbone of the culture out of which the organisation's soul is born.

Vision is a form of futures thinking that is often misused and disregarded with throw-away comments about 'the vision thing'. Our discussion of the David Jones department store chain in Chapter 1 appropriately demonstrates the consequences of an absence of long-term strategic thinking which is ideally encapsulated in strategy and articulated through a description of a vision. The absence of a vision in particular was found to lead to short-term decision making and ultimately a calamity at the department store; David Jones. Senge (1990) is supportive of a *shared vision* as a basis upon which organisational learning can occur. Shared vision, according to Senge, is a 'force in people's hearts' that becomes 'a force of impressive power'. A shared vision and a notion of *personal mastery* (defined by Senge as 'the discipline of continually clarifying and deepening personal vision, of focusing energy, of developing patience, and of seeing reality objectively') combine to become the two key disciplines that provide inspiration to participants in a learning organisation. I explore the value of organisational learning and its contribution to strategy and organisational renewal as part of the people component of strategy practice throughout this book. Learning, Senge suggests (1990) may in fact be 'the only source of a sustainable competitive advantage' which as I have noted previously, can now be seen to be the premise of a *renewable* competitive advantage.

Another key attribute of a learning organisation is provided by Senge (1990); it is the discipline of *systems thinking*. Systems thinking was defined in Chapter 1 as being an integration of a combination of unknown, unseen phenomenon into a whole. Flood (1999) extends Senge's view of systems thinking to include the notion of *systemic evaluation*. Flood's application of two different aspects of evaluation allowed me to adapt his views for application to the construct of the strategic planning component of the Strategic Management Framework. In my exploration of this terminology so far I have referred to Flood's (1999) explanations of *systemic evaluation* in the context of *strategy evaluation shaping* and *strategy evaluation reviewing*. Our discussion here follows each form of evaluation within the context of an integrated and aligned strategising system. This, I believe, enforces the legitimacy of the application of the fully integrated Strategic Management Framework as a valid and integral component of strategy as practice. It is also the basis upon which reinvention of strategic planning can be effected. The topic of strategy evaluation is discussed later in this chapter in the context of the Strategic Management Framework and again in Chapters 3 and 7.

Strategic Architecture: Providing Structure to Long-term Strategy

The fully integrated Strategic Management Framework assists practitioners to understand the content of strategy in one page, as demonstrated in Appendix 2 of this book. This is an important feature; as we will observe later, the area of greatest-short term influence is the differentiating/transformational activities that are representative of activities over ownership. Activities are more readily changed than are resource-oriented assets and competencies (for example) or the market-oriented assets of brands or 'positions' in the market (the primary measure of which is market share).

The strategic architecture (see Figure 2.1) is one of the key features of the Strategic Management Framework, defining the structure of long-term strategy and providing the basis upon which practitioners are able to manage and review strategy and strategic plans continually. In particular, the hierarchy helps us to do five things:

1.   define clear and concise outcomes from strategy – stakeholder outcomes;

2.   clarify the 'blue ocean'- oriented market opportunities, or at the least market spaces that offer at least a sustainable, or better; renewable competitive advantage;

3.   appreciate and evaluate some of the different strategic tensions that exist between the polarities of the outside-in (market-driven) versus inside-out (resource-driven) activities through an articulation of the transforming activities and differentiating activities identified as key components of strategy;

4.   provide insight through the brief, but purposeful statement of strategic intent;

5.   make a valid assessment of the resource base, comprising the intangible elements of capabilities, competencies, values and culture, as well as the physical, tangible assets such as plant, buildings and machinery.

Tensions in strategy, as demonstrated in the construct of a strategic architecture (Figure 2.1), are evident between the outcomes or effect of the strategy that can only be realised when the causal activities (the differentiating/transformational activities) are conducted to either ensure visible differentiation exists between the firm and its competitors, or when they are deployed to build and enhance organisational competencies/resources. Each will have a strong influence on whether or not a firm remains ahead of competitors. Both forms of activities provide a link between the firm's resource base and the renewable market positions within an industry and within which a firm chooses to compete.

Figure 2.1 summarises a discussion of the application of components of a strategic architecture and the way that the emphasis of the strategic architecture will vary from company to company when they are in the same industry. The illustration here includes an interpretation of the dominant position that various restaurants with global reach in terms of presence or reputation conceptually have in a strategic architecture. A more detailed exploration of the details of a specific restaurant as well as other examples follows the summary.

Strategic Architecture

Demonstration of Different Emphasis from Restaurant Industry

Stakeholder Outcomes

Renewable Industry/ Market Positioning

Transforming Activities | Strategic Intent | Differentiating Activities

Building, Leveraging Resources/Competencies

- **Renewable Industry/Market Position: Starbucks** – As explained in its mission: 'to inspire and nurture the human spirit – one person, one cup and one neighbourhood at a time not just passionate purveyors of coffee, but everything else that goes with a full and rewarding coffeehouse experience'.

- **Differentiating Activities: McDonald's** – Differentiates through low-cost 'self-serve' service and fast/convenient delivery. Sees itself as 'first a job for many, a community partner, a model for other restaurants around the world, and a company seeking new ways to fulfil our brand promise of Quality, Service, Cleanliness, and Value'.

- **Strategic Intent: Hard Rock Café** – Based on a strategy of leveraging an 'experience economy' (Pine, Gilmore, 1998) Hard Rock's strategic intent can be interpreted as 'to provide a dining event that includes a unique visual and sound experience not duplicated anywhere in the world'.

- **Transforming Activities: The Fat Duck** – UK-based with three Michelin stars, voted Best Restaurant in the World in 2005. Self-taught chef and owner, Heston Blumenthal leads his restaurant's charge to build skills in its competencies and techniques. It includes rule-breaking, unusual experiments and an occasional exploding oven.

- **Building, Leveraging Resources/Competencies: El Bulli** – Located in Spain, recognised as the most experimental restaurant in the world. It received up to 1,000,000 reservation requests a year, but only 8,000 got a table.

Figure 2.1   Attributes of the strategic architecture of relevance to the restaurant industry

Illustrative Application of Strategic Architecture and Examples from the Restaurant and Other Industries

STAKEHOLDER OUTCOMES

Located at the top of the strategic architecture, these are the primary performance measures that represent the desired outcomes from strategy (Figure 2.1). Traditionally, this area of focus has centred on financial targets such as return on investment (ROI), measures of growth, and earnings per share (EPS). Increasingly, stakeholder outcomes also include measures of social responsibility in areas that include aspects of community engagement, social respect and environmental concern as well as other related (but non-financial) measures of success. As illustrated in the Cadbury case study that is explored in each chapter of this book, the strategic architecture accommodates a range of stakeholder targets that complement the more conventional, but single focus of financial outcomes. Most targeted outcomes I have observed will not change over a long period, although circumstances may dictate that they vary from year to year, or even month to.

RENEWABLE MARKET POSITION

This defines the markets in which the firm chooses to compete within a given industry. More recent developments in strategy suggest that an organisation should attempt to identify a 'blue ocean' (Kim and Mauborgne, 2004) market position. The term 'blue ocean' is a metaphor used to describe a market position where high growth and profits can be generated through the creation of new demand in an uncontested market space. This contrasts with the more common position whereby firms that have little to offer in terms of competitive advantage are forced to compete head-to-head with other suppliers; a position referred to by Kim and Mauborgne (2004) as a 'red ocean'. I propose that a renewable market position is one that is sustainable in the short term, but evolves over time. As such, it is an illustration of the need for continual renewal of market positioning definitions included in strategy and reflected in the strategic plan.

Porter (1985) proposes that a sustainable competitive advantage is obtained first through the identification of an attractive market position within an industry. The second step is the successful penetration of that market position through the realisation of one of three generic strategies. The three strategies are based on the offer of (1) a unique (differentiated) product or service, (2) a lower-cost product or service than competitors are offering, or (3) the occupation of a focused (market niche) product/service offering. Interestingly, the authors of

Blue Ocean Strategy, Kim and Mauborgne (2006) criticise Michael Porter's idea that successful businesses are *either* low-cost providers *or* provide access to unique products and services. Instead, they propose profitable market positions cross conventional market segments to offer both lower cost *and* uniqueness.

A sustainable market position is often considered to be an adequate outcome from strategy. I suggest here that a more aggressive perspective of sustainability requires the identification and implementation of a *renewable* market position as a means of obtaining and retaining competitiveness on a *continual* basis. Under the regime of a renewable market position and associated competitive advantage, a business's responsiveness to evolutionary and sometimes revolutionary change should be pre-empted and appropriate responses prepared accordingly.

EXAMPLE OF RENEWABLE MARKET POSITION: STARBUCKS

Starbucks' mission, as declared on its website,[1] is 'to inspire and nurture the human spirit – one person, one cup and one neighbourhood at a time', not just as passionate purveyors of coffee, but everything else that goes with a full and rewarding coffeehouse experience. Starbucks believes in continual renewal through leadership:

Our Customers

When we are fully engaged, we connect with, laugh with, and uplift the lives of our customers. … It's really about human connection.

Our Stores

When our customers feel this sense of belonging, our stores become a haven, a break from the worries outside, a place where you can meet with friends. It's about enjoyment at the speed of life – sometimes slow and savoured, sometimes faster. Always full of humanity.

Our Neighbourhood

Every store is part of a community, and we take our responsibility to be good neighbours seriously. We want to be invited in wherever we do business. We can be a force for positive action – bringing together our partners, customers, and the community to contribute every day. Now we see that our responsibility – and our potential for good – is even larger. The world is looking to Starbucks to set the new standard. We will lead.

---

1   See www.starbucks.co.uk/about-us/company-information/mission-statement.

In most instances, corporations will be reluctant to rapidly change the markets in which they choose to compete. Market positioning is therefore a long-term proposition for the business. I note though that from many perspectives it is the primary basis upon which growth is realised. Start-up businesses for example will typically commence with the application of a resource-focused, inside-out strategy, applying a resource and competence leveraging format. Chefs are a good example, they graduate with skills in cooking that can then be translated to their own bistro and later restaurant. They rise to fame through their continual renewal, development and refinement of competencies (enactment of transforming activities) that now include front of house presentation. These are then translated to a high reputation. It is only when they get to the point of real competition that they must turn their business acumen to market focused competition.

As products and markets mature (and as competition increases), businesses are required to focus more on a market positioning-oriented (outside-in) strategy for purposes of growth. Cadbury is an example of this; its transformation from competence-driven (skills in chocolate manufacture) ultimately gave way to toughing it out for market share against global giants, each of whom benefited from their ownership of similar chocolate-making competencies.

Providing the link between organisational resources and a renewable market position are the *differentiating/transforming activities*.

DIFFERENTIATING ACTIVITIES

Differentiating activities provide a point of differentiation when they are deployed to facilitate the way resources are leveraged into a sustainable (or a unique/renewable) market position. They are the physical activity-based elements that provide differentiation in those markets. If there were only one ideal market participant and market position, according to Porter (1996) in his quest to answer the question 'What is strategy?', 'there would be no need for strategy'. In which case companies would face a simple imperative: to win the race to discover (differentiation) and pre-empt it. The essence of strategic positioning, Porter suggests, is to choose activities that are different from rivals' (and if you can't differentiate, he says, then learn to execute activities better). Porter points to the unique 'just in time' supply chain design that the global clothing retailer Gap uses to differentiate itself from other retailers.

McDONALD'S RESTAURANTS AS AN EXAMPLE OF DIFFERENTIATING ACTIVITIES

A global food service retailer with more than 34,000 local restaurants serving nearly 69 million people in 118 countries each day, McDonald's offers a unique value proposition through its variation on traditional supply chain designs.

McDonald's essential business model is designed around the provision of low-cost, self-serve, fast/convenient food of a realistic quality. The company sees itself as 'a first job for many, a community partner, a model for other restaurants around the world, and a company seeking new ways to fulfil our brand promise of Quality, Service, Cleanliness, and Value'.[2]

Altruism and philanthropy is another point of differentiation, always on show through Ronald McDonald, the clown who visits children in hospitals and other places, whilst Ronald McDonald House provides accommodation for parents visiting sick children in nearby critical care facilities.

In his criticism of business's apparent over reliance on operational effectiveness as an emerging phenomenon of the day, to the extent that it was becoming a substitute for strategy, Porter concluded that rather than a focus on cost reduction alone, strategy rests on a firm's ability to deploy a unique suite of activities. Competitive strategy is about being different, he suggests. It means deliberately choosing a different set of activities to deliver a unique mix of value: 'If the same set of activities were best to produce all varieties, meet all needs, and access all customers, companies could easily shift among them and operational effectiveness would determine performance.'

TRANSFORMATIONAL ACTIVITIES

This is an adaptation of the term 'dynamic capabilities' (Teece et al., 1997) to describe the distinctive processes that include the 'honing of internal technological, organisational and managerial processes of the firm'. The way in which the names I give to dynamic capabilities (transformational activities) are shaped, will be dependent upon the nature of the firm's resource base, its asset positions, and the way in which the business chooses to develop its resources (consider the Toyota Way from Chapter 1 as an example). Cadbury demonstrated a very specific development path which was based on a path committed to the development of pure chocolate drink and chocolate products.

---

2   See www.aboutmcdonalds.com/mcd.html (accessed 6 May 2014).

There are three levels of transformational activities, each are related to individual perceptions of environmental dynamism (Ambrosini and Bowman, 2009):

1.   **incremental transformational activities** – those concerned with the continuous improvement of the firm's resource base;

2.   **renewing transformational activities** – those that refresh, adapt and augment the resource base;

3.   **regenerative transformational activities** – those with an impact, not on the firm's resource base, but on its current set of transformational activities in a way that changes the way the firm adapts its resource base.

An appreciation of the existence of both differentiating and transformational activities and the strategic intent (described below) that is usually conceived as being the key purpose of an organisation's strategy are of significant importance as they represent some of the few 'short-term' activities (significant because of their attribute as things people *do,* and as a result more controllable than things they *have*) that can be included in a long-term strategy.

Supported by the managerial philosophy of the Toyota Way (see Chapter 1), this company demonstrates a considerable strength in differentiation through the activities it carries out as a part of its 'agile supply chain'. Toyota's business model requires that its sales and marketing divisions remain highly responsive to customer demands, based on expectations of value – reasonable pricing and high quality in its product and service delivery. These demands are satisfied through the enactment of its competency in 'just in time' manufacturing – the basis of which is the application of lean manufacturing techniques. Through Toyota's integrated supply chain system, customers' orders are afforded a direct link with production schedules which allows Toyota to respond within tight time frames to changes in purchasing patterns as soon as they occur.

EXAMPLE OF REGENERATIVE TRANSFORMATIONAL ACTIVITIES: THE FAT DUCK RESTAURANT

Owned by chef Heston Blumenthal, Berkshire-based The Fat Duck possesses three Michelin Stars and was voted Best Restaurant in the World in 2005. Blumenthal's career path has demanded continual skill development in competencies and technique. This has included, and I quote, 'rule-breaking, unusual experiments and an exploding oven'.

STRATEGIC INTENT

The term 'strategic intent' was coined by Hamel and Prahalad (1989), who used it to describe a method of encapsulating the strategic goals and objectives of a business in its strategy; it was designed as a catch-cry in the form of a statement that was concise, but at the same time seen to be more meaningful than traditional vision or mission statements.

Preferring the term 'strategic intent' to 'vision', Hamel and Prahalad (1994) suggest such a statement 'implies a particular point of view about the long-term market or competitive position that a firm hopes to build over the coming decade or so'. Hence, it conveys a sense of direction. A strategic intent, they suggest, is:

> *differentiated; it implies a competitively unique point of view about the future. It holds out to employees the promise of exploring new competitive territory. Hence, it conveys a sense of discovery. Strategic intent has an emotional edge to it; it is a goal that employees perceive as inherently worthwhile. Hence it implies a sense of destiny.*

As can be observed in Figure 2.1, I adapt the term 'strategic intent' and apply it to the body of the strategic architecture. My reasoning is that whereas a vision, based on an envisioned future is about a future perspective of the business and an outlook upon which the leadership team would like to direct the future of the organisation, a strategic intent is concerned with the underlying *theme* of the strategy.

I propose that in this context a strategic intent is used as a brief description of the general purpose of the *strategy*. Its role is that of an emotive driver of the continual renewal of strategy and ideally the business. An example of a more generic strategic intent is 'conquering *all* global market segments', another is 'transforming knowledge into intelligence'. Another way to look at this application of strategic intent is to incorporate it into the firm's value proposition as a description of the reason why customers will continue to buy the firm's products and services.

The basis for a customer-focused value proposition is usually clear when a firm is first established. It is generally an outcome from the fundamental problem that gave rise to the firm's existence in the first place. Retail stores of all descriptions, for example, were established to provide an outlet for manufacturers to sell their goods and a convenient place for customers to obtain access and choice in the acquisition of those goods. The 1832 version of Cadbury as a retailer is a good example of this, as John Cadbury sought to provide such a solution for his customers in a way that incorporated entertainment as a part of his method of differentiation, he also sought to solve the problem of alcoholism, although it ultimately proved to be beyond his reach. An example of a strategic intent applicable to John Cadbury's retail business therefore, could have been 'delivering health and harmony through purity, taste and entertainment'.

A more specific, industrial example is the mining services company Orica Ltd, founded in 1874 as a supplier of dynamite to miners in the Victorian gold fields in Australia. Today Orica provides blasting services to mining companies around the world that would prefer specialists to handle the highly dangerous components of their mineral extraction activities. A strategic intent for Orica could be described as 'doing the heavy lifting for miners'. This statement, although fictitious could have emerged from Orica's apparent capacity to solve mining companies complex problem of removing rock, dirt and other substances that get in the way of the mining process. Orica was successful because of the realisation of its strategic intent that can be translated into its value proposition. This is the removal of the risk of that activity to mining companies whose own value propositions would be more oriented towards the transportation and delivery of raw materials mined as opposed to the carrying out of the preliminary task of preparing the ground for extraction.

EXAMPLE OF STRATEGIC INTENT: HARD ROCK CAFÉ

This chain's strategy is based on a business model that seeks leverage from the notion of an 'experience economy' (Pine and Gilmore, 1998). According to Pine and Gilmore, an experience economy can be found in situations where companies elect to compete through customer experience as opposed to customer service alone. In order to compete through 'experiences', a service or product offering must include an experience that is memorable to the extent that it will remain with an individual (customer or guest) for a long time.

Hard Rock Café's strategic intent is based on the notion of an 'experience' value proposition, to: 'provide a dining event that includes a unique visual and sound experience not duplicated anywhere else in the world'.

ORGANISATIONAL RESOURCES

At the foundation of the strategic architecture, organisational resources represent the tangible and intangible strategic assets (Amit and Schoemaker, 1993) that must be built, maintained or acquired to satisfy whatever market positioning is to be adopted. Tangible organisational resources may include buildings, plant and equipment, whilst intangible resources include core competencies, brand, knowledge, skills and culture. In some applications, capabilities are considered to be both resources and competencies. I differentiate between a basic capability and transformational activity; a capability included in the resource set is considered a static application, something the organisation *has* in the same vein as a strategic asset. Transformational activities, however, are something the organisation *does*; when viewed as *dynamic* capabilities they are generally being deployed to create an improvement or enhancement to an otherwise static capability, resource or competency.

As with renewable market positions, organisational resources, especially core competencies, are developed over long periods and usually exceed the average annual planning cycle. Acquisition of new resources is an option, leading to the speeding up of the process of resource development. I note, however, that incorporating another business through company acquisition or merger as a means to build a resource base can take time to complete, and integration with the acquiring organisation can be slow, especially the development of intangible assets such as core competencies, culture and knowledge.

EXAMPLE OF COMPETENCIES/RESOURCES: EL BULLI RESTAURANT

Located in Spain, El Bulli recently closed, but in its time was recognised as the most controversial and experimental restaurant in the world. It received up to 1,000,000 reservation requests a year whilst operating, but only 8,000 were successful in getting a table.

Head Chef Ferran Adrià is acclaimed as the best chef in the world. In order to ensure the product offering (menu) was unique and the most exciting in the world, El Bulli closed for half a year in the winter months as the creative team of chefs worked in their food development laboratory. During that period the team would prepare around 500 new dishes for introduction in the next open season.

Resources and markets are in the main fixed over long periods, differentiating/transforming activities however will typically be more accessible in the event that changes to strategy become a short-term imperative, as may be the case during extreme situations that are beyond the control of the executives and directors of the firm. Such situations are not common, but can be imposed on organisations – as we have seen, for example, from the impact of the Great Recession. This event caused many businesses to adapt very quickly from an environment of certainty and a state of long-term renewable growth to one of great uncertainty, forcing the need for dramatic restructuring, renewal or reinvention; enabled through a change in their activities in the short term which in many cases saw an uptake of technology to enable automation or a rationalisation of service offerings and then infrastructure in the long-term.

The development of external market positions and/or organisational resources can be seen, therefore, to be more likely to be *evolutionary* in nature. Differentiating/transformational activities, as something the firm *does*, are naturally more accommodating to *revolutionary* change. Fundamentally, however, most forms of renewal, strategic change and reinvention are carried out at the activity level of the strategic architecture. To change the business model (defined as the manner in which the business enterprise delivers value to customers, entices customers to pay for value, and converts those payments to profit (Teece, 2010)) and the way a business goes to market, it is always necessary to change some component of the resource set, and potentially the way the differentiating and transformational activities interact with those resources (in summation; the management of a system).

SMI Dynamic Model of Strategic Equilibrium

Drawing on the construct of the strategic architecture embedded in the Strategic Management Framework, I propose the notion of a Dynamic Model of Strategic Equilibrium as a concept that defines a state of equilibrium between each of the elements contained within that strategic architecture. Still requiring further analysis of its application in practice, I refer to this proposed construct as the SMI Dynamic Model of Strategic Equilibrium (Figure 2.2). The model depicts a state of equilibrium that can be expected to prevail when a balance is achieved between an inside-out/outside-in strategy and one that incorporates the differentiating/transforming activities described previously; potentially in the form of a micro system. Typically, organisations select an either/or approach to strategising, as shown in the restaurant examples above.

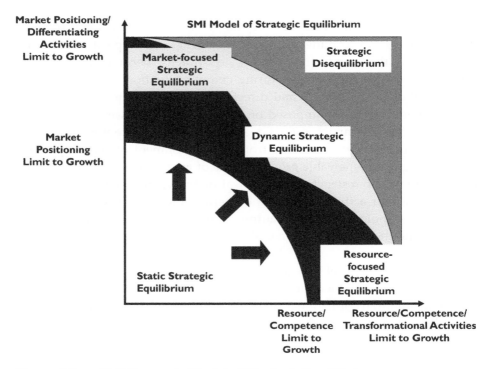

Figure 2.2   SMI Dynamic Model of Strategic Equilibrium

Some, but only a few, achieve a balance between the two; Toyota could be the exception as demonstrated in the example presented previously. Toyota is a Japanese manufacturer that challenged the status quo to become the largest automotive company in the world.

I believe the SMI Dynamic Model of Strategic Equilibrium could be the starting point for the determination of new growth opportunities for organisations operating primarily out of a single dimension (hence the inclusion of the word 'dynamic' in its title). Stand out examples of single focused companies are Red Bull (market positioning), Honda (competence/resource leveraging), Disney (differentiating activities) and participants in Formula 1 car racing (transforming activities) such as Ferrari and Lotus.

It is my experience in particular that few organisations are even conscious of the actual activity component (transforming/differentiated activities) of the elements of a formal strategy structure; it is not well defined or even identified in the mainstream strategy literature to date. As a result, practitioners could significantly benefit from an opportunity (or imperative) to ensure they retain their strengths in areas beyond core resource leveraging or market positioning alone. Points of optimisation for each are shown in Figure 2.2 as areas that represent a limit to growth from either a market positioning or competence/resource leveraging perspective. An appreciation of the existence and strength of transformational and differentiating activities, I suggest, will contribute to the realisation of further ways a firm can compete. This is the case especially in conglomerates, for example, where sibling entities often possess skills in the conduct of complementary or synergistic activities that are not otherwise shared.

McDonald's is highly successful as a provider of convenience foods at low cost and consistent quality. It appears though that it does little to develop its competitive offering further through the development of differentiated or transforming activities. Although there is clear evidence of differentiation in its existing product service and business model, McDonald's adheres to its prevailing static model of equilibrium. Growth is primarily focused on international expansion of markets rather than innovation in its differentiating activities. Continuation of the same business model over a long period has left McDonald's vulnerable to other nimble, less constrained competitors who may be more agile in their approach to building market share.

It is true that McDonald's has explored some points of differentiation and has recently (in Australia anyway) proposed home delivery as a way to grow its business. Although an attractive proposition to customers, this is still not a radically innovative or unique offer overall. We discuss the application of the SMI Model of Strategic Equilibrium in more detail in Chapter 6.

Reinventing Strategic Planning: A Systemic Approach to Strategy Formation, Implementation and Renewal

Senge (1990) informs our approach to the reinvention of traditional strategic planning and enforces the importance of systems thinking as a means to enhance the effectiveness of the activity of strategising. In *The Fifth Discipline* he proposes that the fundamentals of Complexity Theory are sufficient to cast doubt over the claims of traditional strategic planners that a strategic plan in any context is in fact viable. Senge notes:

> *It is doubtful whether the results that happen today are those intended any length of time ago. It is therefore, inconceivable to think that we can plan over any great span of interrelationships or very far into the future.*

The more we try to think global rather than local the more we experience the resistance of complexity. (Senge, 1990)

Through this observation, Senge affords a validity to the Strategic Management Framework; as a system designed to deliberately differentiate between *strategy,* in the form of a representation of an *aspirational,* envisioned future (the validity of which will always be the subject of conjecture) and the *strategic plan* which is the physical instrument that enables the implementation of those aspirations in the short term, and the delivery of change.

The reinvention of the strategic plan into a programme of continual strategy renewal and the inclusion of strategy evaluation reviewing as a fundamental component of that programme is I suggest, a valid solution to the conundrum that arises from the 'doubtful results' that Senge observes as flaws of strategic planning in general. By submitting the strategic plan to continual monitoring and review, strategy practitioners are alerted to those areas of greatest uncertainty and doubt (that Senge suggests arise from the distance of time and space) and as a result, are better prepared to invoke a reactive, proactive or designed response, in time to counter potential adverse outcomes from uncertainty. The more specific the short term objectives articulated in the strategic plan, the more appropriate is the focus of Senge's comments on the short-term planning component of strategy. It is fitting therefore that the proposed mechanism of continual strategy renewal should treat the plan as a dynamic, interactive program of review and re-evaluation as opposed to a static, moribund document.

Senge's proposed notion of 'systemic thinking' is applied to the framework as a means to define 'a way to explore the whole as a means to connect the abundance of events that would otherwise appear to be distinct in space and time' (Senge, 1990). Systemic thinking, Senge suggests, 'provides connectedness, structure and boundaries to our thinking. Boundary judgements help people to formulate viewpoints about issues and dilemmas experienced in their lives'. The Strategic Management Framework was designed to provide a systemic understanding of strategy and is an attempt to apply boundaries to our thinking, enabled where appropriate through the development of scenarios which depict future plausible relationships with the business and its environment. As Senge would hope, the framework 'facilitates construction of incisive insights into each viewpoint', such that 'as a result, we are able to learn within the unknowable' – a useful attribute for any sensible strategy practitioner!

Senge's approach to systemic thinking is based on the premise that single-loop learning (where incremental improvements are made by making adjustments to existing techniques) should be replaced by double-loop learning. According to Argyris and Schon (1978), double-loop learning 'promotes changes to fundamental, preconceived notions and assumptions as the basis upon which learning is carried out, problems are solved and decisions made'.

One application of systemic thinking of great importance to you and me is the interpretation given to it by Flood (1999), who associates systemic thinking with that of a formal process of project management, and by association, *evaluation*. Flood proposes a perspective of evaluation that is centred on systems thinking in a format that he describes as *'systemic evaluation'*. Flood includes an aspect of evaluation that you wouldn't expect outside a book on strategy – specifically that of strategic planning. Its inclusion is unusual because in most instances, evaluation is considered to be about the monitoring and assessment of an operationally focused project or cluster of projects that make up a programme. Rarely is it applied to the context of strategic planning as well, I refer to this concept as Systemic Strategy Evaluation.

Systemic Strategy Evaluation

Flood draws on standard project and programme management concepts of evaluation to draw a comparison with the management and monitoring of each, against the evaluation of the effectiveness strategic planning. As we saw in Chapter 1, Flood proposes two different perspectives of evaluation of relevance to strategic planning. The first perspective is the process that contributes to the formation of the strategic plan. The second perspective applies to plans that are complete and therefore require an assessment of the effectiveness of *outcomes* that include an assessment of the *relevance* of content contained in the strategic plan. The focus of both is typically centred on an assessment of a plan's timeliness, relevance and its efficiency and effectiveness. Each is reviewed in accordance with predetermined people and culture (behavioural) criteria as well as expectations concerned with the plan's financial constraints, time and resource allocations and associated (process-oriented) performance standards.

Flood describes the two components of systemic evaluation, therefore, as being either a part of *formative evaluation* (which in a strategy context can, be defined as *evaluation shaping* – associated with the activity of creating or shaping a strategic plan) and *summative evaluation* (which can be seen to be most relevant to strategy in a context of *evaluation reviewing* – the activity of reviewing the effectiveness and outcomes of a strategic plan).

STRATEGY EVALUATION SHAPING

The notion of strategy evaluation *shaping* is important to us. It is undertaken with the objective of generating information about actions that become the primary outcome from a strategic plan, generally articulated as *strategic objectives*. By definition, the outcomes from strategy evaluation shaping will be based on a number of assumptions, assessments and guesses that contribute to the formation of short term strategic objectives; this is the very nature of strategic planning.

Flood's (1999) view of what I have expressed as strategy evaluation shaping builds on the work of Senge (1990). He suggests that in environments of significant complexity and extreme ambiguity, managers are faced with the need to obtain knowledge about topics that are in effect 'unknowable' – a key challenge of strategy evaluation shaping. Specifically, Flood relies on Senge's method of systems thinking as a way of dealing with the complex nature of the world, which comprises many inter-relationships, but at the same time is resolved through acts of spontaneous self-organisation. It is only possible, Flood suggests, for managers to get to get to grips with things 'that we are immediately involved with', and at the same time are 'not very far into the future'. It is almost impossible, he suggests, to assess and resolve any issues that are future-oriented and strategic (as opposed to planned) in nature.

It is therefore highly desirable for strategy practitioners to obtain as much insight as possible into future eventualities. As an extension of Flood's work I have incorporated the notion of *strategy evaluation shaping* as a key component of the Strategic Management Framework and as such is a form of reinvention of the standard approach to strategic planning. The components of this reinvention contribute to a resolution of Flood's expressed concerns about difficulty with 'seeing the future'. As is illustrated in Figure 1.1 the relevant perspectives of strategy evaluation shaping are addressed through our proposed use of tools that help us to reach into the future, as best we can. The tools and techniques I refer to are identified in the Strategic Management Framework as *environmental scanning, futures thinking* and *responsiveness.*

I suggest that as a result of their inclusion, strategy practitioners are better placed to work in a sphere where decision makers are at the least better informed (through enhanced insight a least) of the unknowable, but are also better equipped to 'manage within the unmanageable and organise within the unorganisable' (Flood, 1999). Each of the perspectives of environmental scanning, futures thinking and responsiveness are explored in more detail in Chapter 3, they are intended to inform strategy through descriptive depictions (such as story) or other similar conceptual means to evoke images of a perspective of what 'could be'. Arie de Geus (1997) illuminates the way in which insight into perspectives of the future can be developed. He proposes the application of scenario analysis as a form of story, in the format of 'memories of the future'. Scenarios de Geus suggests, provide a means for strategy practitioners to come to terms with the degree of unknown futures referred to by both Senge and Flood.

Strategy practitioners can never be sure of what is going to happen even ten minutes into the future. What they can do though is try to second guess it or otherwise influence it through the use of advanced strategy tools. The purpose of the activity of *strategy evaluation shaping* therefore is to provide insight and a basis and content for strategic thinking, strategy formation, strategy renewing and strategy evaluation *reviewing*, and as an outcome, the basis for continual renewal of the material that would otherwise make up the details of the ubiquitous/annual strategic plan.

STRATEGY EVALUATION REVIEWING

There is strong opinion (Rumelt, 1991) to suggest the majority of strategy evaluation *reviewing* activities are evoked solely from the success (or lack of) of predetermined outcomes. A more effective approach to strategy evaluation reviewing, therefore, would surely be to include an assessment of whether or not the underlying assumptions, suppositions and drivers of strategy that were relied upon to develop a strategic plan in the first place continue to retain their relevance on a regular basis, as proposed previously (consistent with a philosophy of continual strategy renewal). As we saw with the David Jones department store chain in Chapter 1, there is not much point in placing a sole reliance on an evaluation methodology that simply waits for the strategic planning period (maybe as long as three to five years) to expire before making any judgement on the effectiveness or relevance of the strategic plan.

A programme of strategy evaluation reviewing therefore must encompass an element of reflection of the strategic plan, with the objective of consolidating what has been learnt through the processes of implementation of the plan, and where appropriate program of continual strategy renewal. I include the formal interactive strategy evaluation and monitoring mechanism as a key component of the Strategic Management Framework. It is an essential component of the strategy evaluation reviewing and monitoring mechanism supporting the overall strategic change agenda shown in Figure 1.1. The interactive strategy evaluation and monitoring mechanism is designed to observe changes in trends and content of assumptions and estimates that were applied to the development of the strategic plan as a result of the strategy evaluation shaping exercise referred to previously. This is illustrated in Figures 3.1 and 5.1 respectively.

Knowledge obtained from these findings is then applied as a mechanism to improve future strategic planning activities – but of greater importance, to reassess the value and contribution of content contained within the strategy and strategic plan itself. Each of these actions can be enhanced through the conduit of a formal learning program, or at a higher level, and as Senge proposes, within the context of a learning organisation. Consistent with Flood's view, I see strategy evaluation as a valid approach to the assessment of the value of a strategic plan's content. When applied to strategy evaluation reviewing in particular it prompts:

> *reflection on actions taken at a strategic level and as a result presents opportunities for consideration of new issues and dilemmas to be addressed. It informs assessments of relevance, validity and continuing commitments to strategy and the strategic plan and plays a central role in keeping all concerned people informed about consequences. This in turn helps them to learn into the future and to facilitate learning within the unknowable. (Flood, 1999)*

The overarching strategy reviewing and monitoring mechanism engages the notion of strategy evaluation *renewing* and incorporates an embedded strategy evaluation *reviewing* capability that will ultimately make the idea of revisiting strategy on an annual or three to five year basis only – obsolete.

The choice of tools used to conduct any form of strategy evaluation activities will be highly dependent upon the prevailing business environment, and as suggested by Courtney et al. (1997), will be influenced by the extent of uncertainty and/or associated levels of risk. Imagine, for example, how different the world could be today had the assumptions behind different scenarios concerning the political stability of the Middle East, environmental stability in the nuclear energy industry in Japan and the potential for imbalance in global financial stability been tested and re-tested over the past few years. An overview of strategy evaluation shaping within which future focused strategy tools are reviewed and discussed follows in the next chapter.

Chapter 3

Strategy and a New Perspective on 'Fit': Directing Desire, Accommodating Fate, and a Catalyst for Transformation and Renewal

> **INCONVENIENT TRUTH NO. 3: MEASURES OF STRATEGY EFFECTIVENESS ARE MISPLACED AND ILL DEFINED.**
>
> The primary focus of strategy evaluation activities is mostly assessed on incorrect measures – an assessment of specific outcomes rather than the 'causal' factors arising from inevitable assumptions/guesstimates that contribute to its formulation and renewal (shaping) and its implementation (reviewing).

Strategy is all about the future, but because the future is unknown, its content is by definition made up of numerous assumptions and guesstimates, each of which are based on a version of the truth that doesn't yet exist. Evaluation techniques that ignore the consequences of the inevitable changes that occur in business after the making of assumptions can be highly detrimental to an organisation's health. This occurs when scant attention is given to the combination of each element of evaluation (as we saw in Chapter 2): systemic strategy evaluation *shaping* and *reviewing*.

In the absence of an agreed and clear definition and purpose for strategy, and as a result of its strong tendency to be treated as a unique and independent process as identified in The First Inconvenient Truth of Strategy, the practice of strategising can now be suitably conceptualised as a specific and independent (although fully integrated) cluster of projects against which normal programme and project management evaluation techniques can be applied. Together, the ensuing programme of strategy and planning combines to form a system which offers considerable synergistic effects. More importantly, when the strategising system acts to integrate strategic planning content with that contained in the strategic architecture (within the construct of the Strategic Management Framework – see Figure 1.1), causal and influential factors interact to form an integrated system. As the time dimensions of each are aligned, the outcome combines to contribute to the formation of a truly dynamic strategy and planning *open-loop system*.

The Third Inconvenient Truth of Strategy

When addressing The Third Inconvenient Truth of Strategy, I therefore propose we explore an extension of the usual strategising infrastructure (the strategic plan) and pursue one that has the added advantage of effectively *bringing strategy to life* (and in a construct worthy of a profession) in the form of a *programme of continual renewal of strategy*. Such a systems-based, continually renewed (dynamic) approach to planning offers a robust solution to the dilemma that is expressed as The Third Inconvenient Truth of Strategy:

> *Measures of strategy effectiveness are misplaced and ill defined. The primary focus of strategy evaluation activities is mostly assessed on incorrect measures – an assessment of specific outcomes rather than the 'causal' factors arising from inevitable assumptions/guesstimates that contribute to its formulation and renewal (shaping) and its implementation (reviewing). The results of this are that in the absence of an appropriate strategy evaluation capability, unforeseen outcomes and unintended consequences arise, including:*
>
> - *incomplete, inappropriate strategy content;*
> - *continued investment in invalid strategies;*
> - *poor responses to unforeseen change.*

The discussion in this chapter, therefore, focuses on the component of the Strategic Management Framework that attempts to identify and quantify those factors contributing to knowledge that informs the effectiveness of strategy and strategic decision making in general; I have referred to these previously (Chapter 2) as the elements of systemic strategy evaluation shaping and reviewing as depicted in Figure 1.1 and Appendix 2.

We commence the chapter again with an update on the developments of Cadbury in the next era of its life which is still characterised by high ambition and exceptional aspiration albeit with an absence of a formal strategy. In which case, it would have been hard to measure the effectiveness of the underlying assumptions that determined its future direction, though some assumptions stand out loud and clear:

- that a method of producing high-quality, delicious chocolate products would be found;

- that a market would exist for those products;

- that the chocolate product would be capable of manufacture on a mass production scale;

- that abusers of alcohol would readily accept a chocolate drink (cocoa) as a substitute for gin;

- that resources would be found to finance and support the mass production of chocolate products.

In a way, the Cadbury brothers were living with, and relying on positive outcomes from assumptions similar to the above each day.

A Second Life and Whisper of Breath at Cadbury

By 1866 the Cadbury Brothers had maintained their commitment to the company values that were so closely associated with their beliefs as well as the foundation of their strategic direction. The Cadbury business itself had reached the point where it was on the brink of bankruptcy, saved only by what can be described as a 'big bet' investment made by George Cadbury, based on an assumption that survival could prevail if he took the decision to invest the remnants of the cash that had been a part of his inheritance from his father.

In a continued belief (assumption?) in the viability and apparent success of other competing manufacturers of products derived from the mysterious cacao nib, George decided that he would continue with the company's commitment to a resource/competence-leveraging (inside-out) strategy and hope the outcome would deliver a step-change increase in production capability – thankfully, it did; his assumption was right. The production technology that was the target of George's ambition was the recently invented

Van Houten press, designed in Europe to extract butter from the cacao nibs in large volumes. It also enabled the production of a less rich and more palatable cacao essence (cocoa drink) than was previously available as a precursor to the ingredients used in the chocolate bars that we enjoy so much today. As a result of the combined benefits of the high volume, flexible production processes that the Van Houten press enabled, Cadbury was now empowered to launch a variety of flavours and mixes – indeed, in some cases, according to press comments of the day (Cadbury, 2010), too many varieties were released.

There was no strategic plan that pointed the Cadbury brothers in the direction of an investment in the Van Houten press, or the number and type of products produced. Their decision was reached through a response to an unstructured, visible operational evaluation programme that would have automatically alerted them to the need to introduce change. In a way, therefore, the brothers were ready to embrace a notion of strategic management. In effect they were following an invisible strategic change agenda, based on an informal strategy blueprint that, had it been real, would have informed decision making about which projects or initiatives would need to be prioritised, progressed, or put on hold. The one significant thing that would have made their leadership capability more effective would have been an indication of potential income and resource deployment demands that would have been incurred as a means of justifying their investment in the cacao press.

Fighting on in what must have seemed like a continual fog of uncertainty, the turnaround in fortune that had been afforded the Cadbury brothers as a result of their subsequent investment in the Van Houten press did make a significant contribution to the future and viability of the Cadbury business. It provided the brothers with a release from the threat of bankruptcy, and subsequently the opportunity to trial new and pure variations of cocoa essence, flavours and more extravagant chocolate products. In the language used in this book, it represented an increase in the conduct of transforming activities as it sought to strengthen its competency in chocolate production, and this in turn allowed further differentiation and the opportunity to explore the products of the future. The fact that the Cadbury brothers neither used this terminology nor had a basic understanding of these basic principles of strategy confirms the extent to which 'intuition' influenced their decisions rather than science. In contrast, we can now see the value the Strategic Management Framework brings to the strategising activity; through its ability to structure and guide strategic analysis in a way that is supportive of an otherwise independently intuitive (strategically oriented) decision making capability.

I propose, therefore, that from the era that commenced with the installation of the Van Houten press, the construct of a strategy plan and strategy blueprint would have provided the Cadbury brothers with a way to frame a strategic plan in the short term whilst still striving to realise their life-long strategic intent of providing a viable alternative to alcohol. Regrettably – as we will see in subsequent chapters – a continual absence of a visible and structured long-term strategy is quite possibly a contributing factor to Cadbury's inability to stave off Kraft's aggressive acquisition of the company in 2010.

Operating in an environment that was filled by large numbers of industry participants but with little industry influence of their own, the Cadbury brothers acted on faith (and on the success of others such as Fry's – a significantly larger business than Cadbury). Supported by that faith, they were able to rise above the competition by default. Based on their religious beliefs as much as commercial acumen, the arrival of the Van Houten press allowed the bothers not only to improve productivity, but also to reduce the amount of objectionable ingredients that disreputable competitors had used in the past in an attempt to reduce costs and camouflage the unpleasant and bitter taste of the cacao fat. Drawing on their inherent values and now confirmed marketing slogan of 'absolutely pure, therefore the best', the Cadbury brothers had stumbled upon a benefit to their brand that wasn't offered by any of its major competitors – that of purity in its product as well as purity in its values.

In getting to this breakthrough, George and Richard had fought off bankruptcy by clinging to a firm belief in the product, and more physically by spending nearly all of their waking hours at work. The driving force for them both was the promise of a secure future, and still, a commitment to the strict values held by members of the Society of Friends. As far as George and Richard were concerned, Quaker values were a greater priority for them than fortune (Cadbury, 2010). Survival and prosperity for the business would enable them to provide ongoing support to their employees as well as the poor and underprivileged.

Financial success, when it did occur, didn't suddenly appear. Seen as a luxury consumer product in these early times, chocolate was, and always has been considered expensive. Perceived to be a comfort food by some, it is considered an extravagance by others. An assumption that this could be over-ridden in the long term was always the basis for hope, but there was no guarantee. Although quality improved considerably as a result of the introduction of the Van Houten press, so did the cost of ingredients. Eventually, though, an increase in consumer wealth and a further reduction in taxes on chocolate did provide sufficient revenue for the Cadbury business to thrive.

Just as the business succeeded, though, so did the opportunity present itself in the early twentieth century to devote time to the search for the perfection of a chocolate product that had already been developed by competitors overseas: the blend of milk and cocoa nibs in a format essential to produce what we know today as Dairy Milk Chocolate. Regrettably, during the course of this search, Richard Cadbury contracted a terminal illness whilst travelling overseas. His subsequent death occurred whilst he was still abroad, in Jerusalem in 1899.

Throughout his career Richard had been operating an inside-out strategy oriented to the maintenance of *what was* – the conduct of transforming activities that were undertaken to improve the competencies Cadbury had and the way in which those competencies could be developed; a program to deliver what *could be*. Cadbury's market definitions were well defined and still limited to an elite consumer represented by the few who were able to afford the luxury of the solid chocolate bars and confections offered by Cadbury, as well as those who could bear the harshness of the bitter component of the cocoa drink. They were also limited to the constraints imposed by known formats and physical production techniques and capacities – the very elements that the Cadbury's assumed would improve one day.

Systemic Strategy Evaluation

Bradley (2008) provides us with some insight into the specifics of Cadbury. We are concerned in this chapter however with his insight into Cadbury's successful turnaround from near bankruptcy to industry leader in their field. As a confirmation of Cadbury's focus on an Inside Out strategy, Bradley observes that their success can be primarily attributable to 'better management of their product range and infrastructure'. Specifically, Bradley observes that Cadbury shined in the areas of customer focus, an ability to rapidly respond to change, an associated speed of decision making and the quality of their product and service that can be seen as a key outcome from their values; captured in the phrase 'absolutely pure, therefore the best'. Cadbury also benefited from another feature of their resource base, following the establishment of a low cost manufacturing capability and an efficient and effective supply chain they had established as a result of their move to a country location out of Birmingham; Bourneville.

From a modern strategy practitioner's perspective, Cadbury seems to have mastered the art of strategy *exploitation*, the mining of existing business to become leaders in their field. This was at the expense though of an effectiveness in strategy *exploration*; an appreciation of future opportunities (other than the quest to perfect a product that was already proven; milk chocolate) that may be the basis for transformation to a more sustainable future. Either way, there is evidence to suggest that there was a place for the application of a formal strategy reviewing and monitoring mechanism to manage the assumptions (and intuitive guesses) that the likes of Richard Cadbury relied upon intuitively at that time to inform decision making into the future.

In this chapter we will review a number of strategy tools and techniques that contribute to our understanding of strategic issues that will have an impact on the future of an industry, a community, a business and most importantly the individual strategy practitioner. They include of course the aspirations, ambitions, assumptions and guestimates that we referred to previously and become therefore, a legitimate subject for review in the next component of the evaluation element of the Strategic Management Framework depicted in Figure 1.1, strategy evaluation reviewing.

Strategy evaluation shaping is the area that the fundamental assumptions, estimates, guesstimates and leaps of faith are *made* as the foundation of the strategy, strategic plan and futures thinking in general. The output is of course subjective, its validity highly dependent upon less tangible attributes of strategy; anticipation, adaptation, expectations, hope, enthusiasm and optimism. One description of the notion of strategic uncertainty as an aspect of subjectivity was identified by Hubbard et al. (2007) who found that senior leaders of the eleven most highly regarded Australian Corporations benefited from 'clear, but fuzzy strategy'. This feature of an organisations strategising capability Hubbard et al. observed, provided the senior leaders they interviewed with a clarity of purpose, as well as a level of flexibility that (they thought) ensured no opportunities were missed.

> *Strategy needs to be clear enough to provide guidance to current activities. At the same time it can be fuzzy so that opportunities that are related or are incremental can be taken up'. Characteristics of organisations operating clear but fuzzy strategy included attributes of adaptation, continuous improvement, and innovation. The organisations were also structured to ensure they were flexible enough to adapt to external change. Strategy was seen as an art; managed within a system of continual strategy renewal.*

> *Strategy for winning organisations is clear, but slightly fuzzy.*
> *It is communicated with a high degree of clarity and consistency, but*
> *in different ways and it develops and changes incrementally over time.*
> *(Hubbard et al., 2007)*

Each of these attributes are I suggest, sufficient to justify the necessity for the ensuing activity of systemic strategy evaluation reviewing, to become a formalised component of any strategising programme.

Systemic strategy evaluation reviewing is the term I use to refer to the monitoring of two aspects of strategising within the boundaries of the Strategic Management Framework. The first is the programme and project-oriented aspect of strategy implementation; its efficiency and effectiveness and the measurements and analysis related to the realisation of desired outcomes from short-term strategy, as expressed in the strategic plan. The second is the specific outcomes from strategy (strategic objectives and associated projects and performance expectations) as well as the less certain component of strategy that may or may not prove to be accurate, reliable or sustainable in the future; the assumptions and guesstimates referred to previously. The former relates primarily to programme and project management issues such as project costs, completion dates and actual versus estimated return on investment; the latter relates to less clear-cut issues of strategic planning that could include an assumption, for example, that people will be attracted to a tastier version of chocolate, that supply of the precious cacao nib grown in the Tropics will always be available, and that we will be able to ship the resulting products around the world at a viable cost. The mechanism that is illustrated in Figure 3.1 demonstrates the integrated nature of the elements of strategy evaluation shaping and reviewing.

The topic that makes up the bulk of our discussion in this chapter is systemic strategy evaluation shaping. This is the activity where we create the decisions that are based on the risky factors of uncertainty in strategy; the leaps of faith based on assumptions, guesstimates and estimates.

Systemic Strategy Evaluation Shaping

Systemic strategy evaluation shaping (Figure 3.1) consumes the majority of work to be conducted in the development and/or the review and renewal of strategy and the strategic plan. This method of evaluation relies on a big-picture direction from the firm's vision and mission and its *integration* and *engagement* with long-term strategy as expressed in the form of a strategic architecture, as discussed in detail in Chapter 2. In reviewing the topic of strategy evaluation shaping, we address the three categories of *environmental scanning, futures thinking* and *responsiveness*. Environmental scanning is used to deliver insight into trends and cycles of possible events and areas of influence that may or may not occur in the future, futures thinking refers to the use of specific tools to develop and evaluate stories of alternative (possible) future scenarios. Responsiveness accommodates either one of three actions and reactions to foreseen or unforeseen events. One is a reactive response to unforeseen, unexpected change (accommodating fate) second is a proactive response to anticipated change (anticipated response), third is the design of a hoped-for response to deliberate change (directed desire).

The strategic plan is very much a 'static' instrument, it is still though one that provides a viable basis upon which implementation and an associated programme of strategy renewal can be based. Future iterations of the strategic plan however may now be avoided as I would expect the notoriously static planning document would become an interactive monitoring mechanism; reviewed and renewed on a regular basis, its frequency subject to the discretion of the leadership team and the circumstances of the organisation within which such a mechanism is deployed. This matter and a determination of content is discussed further in Chapter 5 under the topic of 'programme of continual strategy renewal'. We propose that in any format, the strategic plan is a primary contributor to a programme of continual renewal of both strategy (directly) and the business (as an outcome). Fundamental to our discussion here therefore, is the inclusion of the various assumptions and 'unknowns' identified as part of The Third Inconvenient Truth of Strategy that are also considered in the context of strategy evaluation reviewing.

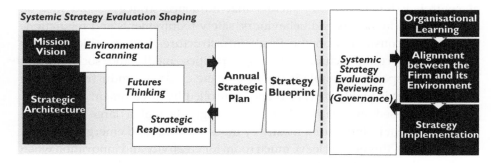

Figure 3.1   Extract from Strategic Management Framework: combined programmes of systemic strategy evaluation

The more specific professional attribute of strategy evaluation reviewing is the issue of *strategic governance*. This remains a vital aspect of strategy that we will explore in detail as an element of strategy as a profession in Chapter 7. As we will see at the conclusion to this and subsequent chapters, the strategic plan, when treated as an ongoing programme of continual strategy renewal (see Figure 1.1) becomes the catalyst rather than inhibiter for strategising, and indeed the driver of strategy, strategic change and ideally organisational renewal.

INSIGHT INTO SYSTEMIC STRATEGY EVALUATION SHAPING

In our review of the concept of strategy evaluation shaping, I propose to explore the major elements located on the left of Figure 3.1. As you will observe from this diagram, the practice of evaluation consists of a constant alignment and realignment of fit between each of the three elements of environmental scanning, futures thinking and responsiveness. Each contribute to our appreciation of the nature of the external environment and ways in which it can and should be revisited, reviewed and reassessed on a regular basis. The process or system itself can be incorporated into the same management reporting and control system within which a firms other topics of evaluation are being monitored. These include the assumptions that were made when the firm's vision, purpose and long-term strategy were developed and subsequently became embedded components of the firm's strategy, as reflected in its strategic architecture.

STRATEGY EVALUATION SHAPING, ELEMENT I: ENVIRONMENTAL SCANNING

A key influence on an organisation's strategy is the extent to which external industry-specific factors will influence the firm's capacity to exert any form of control. External industry factors that influence strategy could include regulation, social norms and behaviours, safety requirements and regulations that impose constraints on the firm's infrastructure. Less specific industry related forces could include technology, politics, media and social unrest. An industry specific example is utilities, or the electricity industry, which in most countries is highly regulated and controlled by government authorities. As we discussed in Chapter 1, research suggests that a large portion of strategy content is 'influenced mostly by industry forces and emerging trends'. On the surface, this doesn't leave much room for creativity and innovation when assessing the competitive advantage of a business in the electricity market. It does, though, require the firm to maintain a good appreciation of where the industry in which it operates is headed.

An example of a business that is in this position is Asciano, a rail freight transport and port management company that operates in Australia well under the radar of better-known consumer-oriented brands. Asciano's success is highly dependent on ownership of and access to sea ports and rail tracks, most of which it does not own. In most cases, they remain the core assets of governments, or mining companies which in turn may also be leasing the tracks from the government. Similarly, Amcor, a global packaging company and primary supplier to the tobacco/cigarette industry, has no influence over the sale (or otherwise) of the end product – cigarettes. Its fortunes are therefore largely tied to the fluctuations of the industry and the marketing efforts of its customers, who, because of consumers' health concerns, are understandably under constant pressure to exit that business. Other examples of organisations occupying this space are utilities, government departments and agencies, hospitals, not-for-profit organisations and educational institutions.

For organisations that are not tied to industry influences, it is just as important to be aware of future trends and factors of influence that could emerge as a threat or opportunity for them in the future. However, such organisations can benefit from a capacity to influence the structure, or shape of their industry environment as opposed to having to conform to it. In fact, many of the more successful firms have been able to carve out their own future within an industry, and as a result benefit from at least a renewable competitive advantage, or better still, global domination of that industry. Examples of individuals and companies that have realised such an outcome include Anita Roddick (who as founder of the Body Shop is famous for her observation that she looked at what others in her industry were doing and deliberately 'walked in the opposite direction'). Others are Richard Branson (Virgin), Henry Ford (Ford) or even early twentieth-century inventor Thomas Edison. We shouldn't forget either the vast number of inventors and entrepreneurs who literally invented new spaces in an industry, and sometimes a new industry altogether, such as Zuckerberg with Facebook.

Each of these individuals and the companies they founded benefited from their ability to *define new rules* of the game as opposed to *playing by the rules of the game*, as many industry incumbents tend to do. Whereas some opportunities are sourced as a result of deliberate attempts at creativity, innovation and invention, other initiatives that have led to success are driven by the opportune and timely application of *what is* (an existing set of resources) or *what will soon be in existence* (emerging). One of Steve Jobs's attributes, for example, was his ability to spot emerging technologies and to ensure that Apple was working to capitalise on them before anyone else – that is, before the new wave of technology advancements became the norm.

Another example of an entrepreneurial company that is writing its own future is a small women's fashion retailer based in Melbourne, Australia called The Ark. At a time when the highly labour-intensive textile industry has long left Australian shores in favour of higher-volume, lower-wage countries such as India and China, the owners of The Ark have thrived under their own unique value proposition realised through a clothing range that is designed and made in Melbourne. As with Apple, the owners of The Ark found that control over design and manufacture allowed the company to respond to and largely influence customer demand. The number of retail outlets operated by The Ark is deliberately limited to only three stores. Offering contemporary (fashionable, but unique) designs, production runs are also limited so that customers won't be embarrassed by seeing other women in the same dresses around town.

Described on its website as a business run by women for women, The Ark adds extra value to its customers:

> The Ark wishes to keep understanding and educating our valued customers positively. We have staff with skills in the areas of design, patternmaking, e-commerce, wholesale, customer relations, graphics, marketing, sales and accessories who all work cohesively together to bring the best from The Ark product, season after season.[1]

Most importantly, The Ark is all about the customer:

> If you've lost confidence in your body and its ability to make you feel good, indulge in the often hilarious but always informative WORKSHOP YOUR SHAPE nights. Here the staff themselves strip down to the bare essentials to help you understand how to make the use of the best bits and disguise the less loved parts. So which shape are you? CURVY, SQUARE, TRIANGLE, DIAMOND or STRAIGHT?[2]

---

1   See https://www.smiknowledge.com/blog/2012/05/the-mainstream-retail-business-model-time-for-reinvention/.
2   Ibid.

Environmental Scanning Tools: PESTE Analysis

The primary tool used for environmental scanning in its most simplistic form is PESTE analysis (or a variation thereof), an acronym for the Political, Economic, Social, Technological and Ecological issues that face a business. The purpose of PESTE analysis is to develop an overview of the different macro environmental factors the company has to take into consideration when conducting an external environmental analysis contributing to strategising activities or market research. It contributes to strategy evaluation activities because it provides insight into the strategy practitioners' understanding of the specifics of the future, and informs decisions on market growth or decline, its position in that environment, and an indication of the future potential and direction for proposed or existing operations. PESTE analysis also offers increasing value as environmental or ecological factors continue to have greater impact on corporate social responsibility (trends), serving as an early identifier of potential opportunities and/or threats to the business.

PESTE is a vital component of standalone strategic analysis, or a contributor to the conduct of scenario analysis (discussed in the next section). Table 3.1 gives an example of the application of PESTE analysis by examining the mid-term (ten- to fifteen-year) trends within the political, economic, social, technological, and ecological dimensions. To complete the analysis, a list of at least five changes in each element is required to be identified (a total of 25 items).

Table 3.1   Example of application of PESTE analysis

Dimensions	Areas of greatest uncertainty impacting our industry
Political (e.g. change in balance of power in Governments)	
Economic (e.g. continuing repair of effect of Great Recession)	
Social (e.g. impact of mass cross-border migration)	
Technological (e.g. emergence of analytics, big data and social media)	
Ecological (e.g. impact of climate change, incidence of obesity)	

Environmental Scanning Tools: Porter's Five Forces Model

A second tool used to assess and review the external environment within which a firm operates is Porter's Five Forces Model (Porter, 1980). Developed by Harvard Strategy Professor Michael Porter, this model is mostly an econometrically based environmental analysis (industry attractiveness) assessment of the strength that the five forces that prevail within an industry will have. The five forces are: the bargaining power of buyer's, the bargaining power of customers, the threat of new entrants, the threat of substitutes and the extent of rivalry among existing participants in the industry (your competitors). Porter refers to this model as the Five Forces Model of Competitive Advantage. It is used to compare the impact each force will have on competitive intensity, and therefore the attractiveness of an investment in an industry.

It also provides information contributing to an understanding of a firm's current or potential strategic market position in an industry. Another application is to use it to highlight specific issues of industry attractiveness, which in this context refers to the overall industry profitability. An unattractive industry is one in which the combination of these five forces acts to drive down overall profitability. A very attractive industry would be one approaching pure competition in which available profits for all firms is driven down to zero. However, the overall industry attractiveness picture does not imply that every firm in the industry will return the same profitability. To some extent, the effectiveness of a firm's strategy will have a direct influence on this.

Porter's Five Forces Model is useful because it assists firms to assess and develop strategies that could deliver profits above the industry average. It prompts industry participants to reassess the marketplace, dependent upon any given changes in industry information that become observable from changes in any elements of the five forces. It also complements other elements of Porter's analytical toolkit, which also includes the notion of a value chain and the three generic strategies referred to in Chapter 2. As we saw in Chapter 2 also, blue ocean strategy (a derivative of an analysis of 'value curves') is a more recent and highly valuable method of assessing market opportunities and is discussed later in this chapter).

Environmental Scanning Tools: Competitive Intelligence

A step beyond the more simplistic competitor analysis, a *competitive intelligence* (CI) system is a methodology that is sometimes viewed as a knowledge management system in its own right. Embedded within an organisation's intranet (or similar knowledge management technology), CI becomes a knowledge base of competitive activity that is interactive and visible. The management of a CI system is similar to that of a customer relationship management system or business intelligence (big data) system. Rather than an isolated analysis of competitor's traits or similar kinds of analysis, CI is managed as an interactive monitoring mechanism that has various live sources of data. A CI methodology is conducted as formal management capability and can be embedded within the firm Strategy Evaluation Dashboard Monitoring Mechanism discussed within the context of the programme of continual strategic renewal in Chapter 5.

In Table 3.2 I summarise the differences between the content of the better known, but higher level competitor analysis study as opposed to that of an in depth competitive intelligence system. In Table 3.3 I provide a summary of possible sources of data from upon a CI system can be based.

Table 3.2   Competitive intelligence characteristics

Competitor analysis: Information	Competitive intelligence: Knowledge
'One-off' analysis of: • comparative cost structures • location analysis • price and promotion activities • new product launches • number of employees	Competitor analysis *and* embedded (intranet portal) programme of monitoring and planning of competitor strategy and activities relating to: • future strategies • core competencies • investment programme • diversification opportunities, etc.
Orientation: Comparative advantage	*Orientation: Competitive advantage*

Table 3.3 summarises data sources with a focus on the external business environment.

Table 3.3   Alternative sources of competitive intelligence data

Areas of focus	Sources of information
External environment:	
• the economy • the marketplace • consumer trends • industry trends • technological developments	• professional service providers (Factiva, IBIS) • media, especially the Internet • general media: newspapers, TV etc. • internal sales force: price changes, people moves

Table 3.3   Alternative sources of competitive intelligence data *concluded*

Areas of focus	Sources of information
Competitor-specific information:	
• potential expansion of plants and operations • fundraising for future investment (share offerings, debt etc.) • moves of overseas competitors/company acquirers (predators) • parent company announcements	• public notices: annual reports • advertising and media agencies: advertising campaigns • business analytics: trackers and predictive analytics • trade shows • soft sources: sales, existing and former employees etc.

The effectiveness of a competitive intelligence system is optimised when implemented on a large scale. In this capacity, input is encouraged from employees who may hear things about competitors' activities from various sources, these could include social occasions such as parties or sporting events. Specialist staff can be asked to trawl the Internet and other media for information, whilst formal industry reports published by research companies can also be a useful source of information. Outputs may be presented simply though emails, a formal interactive strategy evaluation and monitoring mechanism or a more comprehensive dashboard reporting mechanism. More complex, dashboard reporting mechanisms are potentially the most effective method of reporting. An alerting mechanism incorporated into the firm's dashboard reporting system enables an automated response in especially volatile and competitive environments where changes in price, product/ system designs, pricing and availability may occur over short time spans. Petrol and alcohol are examples of this situation, where prices for petrol in particular can change hourly.

A competitive intelligence monitoring capability is operated through an alerting mechanism that can be linked to the strategic risk system referred to in Chapter 7. The CI system in general provides a means for managers to be more proactive than reactive in response to the activities of competitors.

STRATEGY EVALUATION SHAPING, ELEMENT 2: FUTURES THINKING

'Futures thinking' is the activity of looking into the future as an attempt to better prepare for whatever that future may bring, good or bad. Strictly speaking, of course, the future doesn't exist, so any conclusions that may be drawn about it can't be guaranteed.

Just as the researcher Igor Ansoff is now referred to as 'the Father of Strategy', Royal Dutch Shell and its pioneering strategy team, in particular Pierre Wack and Ted Newland, can be accorded the title 'Fathers of Structured Thinking Around Strategic Foresight'. As early futurists, Wack and Newland contributed to Shell's version of a methodological approach to futures thinking through the use of scenario planning. One of the strengths of the scenario planning practices developed by Pierre Wack in particular is the ability for Shell to transform quantitative and qualitative insights into descriptions of plausible but not necessarily probable futures by explaining their observations in the form of stories. In this format, the entertaining nature of their findings facilitates the capture of interest and enquiry, which literally builds *memories of the future*.

The term of 'memories of the future' is attributable to another of Shell's team of scenario planners, Arie de Geus. As author of the book *The Living Company*, de Geus (1997) describes memories of the future as being grounded in perception which in itself is not simply a matter of collecting information, but rather a way of looking at an object/event as 'an active engagement with the world; it requires the deliberate effort by management groups within the company to visit their future and develop time paths and options. Otherwise, the observations and data that are collected will have no meaning'.

Scenarios are used as a means to visit the future, but not one specific predictable future. Rather, scenarios are stories that are developed around a range of plausible futures to invoke strategic foresight, inform decision making, and in turn, induce action. The strength of scenarios is emphasised by de Geus as being its application to a learning organisation, to the extent that he is widely recognised as the originator of the concept. In that capacity, he is also recognised as providing the inspiration to Senge to go on to research and publish the book I have referred to previously *The Fifth Discipline* (1990).

In introducing the notion of organisational learning, de Geus bridges the divide between its application to individuals and teams. Individuals physically learn and retain knowledge, that wisdom is then retained in teams through formal and informal means (de Geus, 1997). Formal systems and processes, policies and procedures act as repositories for explicit knowledge, whilst folklore, story and collective wisdom remain the repositories for tacit knowledge. Explicit knowledge can be physically presented in a form that has been articulated, codified and stored in various media formats, tacit knowledge is presented in a format that is difficult to transfer to another person by any other means than verbalisation or in writing.

De Geus applies his concept of organisational learning to an understanding of the value it brings as a motivator for a response to the potential of change. De Geus suggests that memories of the future are a useful method of promoting change as a result of their ability to 'reduce uncertainty through prediction' (de Geus, 1997). Making any predictions about the future is, of course, a fatally flawed procedure. In recognition of this reality, de Geus has observed that memories of the future are more likely to evoke a response from managers because they are less specific, less certain, and as a result 'allow the manager to learn and to anticipate alternate, possible futures'. The importance of this capability is that knowledge captured in our memories is usually acted upon, whereas certain knowledge applied to a predicted/probable outcome, whilst interesting, is not necessarily believable, and even if it is, it is less likely to be acted upon. Developing plausible memories of the future, de Geus suggests, 'better allows us to prepare for them'.

An unfortunate but powerful example is the US government's response to the threat of terrorist attacks in 2012, when the US consulate in Benghazi was penetrated and torched. This is an episode that resulted in the loss of lives, including the highly respected Ambassador Christopher Stevens. Subsequent to the event it was rumoured that the embassy had insufficient defence, even though forewarning and advanced intelligence indicated an attack was imminent. Later, in August 2013, US agencies were rallied to action when their memories of the future prompted them to respond proactively to a non-specific threat (created as a result of an increase in Internet 'chatter') by moving to close all embassies in the Middle East even though they didn't have any specific information about the target or timing. The Benghazi episode was the trigger for this demonstration of proactive responsiveness.

Futures thinking: Scenario planning

Scenarios are the specific stories of the possible eventualities that are the output from scenario planning exercises. They provide a useful context for debate, contribute to informed decision making, and in that way help to facilitate the development of better policy and strategy. They also provide a shared understanding of possible future environments upon which a commitment to action can be based. As an exploration of the possible, not just the probable, they provide a relevant challenge to the conventional wisdom of their users and help them prepare for major changes that may lie ahead. They provide the content which feeds the previously mentioned memories of the future.

As a basis for strategy evaluation, scenarios are valuable attributes which can be applied to:

1.   test the validity of assumptions made in the strategy and the strategic planning process – a key part of the process of strategy evaluation;

2.   conduct a 'reality check' – providing insights into the question of reasonableness of assumptions and expected outcomes made in any situation, not just a strategy renewal;

3.   pre-empt the future – providing insights into potential outcomes and possibilities;

4.   inform decision making now – providing insights into the future, allowing us to make decisions now, in the context of possible (but not necessarily probable) outcomes;

5.   carry out risk assessment – analysis of potential and highest risk outcomes from a portfolio of strategic options-supporting activities that could include business cases, joint ventures, acquisition analysis and global expansion;

6.   facilitate leadership development – working in teams to develop shared visions of the future.

Futures thinking: Data analytics (big data)

As an emerging industry in its own right, data analytics is focused primarily on an analysis of internal trends and circumstances. Big data provides an 'evidence'-based approach to research that makes a significant contribution to strategic decision making because of its insight, which had previously been 'lost in the detail'. Designed to provide support to what would otherwise be considered to be gutfeel or intuitive decision analysis, data analytics utilises an increasingly complex array of software packages that are designed to mine the quantum of information contained within the mountains of data stored in enterprise-wide transaction processing systems. Collected over many years of transaction history, the information includes a summary of trends, anomalies and patterns in existing data, as well as an estimate of the potential outcomes using predictive analytics and trend analysis.

A primary purpose of the application of these tools is the development of the formal interactive strategy evaluation and monitoring mechanism we referred to previously as a basis for the measurement, management and reporting of data and content contained within various alerting mechanisms, strategy implementation and the continual renewal of strategy.

Futures thinking: Strategy as serious play, storytelling

Relaying sometimes dry factual content in the form of a more entertaining story has proven to be an effective way to considerably improve communications within a company, community or other organisation structure. An example is the relaying of a communiqué from head office. Rather than an hour-long presentation of the facts associated with poor plant performance, users of story would suggest that the issues be presented as a narrative that could, for example, involve players responsible for plant performance. This could include the recollection of the CEO, who, when faced with a similar problem during his or her period as factory leader, experienced similar faults – ideally re-told in a humorous way to ensure the current audience members are left in no doubt about ways to fix the problem.

In some instances humour is less appropriate as the situation being addressed is more serious in nature, in which case demonstrations, pilot programmes, beta releases and scenarios offer alternative ways to create awareness, manage mistakes and enable learning. Similarly, in a strategic context, the use of toys or plastic building blocks is sometimes seen as a viable method of illustration. Rather than slides, numbers and reports, the use of alternative mediums of communication and visualisation allows us to present and look at different perspectives on a problem. One of the reasons this works is that the method engages all the body's senses, not just the eyes and brain. In their paper 'Playing Seriously with Strategy', Johan Roos, Bart Victor and Matt Statler describe the use of LEGO bricks as a method of articulating strategy rather than words alone (Roos et al., 2004). Business simulation tools such as 'war games' provide another way of using theatre, intrigue and competition to get people more involved in strategy.

STRATEGY EVALUATION SHAPING, ELEMENT 3: RESPONSIVENESS

We have observed previously that all of proactive, reactive and designed forms of responsiveness are important and critical components of strategy. The formal 'Strategy Evaluation Reviewing and Monitoring Mechanism' discussed in Chapter 5 (Figure 5.1) is deployed to provide insight into potential activities or events that will provoke a response to proactive and reactive change. Designed change on the other hand is articulated as actions, projects and programmes that are the intended outcome from the strategising activities that contribute to, and are part of the strategic plan. There are numerous tools applicable to the broadly defined category of responsiveness, we will cover only a few here, with an emphasis on growth; specifically internally generated, organic growth rather than growth as a result of merger and/or acquisition.

Responsiveness: Strategies for growth

There are numerous models that help organisations to identify opportunities for growth, and Table 3.4 provides details of a few.

Table 3.4   Models that contribute to strategies for growth

Three Horizons and Capability Staircase (Baghai et al., 1996; Baghai et al., 1999)	**Purpose:** To provide a method for mapping future growth strategies in accordance with three time horizons. **Why it is useful?** It overcomes common pitfalls of growth strategies which do not include dimensions of time and the ability to anticipate resourcing/investment requirements. **How is it used?** Three Horizons Growth – a continuous pipeline of growth initiatives allows: • a staircase for building new resources, capabilities, and management systems; • borrowing from the existing core business(es); • learning and developing new capabilities (a stepping-stone approach).
Ansoff Product–Market Matrix (Ansoff, 1957)	**Purpose:** It allows strategists to consider ways to grow the business via existing and/or new products, and existing and/or new markets – there are four possible product/market combinations. **Why is it useful?** It illustrates how the element of risk increases the further strategy moves away from known quantities – the existing product and the existing market. **How is it used?** As a matrix, it provokes new ideas about ways to build on existing product strengths by: • being open to new product development (requiring, in effect, a new product); • market extension (a new market) typically involving a greater risk than 'penetration' (existing product and existing market); • diversification (a new product and a new market).

Table 3.4   Models that contribute to strategies for growth *concluded*

BCG Growth-Share Matrix (Henderson, 1979)	**Purpose:** It helps the company to allocate resources, and is also used as an analytical tool in brand marketing, product management, strategic management, and portfolio analysis.

Why it is useful: It is useful to graphically illustrate the potential of future cash flows from the portfolio suite.

How is it used? When used appropriately this matrix provides insight into ways to invest in various portfolio's of Business Units or products, however it:

- only ranks market share and industry growth rate, and only implies actual profitability;
- overlooks other elements of industry influences;
- has a subjective element involving guesswork about the future, particularly with respect to growth rates;
- is susceptible to over-enthusiasm of managers, who may claim that cash must be thrown at businesses that are not ready to generate the kinds of returns the proposed investment would otherwise warrant.

As a result, a poor definition of a business's market leads to some poor performers being misclassified as high cash generators when they are not.

Blue Ocean Strategy vs. Red Ocean Strategy

Purpose: Used to determine where high growth and profits can be generated through the creation of new demand in an uncontested market space, or 'blue ocean', rather than by competing head-to-head with other suppliers for known customers in an existing industry 'red ocean'.

Why it is useful: Value curves are used to help explore the value 'tradeoffs' firms impose on their customers, the value proposition generated by a firm's key attributes that specify the benefit to the customer. Dramatic increases in this value typically lead to discontinuous changes and:

- an expansion in the total size of the market;
- obsolescence of existing business models, making incumbents especially vulnerable as their way of doing business becomes increasingly obsolete;
- target specific (often unfulfilled) customer needs and increase market space.

How is it used? The cornerstone of 'blue ocean' strategy is value innovation: the simultaneous pursuit of differentiation and low cost. A 'blue ocean' is created when a company achieves value innovation that creates value simultaneously for both the customer and the company. The innovation (in product, service or delivery) must raise and create value for the market whilst simultaneously reducing or eliminating features or services that are less valued by the current or future market. The Strategy Canvas is both a diagnostic and an action framework that uses value curves to illustrate compelling opportunities for 'blue ocean' strategies. It serves two purposes:

- it captures the current state of play in the known market space;
- it provides a canvas upon which proposed value innovations can be evaluated.

Measures of Responsiveness: Organisational transformation and renewal

Organisational transformation and renewal is an outcome from a consciousness of the need for responsiveness (change). Intuition (again) plays a big part in knowing why to change and when it is important to change. Knowledge about the detail of change – the who, when, how and what to change – is informed by data. However, knowledge from data doesn't come directly from an enterprise-wide reporting system, nor directly from any transaction processing system, for that matter. It is, therefore, necessary to design a method of mining this data source, and that, as we have identified, can be derived from the mechanism we are proposing as strategy evaluation reviewing (discussed further in Chapter 7), which in turn is based on the design of a strategy evaluation monitoring mechanism, each of which are located in the fully integrated Strategic Management Framework illustrated as Figure 1.1. This monitoring mechanism can include data on competitive intelligence, analytics (trends and alerts), strategic risk (discussed as part of the topic of strategic governance in Chapter 7), scenario analysis, the strategy blueprint, assumptions made as part of strategy evaluation reviewing and all other knowledge of strategic importance.

The Cycle of Organisational Transformation and Renewal

In any discussion on the topic of organisational transformation and renewal, it is useful to understand the environment within which change will take place as much as the alerting and management of change itself. Previously I have observed that a firm must continue to find a position of fit within an increasingly dynamic, uncertain and sometimes irrational *external* environment. Similarly, events that occur *within* a firm will also have a significant impact on the content of businesses strategy and the strategic plan. I have also observed from research (Hunter, 2000) that a firm's position within its Cycle of Organisational Transformation and Renewal will have a significant impact on the management of a business, as shown in Figure 3.2 (overleaf).

As observed from my own research (Hunter, 2000) and in expanding the work of Ghoshal and Bartlett (1999) and earlier Gouillart and Kelly (1996), the existence of a Cycle of Organisational Transformation and Renewal was found to introduce insight into a far more complex programme of change in organisations, in stark contrast to the more familiar single-step approach to change of freeze–change–unfreeze proposed as early as 1947 by Kurt Lewin.

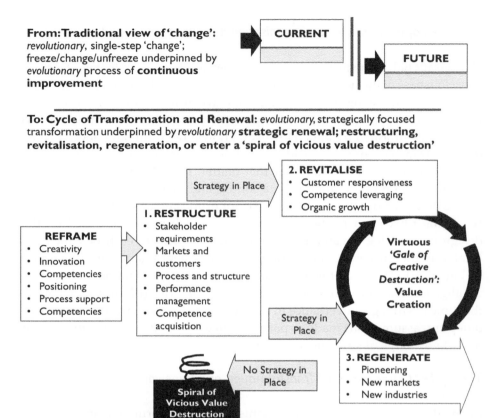

Figure 3.2   The four steps in the Cycle of Organisational Transformation and Renewal

The importance of understanding the impact of change in relation to alignment is attributable to the fact that whilst changes in the external environment are usually appreciated and understood, the impact of change internally is generally only appreciated when a tipping point or awakening from a dominant logic, for instance, has been reached and a recognition emerges that some form of change is required, usually quite quickly.

A dominant logic is a prevailing point of view among a leadership team, for example, which is often erroneously based on a prevailing commitment to competencies and capabilities that are seen as sacrosanct reasons for the team's past successes. It is a description of the culture and system of beliefs that the company leaders in particular hold to be true. A dominant logic can be useful when applied to strategic decision making in environments of little change; it can be devastating when the tried-and-true 'old normal' dissipates and a new way of thinking is required, but doesn't eventuate. This form of static, single-step change is contrasted with the Cycle of Organisational Transformation and Renewal that makes up the bulk of Figure 3.2.

The first stage of the Cycle of Organisational Transformation and Renewal – *reframing* – is described by Gouillart and Kelly (1996) as 'the shifting of the company's conception of what it is and what it can achieve'. Reframing, they suggest, addresses the corporate mind, the objective being to open it up to new visions and new resolves and to break out of existing mindsets. Similarly, Prahalad (2010) suggests: 'Leaders must also remember to focus the organisation on the forgetting curve. They must identify the behaviours, practices, and beliefs that are increasingly becoming dysfunctional or counterproductive and put in place ways of discarding them.' Senge (1990) describes the essence of reframing in the context of a learning organisation. He attributes it to a breaking down of mental models, the fundamental component of which is reflection. From my own experience, I cannot emphasise enough the need for business leaders to break out of their preconceived mental models and to engage in regular exercises in reframing.

Few groups can express an experience that led them to reframe their mental models more than those who have experienced an imperative to do so first hand. They are the returning astronauts who have viewed the planet Earth from outer space and assessed its fragility within the context of the entire Universe. They describe the impact of this experience as an 'overview effect'. This, they explain, has a 'transformational impact on their perspective of the planet and mankind's place upon it'. It is one that enables astronauts 'to appreciate Earth as a shared home, one without boundaries between nations or species'. So insightful is their experience that they have combined to form The Overview Institute, an organisation charged with the challenge of addressing the stark situation that they describe as 'a critical time' for Earth:

> We live at a critical moment in human history. The challenges of climate change, food, water and energy shortages as well as the increasing disparity between the developed and developing nations are testing our will to unite, whilst differences in religions, cultures, and politics continue to keep us apart. The creation of a 'global village' through satellite TV and the Internet is still struggling to connect the world into one community. At this critical moment, our greatest need

is for a global vision of planetary unity and purpose for humanity as a whole.[3]

We return to the imperative for reframing in Chapter 7, where it is identified as a crucial element of strategy as a profession.

The next stage of the Cycle of Organisational Transformation and Renewal is *restructuring*, an activity undertaken to re-focus and strengthen the performance of business units through evolutionary or revolutionary change. Actions to bring about organisational restructuring include downsizing, redundancy and divestment programmes. It is a process that is undertaken primarily to realise cost reduction targets, but is also often seen as vital as a driver of organisational renewal.

The following stage is *revitalisation*, a process that naturally follows a restructuring activity as it entails building and rebuilding an organisation's strength following the changes demanded by restructuring. It includes rebuilding the morale and culture of the business that is an inevitable outcome from a restructuring programme. The primary objective in this phase is to capitalise on opportunities across business units by exploiting economies of scale, leveraging individual resources and capturing opportunities for cross-unit learning.

Regeneration is the most comfortable stage in the cycle, and is characterised by its emphasis on wealth creation and continual renewal as a basis for continual growth. It is reached when an organisation is able to embed its ability to 'continually replenish and renew itself' (Ghoshal and Bartlett, 1999).

Hunter (2000) observed that the cycle shown in Figure 3.2 is breakable. When an organisation entered a period of restructuring for the purpose of cost reduction alone and in instances where there wasn't a conscious strategy for revitalisation and regeneration, it was apparent that the organisation was susceptible to enter a vicious spiral of value destruction – in the form of continued attempts to reduce costs rather than rebuild and move towards the creation of new wealth. On the other hand, those organisations that entered a transformation programme with a clear strategy of renewal (those which had a good understanding of what they were restructuring to become – a renewed purpose), they usually went on to enter a virtuous cycle of value-creation, one of revitalisation followed by regeneration.

---

3   See www.overviewinstitute.org/about-us/declaration-of-vision-and-principles.

The period in the life of Cadbury (1866 to the early 1900s) is characterised by each of the stages of the Cycle of Organisational Transformation and Renewal. Whereas the long-term strategy remained consistent, the change in fortune that was brought about by the purchase of the Van Houghton press was significant and enabled Cadbury Brothers for the first time to migrate from a stage of restructuring to one of revitalisation and then renewal – as might be expected in a business where long-term imperatives are well understood and the outcome from revitalisation strongly appreciated.

The validity of the practical working of the cycle demonstrated in spades at Cadbury. In view of the strength of the brothers' understanding of their long-term imperatives, John and Richard were able to move quickly into a mode of revitalisation – invigoration and motivation of the team – then on to a period of regeneration. The ease of transformation was enhanced considerably when in 1879 the machines were turned on at Cadbury's new production operations at a location they named Bourneville. This facility included many features designed specifically and directly to boost morale and at the same time improve the health and welfare of employees. In view of Richard Cadbury's death in 1899, it is interesting to assess the impact of this unforeseen event on the business; the answer will become apparent in Chapter 4.

The Strategic Plan and Strategy Evaluation Reviewing

Ultimately it is the value and quality of the content contained in the strategic plan that is of primary concern to us in this chapter – more so I think than the means by which we obtain that content. The content we do develop is articulated in the form of a description of the specific strategic objectives that are identified as its outcomes. These are typically project- or programme-oriented in nature; examples include a determination to enter new markets in a foreign country, to implement a new management information system or to embark on a programme of cost reduction and restructuring.

It is these specific strategic objectives that are included within the construct of the strategy blueprint, a structure referred to in Figure 3.1 and illustrated in Appendix 2. An illustration of a Strategic Architecture and Strategy Blueprint derived from the Cirque du Soleil case study is presented in Chapter 5. In the next chapter we review the most critical aspect of strategy, individual stakeholder engagement and strategy as practice – enacted in teams.

Chapter 4

Strategy in Teams: Empowering Teams as Business Leaders and Enablers of Continual Renewal

INCONVENIENT TRUTH NO. 4: INDIVIDUAL SUBCONSCIOUS PREFERENCES EXERT AN INVISIBLE, ADVERSE INFLUENCE ON DECISION MAKING.

Strategy is dominated by individual subconscious preferences and an often destructive dominant logic that prevails in groups/teams.

There has always been a lack of appreciation of the importance of cognitive aspects of strategy, especially in the *doing* context of strategy as practice. In the absence of a clear understanding of the *purpose* of strategy, though, practitioners, managers and leaders will often resort to a structured planning regime that is more about form-filling and documentation rather than the undertaking of rigorous research and analysis that is required by the challenging and sometimes arduous task of problem solving and structured strategic thinking.

To be effective, individual strategy professionals need to engage in deep strategic thinking (strategising), creative strategic thinking (design, integrative thinking), problem solving, strategic analysis, planning and assessments of the implications of a programme of strategy renewal. As an emerging profession, strategy practitioners should not feel it's OK to take short cuts – it's not.

Even though we focus on individuals when promoting the notion of strategy as a profession, strategy in an organisation is rarely the responsibility of individual practitioners alone. Rather, in most instances it is conducted in groups or teams. The success or otherwise of that team is highly reliant on effective teamwork and the guidance of a strong leader, so motivating, cultivating and rewarding individuals in order to get them to strategise effectively *together* is critical to the success of that leader. The problem is that individuals in teams don't always work well together, for a variety of reasons.

The Fourth Inconvenient Truth of Strategy

The issue of the effectiveness of individuals working together in strategically oriented teams is the focus of The Fourth Inconvenient Truth of Strategy:

> *Individual subconscious preferences exert an invisible, adverse influence on decision making. Strategy is dominated by individual subconscious preferences and an often destructive dominant logic that prevails in groups/teams. The consequences are that a dominant logic leads to hubris and myopia, which contribute to tensions within teams. This leads to discontent, conflict, organisational discord, and inevitably, suboptimal strategic outcomes.*

In addressing this Fourth Inconvenient Truth of Strategy, we will explore the issue of adverse influences on teams. This includes the topics of *dominant logic* among team members, *strategic drift* of teams and the notion of *strategic agility* as a solution. We also explore the primary team activity that is followed (usually by tradition and convention) in the form of a praxis – the way we physically prepare the annual strategic plan and the way it is managed and evaluated on an ongoing basis.

In particular, we will address the need to challenge conventional wisdom and assess the value of the content and construct of team-focused, generic 'away days' (or 'off sites') for the purpose of strategising. An alternative, I propose, is a more thorough and comprehensive approach to the workshopping component of planning, and potentially, a transformation of the omnipresent 'off site' routine as an alternative method of strategising, through the application of the formal and embedded programme of continual strategy renewal, as discussed in Chapter 2. This is followed by an introduction to an *automated strategy evaluation dashboard monitoring* mechanism that gives visibility to strategy and informs the decision making activities undertaken by the various leadership teams.

Our story of Cadbury does not directly address the issue of teams per se, we can see from this next instalment of the Cadbury case study that newly invigorated teams, the breaking down of hardened values and cultures and the strength of leadership are all at the fore of a successful business.

Launch of Cadbury Brothers Ltd: Realising the Power of Teams

Richard Cadbury's untimely death left his brother George as the sole Managing Director of the business. Acting upon a prior agreement with Richard, George immediately moved to turn the family-owned business into a private limited company. Illustrative of an act of *reframing* (thinking differently), followed by a programme of *restructuring* (a programme of change in a business model or physical structure) – both identified as components of the Cycle of Organisational Transformation and Renewal described in Chapter 3 – George acted rapidly. A new leadership team was formed, with George appointed as Chairman. In the implementation of decisions expressed in Cadbury's newly defined long-term strategy, formal or otherwise (but at any rate articulated as a result of team based collaboration – and learning) the transformation began. No doubt an informal plan was developed, it wouldn't have been called a strategic plan, it would though see the business implement a purposeful program of renewal that would contribute to continued growth and higher profits because of the sense of purpose and direction now adopted by the recently invigorated, focused leadership team. Changes included a revision of its company structure which saw the launch of Cadbury Brothers Ltd in 1899. George's fellow directors were Barrow and William A. Cadbury, sons of Richard, and two of his own sons, Edward and George Cadbury Junior.

Prior to Richard's death, both George and Richard had sought to satisfy two complementary needs: to further indulge their deep Quaker commitments with a focus on employee welfare, and to find a location to build new manufacturing plant that would cater for increased production demands from an ever-growing sales base. The brothers sought to satisfy both requirements through the establishment of a new manufacturing facility which they completed in 1879. It eventuated with the construction of a production plant in the countrified atmosphere of Bourneville, located 6.4 kilometres to the south of their previous address, Bridge Street in central Birmingham. Employee conditions were so good at Bourneville it would become world-famous. Benefits afforded to employees included the provision of modern amenities that ultimately included a swimming pool, tennis courts and company-sponsored housing.

There was also another side to the investment the brothers made in Bourneville that is reflected in the realisation of significant efficiencies in the supply chain. Situated on a canal and in close proximity to a railway line, Cadbury's was able to haul imported sugar and cacao beans from the coast directly to the factory by barge, and to distribute its finished goods to its major markets by rail. The notion of employee benefits also had a spin-off that had a positive impact on efficiency. As a result of the move, staff morale was boosted by the provision of amenities and housing and an end to the Dickensian-era working environment. The company was in turn able to benefit from its access to a loyal, fit, healthy and dextrous employee base whose primary contribution to the organisation was the provision of unskilled manual labour.

The commitment, discipline – and some would suggest, devotion – that became the hallmark of the Cadbury business reached a new level of success after another product innovation was made in late 1897. After a considerable period (over 10 years, in fact) George's son, George Cadbury Junior, was able to announce that his research and development team had finally been successful in blending milk with raw chocolate to produce a prototype milk chocolate product – a precursor to the melt-in-the-mouth milk chocolate bar we enjoy so much today. Cadbury's final version was called Cadbury Dairy Milk Chocolate. The ultimate saleable version, however, did not materialise until 1904. This breakthrough, as good as it was, was still some eighteen years behind the Swiss and other competitors, which had first developed a milk chocolate product as early as 1886.

The lateness of the release of Cadbury Dairy Milk Chocolate into the consumer market afforded its global competitors a considerable head start, and this hurt Cadbury the most in its home market, the UK. Just as the Swiss company Nestlé had already stolen a considerable march on its international competitors with the manufacture of milk chocolate, other chocolate manufacturers in the UK and Hershey in the USA had developed their own versions of the revolutionary bitter-free (or sweet-tasting) milk and cacao chocolate product.

Entering a new period of revitalisation following the restructuring that took place as a result of the appointment of the new leadership team, the new breed of leaders made up of George and Richard's descendents introduced a new burst of energy into the businesses leadership profile – and an ethos of working as a team which had not been a predominant characteristic of the management style practised by Richard and George. Having finally cracked the secret to the mass production of Dairy Milk Chocolate, Cadbury was poised to enter a new era of market competitiveness representing a significant shift in its state of market equilibrium. The change represented a *transformation*, from an inside-out resource-based push to one of an outside-in market-driven pull as its primary focus of competitiveness.

Upon entering this new era of ownership, the leadership team introduced new ideas to improve the business. They had the creativity, the energy, the freshness and enthusiasm to make a difference. Perhaps more importantly, they also had a shared vision, a shared mental model (unencumbered by the strength of traditional Quaker values) and an ability to learn and reinvent the business where appropriate.

However, the actions they took to improve the business didn't need to focus on an overly aggressive reinvention of strategy per se. More likely it was a focus on implementation – as is often the case in business, although, as we will see in Chapter 5, implementation of strategy is judged by many to be notoriously unsuccessful (Mankins and Steele, 2006). Rather, as a group of enthusiastic and motivated leaders, the new Cadbury leadership team focused on the more obvious areas where systems, processes and infrastructure could be improved. We can now identify these as being a refocusing of transforming activities that were redirected intuitively by the new team, away from a sole focus on production capability, towards broader based issues with the purpose of allowing the business to maintain and grow its strategically important resource base. Improvements made to operational effectiveness were centred on the most critical areas of operations. These included the introduction of analytical laboratories, increased expenditure on brand recognition (through advertising) and the establishment of a costing department, a sales department, a works committee and a medical department. These changes were followed by the introduction of pension funds as well as education and training programmes for employees (Cadbury, 2010). The results were noticeable, and as sales in exports grew, additional significant decisions were made to improve the efficiency and effectiveness of manufacturing operations of the factory itself.

As an indication of the awakening of the need to re-focus attention on markets and customers and not the Cadbury resource base alone, investments were also made in the areas of new product development and the introduction of new ideas in product presentation and marketing programmes. These included a new focus on the use of marketing techniques such as the attendance of mobile sales booths at sporting events, increased sales representation in stores, outdoor advertising and in 1920, the launch of the now famous purple packaging (with gold lettering). As a result of the fresh and invigorated thrust of energy that was generated by the leadership team, the newly derived efficiencies and promotions significantly improved competitiveness, to the point where chocolate had become much more affordable, accessible and available for the majority of the population.

The considerable disruption from world events that took place in the first half of the nineteenth century proved to be a huge distraction to the Cadbury business. These events though turned out to be both a blessing and a curse. Just as orders from the armed forces for chocolate and the disruption of supply from European based manufacturers afforded Cadbury a leg up in profitability, a spike in the price of imported raw materials sugar and cacao had the opposite effect. Similarly, just as the UK Ministry of Supply assumed control of the Bourneville factory, and in the First World War used the premises to produce war supplies that included gas masks, aeroplane wings and machine tools, this event forced Cadbury to do more with less. This meant that Cadbury was forced to significantly reduce product variety and rationalise its production to a much more efficient base. Learnings from these disruptions counted in their favour though, as the manufacturing capability that was already their competitive advantage was enhanced even further as a result of this experience.

When combined with the considerable unrest in the first half of the twentieth century that was also under way around the world (in the form of revolutions in places such as Russia and China, and the Great Depression that swept the Western world in 1930), Cadbury was faced with greater complexities and challenges than we could ever imagine today. It took eight years for all forms of rationing to end in the UK following the declaration of victory in the Second World War on 8 May 1945. The pace of recovery from this final war episode was so slow that it drove the newly appointed chairman of Cadbury Brothers Ltd, Laurence Cadbury (son of George Cadbury's second wife), to focus on identifying new ways to grow the business through an expansion of the markets for Cadbury chocolate products overseas.

Under his guidance, Cadbury expanded its Canadian, South African, Australian, New Zealand and Irish businesses significantly. In 1953 further developments saw a second-term reinvigoration of Bourneville and the establishment of a new factory in Moreton, on the Wirral Peninsula near Liverpool. Market-based competition was now stronger than ever, and differentiation more difficult to achieve. At the same time, a game changing marketing weapon had arrived in the form of a new communications medium, television that saw advertising become the key driver of growth in sales volumes and market share for all consumer-oriented products. The focus of Cadbury's strategy now moved from the development of a competency in chocolate manufacture towards the realisation of growth in profitability (efficiency and effectiveness) and the expansion of markets overseas.

For more than 100 years, Cadbury had remained essentially a family business, non-family directors being appointed to the board for the first time in 1943. Company fortunes went from strength to strength, benefiting from new technology that made it one of the most efficient chocolate manufacturers in the world. In 1961 pressure from Cadbury family shareholders began to emerge, seeking relief from a lack of access to cash that was tied up in the form of shares. The best way to unlock this cash, the family members reasoned, was to take the company public. In 1962, therefore, the Cadbury business was reorganised and a publicly listed company was formed – Cadbury plc. The family team that had thrived on the challenge of growing a multinational company had finally succumbed to the reality of handing the baton over to professional managers and directors. This move brought greater individual freedom for family member shareholders, the business now came under significant public scrutiny and was deemed by many in the stock market to be under-performing.

By this time, however, the chocolate confectionery industry had matured significantly, forcing Cadbury's directors to accept the need to look further afield, at new international markets, if the company was to increase share price whilst also maintaining or growing its dividends. Fundamental to the state of decline was an easing in Cadbury competitiveness that prior to the onset of war had been a competency in efficient and effective manufacturing (Bradley, 2008). Up until the disruption of the wars that occurred in the first half of the twentieth century Cadbury had been relying on a comparative advantage of low cost and high quality, to compete. In between and in the post war period, their competitors had caught up, Cadbury's past competitive advantage had been significantly diluted. At the same time the maturation of the confectionary industry not only saw a consolidation of suppliers, it also (unusually) saw a consolidation of consumer preferences. Chocolate, as it turns out, is a product where taste is of paramount importance. Once a preference is established amongst consumers, it is very difficult to introduce any kind of variation. That is why some chocolate brands enjoy a perennially higher market share in some countries over others.

Strategising in Teams and the Effect of a Dominant Logic

As a family owned company, most, if not all of the key decision makers at Cadbury would have been related. The implication being that just about every aspect of interpersonal behaviour between team members (that normally exist in non-familial environments especially), would be accentuated. At the same time there would have existed a level of familiarity that allows team members to cut through the niceties of civil interaction that is mandatory for those in a more public corporate environment. The dynamics of team interactions at Cadbury therefore, may have been challenging if not fiery from time to time.

Evidence of areas where leadership intimacy did work well in the company was in the team's ability to make quick decisions, adaptiveness and a passion for quality (Bradley, 2008).

In a broader context, one can appreciate the necessity for team members in business organisations to conform in some way, although a degree of familiarity and cohesiveness inevitably evolves over time. The question though, is: 'How well can this team work together in order to ensure optimal levels of performance?' As an illustration of the difficulties of working in teams, I refer to the popular movie *As Good as it Gets*, which features an example of a team thrown together under tenuous circumstances. The storyline explores the interactions that arise between three insecure and diverse personalities residing in New York who are forced to collaborate to achieve specific goals and outcomes. The unlikely trio includes Melvin Udall (played by Jack Nicholson), a middle-aged, successful author who suffers from an obsessive compulsive personality disorder as well as unfortunate personality traits that include homophobia, anti-Semitism, racism and an intense dislike of people and dogs. The second character is Simon Bishop (Greg Kinnear), a gay, agitated, highly creative but emotionally detached and demoralised character who appears to suffer from depression. Simon lives in the apartment opposite Udall and owns a dog. The third is Carol Connelly (Helen Hunt), who presents as a calm, responsible and capable woman who is overburdened by a lack of money and a requirement to support a young son who carries a permanent debilitative disease. Carol is adopted by Melvin as his personal waitress in the local restaurant where she works, as no one else can relate to or tolerate him. Carol lives with her mother and ailing son on the other side of town. A rational individual, she is quite stable, she just needs a break.

When Simon is assaulted, robbed and nearly killed in his apartment, Melvin, in an unusual display of sympathy, offers to look after his dog whilst he is in hospital. When he later offers to drive him to Baltimore so that he can visit his parents following his release from hospital, the necessity for slick teamwork begins – or rather, it doesn't. As an example of the ensuing disharmony, Melvin invites Carol to join them on the journey, and once they arrive in Baltimore, Carol inspires him to take her to dinner. Her patience with his behaviour is short-lived. His comments about her clothing in the restaurant become too offensive for her to bear, so she leaves and doesn't talk to him again for the entire trip home. Simon remains neutral but naturally orients towards Carol's side, so it is a subdued journey.

As independent individuals, Melvin, Simon and Helen lead happy (albeit lonely) but very different kinds of lives. Working as a team, they achieve their collective goal of getting to Baltimore and back, even though there is conflict and their combined efforts are mostly ineffective. The divergent personality types depicted in this movie can all too often be witnessed in leadership teams, each of which are generally made up of people with strong, individual personalities, and all of whom will in some way present with extreme personality traits just like the main characters in the film. Our understanding of the impact of individual personalities and traits in the adverse environment that is the backdrop to *As Good as it Gets* is important. No matter how similar team members are to the personalities of Melvin, Helen and Simon, most of the time the primary drivers of strategy are the members of the senior leadership team, which is bound together by some form of bond. For all activities outside specific functional roles, the team you have is the team you get. The imperative to work together to realise results really is *as good as it gets*.

Most often, the final document or stamp of approval – or in an open strategising community, the overall strategy content, commitment and approval – is developed by a small group of individuals working in a team that develops and confirms the strategy of the organisation. In too many cases, though, ill-prepared teams, ill-informed teams, badly structured teams or teams that are simply dysfunctional fail to develop strategy content that is anything more than a reflection of the status quo. The worst-case scenario is a team whose members live, eat, breathe and think the same way.

In many instances, a team that has not changed its makeup for a sustained period is known to be susceptible to the syndrome of dominant logic. As Prahalad (2010) explains, leadership teams in successful enterprises will over time create distinct business ideologies – such as the Hewlett Packard (HP) Way and the Xerox Way. These doctrines embody specific ideas about how to compete, define performance measures, design organisational structures, and assess how and who to reward, and the beliefs and practices that constitute the company's dominant logic (Prahalad, 2010). Prahalad warns:

> *Adhering to one best way of doing things worked well during the industrial era, but the forces of globalization, digitization, mobile communications, and sustainability pose a different set of challenges today. However, many leaders remain in denial, claiming that consumers don't change quickly, that existing products are superior and that people won't give up on familiar experiences and so on. They don't accept in time the need for change. (Prahalad, 2010)*

A dominant logic can be seen to arise in successful companies, to the point where the more successful they become, the more embedded a leadership team's collective frame of reference also becomes. Success breeds success – until it doesn't. At that point the team becomes overwhelmed by hubris. The more rigid the frame of reference, the more influence the dominant logic of that team will have. Similarly, continued success can result in a company physically embedding its distinct business ideologies into rigid systems and processes or formalised policies and procedures, creating a situation where entrenched continuous improvement programmes such as the Toyota Way can have a negative impact on business effectiveness. As observed by prominent researchers Prahalad and Bettis (1986): 'those things that underpinned past successes eventually become the cause of failure'.

A dominant logic operates beyond the conscious awareness of teams. Individual team members remain oblivious to its existence, often until it is too late. Ultimately, arrogance and overconfidence become inevitable outcomes from successful teams which continue to be rewarded for remaining stubbornly committed to the status quo – until the status quo becomes irrelevant, as does the team. Inevitably, as observed by Prahalad and Bettis (1986), 'any form of challenge to continually successful teams is seen as being anti-social'.

Perhaps there is a degree of dominant logic evident in many teams. Although our research has shown that 83 per cent of survey respondents think that their strategy and strategic planning are useful and worth preserving, other results as shown Table 4.1 suggest that many aspects of individual and team effectiveness in practice are in fact a lot less than perfect, and as a result, effectiveness in strategy suffers.

Strategy in particular succeeds or does not depending on the calibre, knowledge and experience of individual strategy practitioners, the extent to which they are competent strategic thinkers, and their ability to work and, when necessary, lead teams. In these circumstances, adopting the principles of a learning organisation becomes even more appropriate. As I have said before, strategy is about the future, and the future is unknown. In order to respond to the unknown, individuals and teams must *unlearn* the wisdom of the past and *learn new things* that are potentially going to deliver greater value in the future.

Table 4.1   Survey results from SMI/Swinburne University research into strategy practices conducted in 2013

Strategy limitations and effectiveness of teams and individuals	Strongly agree/agree
Scene-setting:	
• Strategy is limited by our capacity for change.	57%
• Strategy and strategic thinking is one of our main strengths.	21%
Strategy effectiveness:	
• All of our managers act in accordance with the direction identified in the strategy.	47%
• Strategy prepared in groups tends to impede progress as a result of conflict that occurs within the group.	32%
• We implement strategy effectively.	26%
• All of our senior managers are competent 'strategic thinkers'.	19%

Organisational learning (and unlearning) therefore provides a means to capture individual knowledge and skills and apply them to the advantage of the team. The notion of unlearning is also explored as a discipline of Senge's (1990) concept of learning organisations. This is realised through the recognition of the problem of individuals' preconceived mental models that influence subconscious preferences and lead to bias in decision making. Very often, Senge (1990) observes, individuals are not consciously aware of the existence of their personal mental models, or the effects they have on behaviour. The outcome is that 'many insights into new markets or organisational models fail to get into practice because they conflict with powerful, pre-existing tacit mental models'.

The Environment Within Which a Systemic Strategy is Enacted: From Strategic Drift to Strategic Agility

All too often the reality of a shift in the environment within which a business succeeds eludes the conscious awareness of leadership teams. Strategy authors Johnson et al. (2011) compare the extremity of the unfortunate impact of such a situation to that of a business that, similar to strategic inertia, has entered a state of a strategic drift. An example of strategic drift can be found in what was once one of the two premier domestic airlines in Australia, Ansett Airlines, which collapsed over ten years ago. Once the owner of a 50 per cent share of Australia's domestic airline market (with Qantas), Ansett Airlines' demise (considered to be one of Australia's biggest corporate collapses) provides a strong opportunity for learning.

Writing in the *The Australian* newspaper, journalist Robert Gottliebsen appears to have hit the nail on the head quite early (9 September 2001) following Ansett's demise. Gottliebsen observed:

> *Ansett's sins were many. It had work practices that reflected poor management, too many aircraft types, a seat configuration in aircraft that did not maximise returns, and it was loaded with borrowings from bankers who had never checked the calibre of the management. (Gottliebsen, 2001)*

This sentiment was confirmed later by CEO of the day Sir Rod Eddington, who described Ansett simply as 'a great airline, but a poor business'. Similarly, one former Ansett employee observed on reflection that: 'Ansett suffered from the industry's highest employee cost base, inflexible trade unions and a Noah's Ark Fleet of planes.'

Ansett can be seen to have been in a state of strategic drift – a situation that arises when a dominant logic afflicts critical decision making, which in turn inhibits an leadership team's ability to respond adequately to changes in its operating environment. Such a situation lets teams continue with that strategy for too long, even when the decisions and activities of the company are obviously increasingly out of touch with external trends. Just as low-cost airlines globally (and in Australia now with Virgin) were emerging, Ansett seems to have been oblivious to the consequences, by way of example, it was observed that at the time of its greatest threat a former CEO wanted to include gold plated ashtrays in the new Airbuses.

Johnson et al. (2011) identify four phases of strategic drift. Phase 1 is represented by a period of incremental change – in the wrong direction. Signs of trouble at Ansett emerged as early as 1994 when one of its international Boeing 747 Jumbo jets landed in Sydney with only three engines working and a warning sound alerting the pilots that the nose landing gear had also not extended. That, though, was not the real problem. The real problem was that the flight crew had been unsuccessful in establishing the reason for the warning, so they ignored it. Why? They did not believe that a mechanical fault existed. They simply proceeded to land the plane with its nose gear still retracted. Fortunately, there were no injuries.

In Phase 2 of strategic drift the inevitability of failure to change becomes more noticeable. At Ansett, the company was increasingly experiencing bad publicity. Compounded by its ageing fleet, Ansett started to buckle under the weight of increasingly ineffective maintenance measures. The outcome was a decline in overall market share, with customers becoming less trustworthy and loyal as the young, fresh, low-cost Virgin Blue Airline became increasingly more attractive as a viable alternative to the top two, Ansett and Qantas.

In Phase 3 of strategic drift organisations are noted to be in a state of flux. At Ansett, this meant that the problems continued, and in fact compounded, whilst the threat of competition from Virgin and other low-cost carriers was still being ignored. When the Australian Civil Aviation Authority forced the grounding of Ansett's entire Boeing 767 fleet because of more maintenance concerns, things really started to turn sour. The impact of the forced landing was compounded by the distraction of finding ways to restructure and reduce costs as the company was becoming increasingly short of cash. It was reportedly losing up to AU$1.3 million a day.

In the final phase of strategic drift, businesses either end up with a resolve to make dramatic moves to restructure, or face the inevitability of takeover or collapse. Ansett was by now assessing drastic options for survival associated with an immediate (revolutionary) transformational change. As observers noted at the time, though, Ansett's parent company, Air New Zealand, simply didn't have the resources to hold it up. Just as major cost reduction measures were being implemented, it became apparent that adequate levels of revenue could not be maintained, receivers were appointed and the entire fleet was grounded. The fight for survival had been lost, and Ansett's planes were later sold for spare parts.

Had Ansett's leadership team possessed a capacity for *strategic agility* instead of falling into the trap of strategic drift, things might have been different. Strategic agility represents a management mindset that leads a business towards a state of transformation and reinvention as opposed to decline and extinction. The identification of the construct of strategic agility can be attributed to academics Doz and Kosonen (2008), who studied nine successful high-technology firms to determine how management teams could succeed in transforming organisations. The need to do so, they suggested, arose because of their view that firms fail not because they do something wrong, but because they keep doing what used to be the right thing for too long, and end up falling victim to the rigidity of their prevailing business model.

The three vectors of strategic agility have nothing to do with strategy systems and process, but rather a state of leadership – and mind. The cognitive aspects of strategic agility include:

- **strategic sensitivity** – the ability to mount proactive and reactive responses to changes in the business environment;

- **leadership unity** – the capacity for the leadership team to make short, sharp, responsive decisions without being bogged down in bureaucracy;

- **resource fluidity** – the internal capability to reconfigure and redeploy resources rapidly and effectively.

The promise from strategic agility, according to Doz and Kosonen (2008), is: 'Continuously adjust and adapt strategic direction in core business as a function of strategic ambitions and changing circumstances; create not just new products and services, but also new business models and innovative ways to create value'.

The organisations that participated in Doz and Kosonen's research included IBM, SAP, Intel, Kone and Cisco. Characteristics of strategic agility include the operation of an open (visible) strategy process, heightened strategic alertness (at senior leader level), high-quality internal dialogue, mutual dependency (among the senior leadership team) and an adaptive (inclusive) leadership style. But none of these can exist or be conducted in isolation. In order to be successful, the enactment of all three is essential: 'Being good at one, or even two, or working hard to rebuild selectively some capabilities and not others, will not help much. It may even lead you to a dead end.'

As we discussed in Chapter 2, Senge (1990) observed that the discipline of *team learning* is an important component of learning and the operation of a learning organisation. Its application that is relevant to this chapter comprises the apparent synergistic effects that are available from combined knowledge rather than individual knowledge. In particular, Senge (1990) promotes the activity of dialogue between team members as they interact and learn from each other – and I have observed that this is an attribute of excellence in the executive education programmes I have conducted as part of the SMI. Dialogue, Senge suggests, is one of the most important elements of communication within teams. He sees it as being rather more powerful than simple conversations. Senge describes dialogue as being optimised when the capacity of team members reaches the point where they are able to 'suspend assumptions and enter into a genuine "thinking together"'.

Teams that think and learn together are in a position to share their knowledge more widely, and thereby encourage learning by other teams whilst at the same time invoking a demand for innovation. Teams that learn together and are innovative will no doubt also be successful teams. Team learning, according to Senge (1990), has three dimensions. The first is the need for teams to think insightfully if they are to solve those 'wicked' problems we referred to in Chapter 1. The second is the need for innovative, co-ordinated action, the art of working together seamlessly, effortlessly and effectively. In a precursor to the potential role of the chief strategy officer and his or her team (see Chapter 7), the third dimension of team learning is that it is the role of team members on other teams who undertake much of the learning, for example where many of the actions of the most senior teams are in fact researched and developed by other (usually subordinate) teams.

An excellent example of this team-based approach to learning at the most senior level is provided by Grove (1999), whose story, described in his book *Only the Paranoid Survive*, describes the close relationship he had with his co-founder and Chief Operating Officer at Intel, Gordon Moore. Over time, according to Grove, his and Moore's relationship grew uncannily deep. In contrast, his relationship with his other co-founder, Robert Noyce, never rose to those heights. When asked how he, Moore and Noyce worked together at Intel, though, Grove referred to Peter Drucker's 1954 book *The Practice of Management* to accentuate for us the impact of team learning and the role of leader in that team. Drucker (1954), Grove explained, argues that the activities that make up a chief executive's job are too varied to be performed by a single person, but should be divided between three people with different attributes: thoughtfulness, action-oriented and a figurehead. Grove noted that during the 1970s, that description applied to Intel's three co-founders: Moore, with his encyclopaedic mind, was the thought persona; Noyce, a person who had enormous standing in the semiconductor industry, was Intel's public persona or the front person, and Grove, who exhibited a no-nonsense style and 'man of action' persona, was someone who got things done.

Intel's core business, which initially focused on memory chips, changed dramatically over time. The way in which that change came about is now a well-documented part of Intel's history. As Grove (1999) tells the story in *Only the Paranoid Survive*, the company went through a 'crisis of mammoth proportions' as it 'got out of the business it was founded on and built a new identity in a totally different business'. Grove says that although this experience was unique to Intel, the lessons it teaches are universal. When Moore, Grove and Noyce started Intel, their goal was to produce memory chips. By the time the 1980s came, the nature of the business had changed. Japanese chip makers had entered the market in a big way – Grove described them as an 'overwhelming force'. The Japanese were offering better quality whilst also beating the US chip makers on price. In an effort to beat back this competition, Intel tried to ramp up its manufacturing efforts. 'During the 1970s, we were parallel to our competition,' says Grove. 'In the 1980's, the competition became better than us, but we didn't respond until Craig [Barrett] took charge of it.' Even so, in the middle of 1985 a watershed moment occurred. As Grove explains in a frequently quoted passage from *Only the Paranoid Survive*, he was sitting in his office with Moore, then Intel's Chairman and CEO, discussing their situation:

> *Our mood was downbeat. I looked out the window at the Ferris wheel of the Great America amusement park revolving in the distance, then I turned back to Gordon and I asked, 'If we got kicked out and the board brought in a new CEO, what do you think he would do?' Gordon answered without hesitation, 'He would get us out of memories.' I stared at him, numb, then said, 'Why shouldn't you and I walk out the door, come back, and do it ourselves?' (Grove, 1999)*

So they did.

Since 1981, Intel had been supplying microprocessors for IBM PCs. As demand for personal computers exploded, demand for Intel microprocessors grew as well. In addition, its next-generation microprocessor, the famous IBM 386 mainframe, was about to go into production. Grove made the case, which was resisted at first by employees and then gradually accepted, that Intel should leave the declining memory business and concentrate its R&D and manufacturing efforts on producing better microprocessors. As a result, Intel's fortunes gradually swung up again. Grove's leadership in turning Intel away from memory chips and towards microprocessors, enacted through the support of his close colleagues and their teams, helped Intel to retain its market lead. It might otherwise have gone the other way.

Strategy developed by teams also benefits from the input and often insight from new staff and external advisers. They can bring a degree of naivety (a useful contribution in many cases where accepted wisdom is often a cause of close-mindedness and negativity), an undistracted discipline of focus, a propensity to challenge and a fresh perspective to the really wicked strategic problems. At a recent dinner my wife and I attended to welcome home a friend from a seven-year international posting, I was reminded of the value of this input. Having returned to Australia from the position of global manufacturing leader based in Europe, my friend carried the authority, respect and knowledge that is automatically associated with that level of experience. As part of his portfolio of manufacturing operations upon his return to Australia he inherited one plant in particular that, he explained, was struggling to get enough volume to justify its existence. As a proactive, action-oriented kind of person, my friend immediately used his initiative to trial new products at that factory. Rather than get upset, the marketing department (with which my friend had become quite frustrated because of its lack of initiative) expressed delight at the innovative products the factory came up with. Hopefully, as a result of this man's leadership, the factory that was in danger of coming under threat of closure will remain bountiful and viable, and its management team will become more interactive and engaged.

Team involvement can be extended to include the engagement of entire communities of stakeholders to be most effective. Depending on the specific circumstances of the strategising activity, it should include input from as broad a range of talent as possible. Once included, however, engagement must continue throughout, otherwise the feelgood factor of inclusion will soon turn to disappointment and doubt amid a feeling of rejection and exclusion. As discussed previously, a primary attribute of agile strategy, according to Doz and Kosonen, is collective commitment, and collective commitment can only come from successful teams.

Sam Palmisano, formerly President of IBM, successfully applied the power of teams. One way he used teams to advantage in particular is of note. In order to break down the impact of traditional one-on-one reporting and a prevailing dominant logic associated with a strict hierarchy of individual performance reporting, he encouraged senior leaders to work together in teams. Their objective is to facilitate the breaking down of the silo mentality that often arises between various fiefdoms, to encourage open dialogue that is cross-functional and cross-business unit in scope. Reporting on this phenomenon after their interview with Palmisano, Doz and Kosonen (2008) observed that the benefits from this form of teamwork are clear: 'more cognitive diversity, more depth and breadth in substantive dialogue, and, most importantly, more leadership unity across the top team and the whole organisation'.

The Case against Teams: Why Teams Don't Work

As a fundamental component of this Inconvenient Truth of Strategy, we have assessed the issues of the problem of dominant logic, the threat of entering strategic drift, and the importance of a programme of organisational learning and the practice of strategic agility. Each of these elements of good management can be recognised as being highly productive, there is still though the problem of the practical nature of team behaviour. To this end, Professor of Social and Organisational Psychology at Harvard University, J. Richard Hackman (2009), in an interview with the Editor of the *Harvard Business Review*, suggests that rather than being highly productive, significant amounts of research have shown that teams under-perform despite access to multiple resources. The reason for this rather unexpected outcome is that 'problems with coordination and motivation typically chip away at the benefits'. Even when you have a team, Hackman observes, 'it's often in competition with other teams and that dynamic can also get in the way of real progress'. In order to address these concerns, Hackman proposes a number of solutions. These include setting the right conditions and ensuring that at least one member of the team is capable of challenge, limiting teams to no more than nine members, and maintaining consistency by keeping the individual team members together for as long as required or possible.

In order to optimise the chances of success, Hackman suggests that leaders be ruthless about who can and can't join a team, that teams be set a compelling direction, that team leaders should accept their own style rather than trying to emulate others, and that team operating rules be made clear.

Realising Team-based Learning: Rethinking Methods of Strategy and Strategic Plan Formulation

As an emerging topic of research, the use and application of workshops in the formulation of a strategic plan has been the subject of much focus among the academic fraternity in recent times. That research indicates in general that 75–80 per cent of organisations hold two-day 'away days' or 'off sites' as a means of deliberating over the development of strategic plans. In our most recent survey, however, there are indications that such events are less popular than that – the SMI/Swinburne University survey in 2013 indicated that only 45 per cent of organisations used 'off sites' to review strategy.

In itself this is a positive outcome, as shown by research conducted by Chris Clark, who as a doctoral candidate at Macquarie University found the effectiveness of the 'off site' as a means of developing strategy to be limited, although it was very useful as a means of bonding and team-building (Clark, 2005). The latter conclusion can be supported from his research data, which concluded that around 77 per cent of organisations used 'away days' as a means to discuss and/or decide strategy. Of these, 66 per cent of attendees agreed that, on the whole, the sessions they attended were a success. In contrast, however, only 19 per cent thought that the outcome would deliver a considerable change in strategic direction for the business. I suggest that the fact that 62 per cent thought the workshop would evoke some or a moderate change calls the value of workshop effectiveness as opposed to the strategy content itself into question. The result that only 55 per cent of respondees thought the event resulted in an appropriate strategic plan further supports this questioning of value, especially as 26 per cent of attendees were hoping to obtain major operational and structural changes as a result of the event.

As an indication of the propensity of the workshop format to be flawed, the survey result also showed that 57 per cent of respondents thought that attendees devoted no or minimal preparation to the workshop. What is telling is that 72 per cent of attendees thought that they understood the organisation's strategies as a result of the strategic event. This, I believe, points to the value of and need for conducting formal education in strategy, especially strategy practice that has a focus on the unique aspects and content of a particular organisation. We will make provision for this in our proposed strategy evaluation programme to be discussed in Chapter 5. This topic is also covered in more detail in Chapter 7 as part of the discussion of strategy as a profession. The foregoing contributions add to our proposal to dramatically improve the physical planning event and ultimately seek to replace it with a programme of continual renewal (explored further in Chapter 5). The observation of a decline in the use of workshops could be an early indicator that a transformation to this kind of format is already under way.

The astute reader will observe that whilst comprehensive, the extent of change proposed will require significantly more time and resources, especially if we include strategy deployment workshops as a way to communicate, educate and control the implementation of the strategic plan that is derived from the strategising activities that are laid out. The reason we have added additional time and resources though is simple. There is a lot of analysis to be conducted and there are a lot of conclusions to be reached, and this can only be done successfully when sufficient research and dialogue have been completed; this is what makes strategy the task of a professional as opposed to an assignment for an enthusiastic, but most likely part-time, advocate. As demonstrated in Chris Clark's survey data, 50 per cent of organisations hold strategy off site events at least once a year whilst another 29 per cent hold such events more than once a year, presumably for just that reason (Clark, 2005).

Our concern, however, is that the extent of this activity is still not enough. As can be seen in Figure 4.1, a more professional approach would require a strong preparation capability (for the firm and the attendee) followed by a direction-setting workshop to establish the foundations of the plan and information required to make informed strategic decisions which are addressed in the second strategising workshop held a short time later. Broader company-wide engagement is obtained from additional workshops held across the business and data gathered then fed back into a final strategic planning workshop designed to reach consensus. Once agreed, content is assigned to an implementation programme, but in the spirit of making the planning process more continual, we suggest the content be articulated and portrayed within an automated strategy evaluation dashboard monitoring mechanism; reviewed and evaluated on a regular basis.

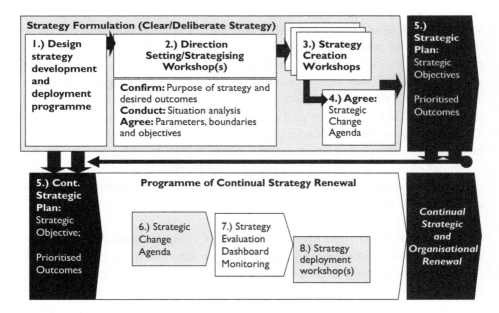

Figure 4.1   A redesigned strategy formulation agenda, from away days to comprehensive review and analysis

Automated Strategy Evaluation Dashboard Monitoring Mechanism

I will be the first to admit that the extent of workshopping described above may be over the top in terms of time demands, but there are ways to truncate the programme. It is my objective here, though, to emphasise the depth of analysis required to develop good strategy, to promote the involvement of as broad a base of stakeholders as possible, to ensure alignment through engagement and ownership and to emphasise that it is all best led by a proficient and qualified professional.

For users of more automated and interactive technology, I propose an advanced version of the format described above and referred to in Figure 4.1. This advanced version is actually far more efficient to operate, enables strategic agility, is based on a formal structure of strategy (the Strategic Management Framework), and introduces a strategy evaluation capability that is designed to be continually renewed and updated. It is also easy to distribute selectively to as many individuals as desired via the intranet or Internet, making access available to appropriate parties on an as-needed basis. Applied through automated performance management software, trends and quantitative data can be viewed via a dashboard reporting mechanism available in most business intelligence software tools.

Where resource and/or budget constrictions apply, a simple manual system will suffice, and automation can be facilitated through standard spreadsheet system. Under either form of automation, I stress that the continual renewal of strategy in whatever format will deliver a team-based, futures-oriented method of redefining strategy.

Whilst the foregoing is taking the strategy professional into a far more 'process-captured' phase of the strategising activity, we must be extremely conscious of the fact that strategy is very much an emergent, intuitive phenomenon that in the form of a structured and deliberate software system could compromise the creative, innovative and emergent content that is typical of emerging strategy. I therefore stress that the treatment of the strategic plan as an automated mechanism is *only* designed to provide information into the strategy evaluation system, and as a result, *still* requires individual participation and involvement. Technology, though, allows this interaction to take place in a broader context, one that is responsive to innovation, strategy education programmes and dynamic strategising programmes as appropriate. The monitoring capability I propose therefore focuses on the development of input, review and outputs that are team-based, responsive to change and interactive, and as a result is contemporary, timely and relevant in use.

To conclude this element of the strategising system, I stress also that the second component of the programme suggests the use of strategy deployment workshops as a means to physically roll out strategy and ensure alignment across the business. We will review the notion and method of alignment in Chapter 6. In Chapter 5 we will explore further the method of strategy implementation.

Chapter 5

Obtaining the Results You Deserve: Strategy Implementation in a Learning Organisation

> **INCONVENIENT TRUTH NO. 5: IMPLEMENTATION IS NOTORIOUSLY UNSUCCESSFUL.**
>
> Terminology such as 'a relentless focus on execution' emphasises redundancy and discontinuity compared to the more positive 'programme of continual strategy renewal'.

Survey data from the SMI show that an average of 73 per cent of respondees consistently say that they could implement strategy more effectively. Perhaps, then, it is no coincidence that our survey results also show that the pervasive strategic plan is deemed to be *the* key method of strategy implementation in practice. At some point practitioners will realise that because of the issues we have already explored in this book, the static strategic plan is not much more than an institutionalised and mediocre management tool that is broken. One of its greatest downfalls in its operation (aside from a loss of relevance in its content) is that there is no feedback loop built into the end-to-end strategic planning process that is capable of flagging a need for change, or indeed enabling any form of responsiveness to change.

Responsiveness, organisational change and evaluation are all things that people *do,* and as such are difficult to build into a system or process. For some reason, though, these critical people factors are all too often overlooked. The implications are significant. Implementation results from the strategic plan are critical, so too is the plan's continuity, renewal and effective engagement of people. It is only people who can ensure that the strategy system is managed effectively and its content remains continually relevant, effective and in constant alignment with the elements of an ever-changing external environment. Conventional methods of strategising (particularly the strategic plan) generally applied to manage and implement strategy are simply not designed to do that. It requires the operation of an interactive, dynamic system *as well as* the skills, experience and capability of a professional to make it happen.

The Fifth Inconvenient Truth of Strategy

In addressing the compelling issues of systems and people in the context of strategy implementation in this chapter therefore, we will address The Fifth Inconvenient Truth of Strategy:

> *Implementation is notoriously unsuccessful. Terminology such as 'a relentless focus on execution' emphasises redundancy and discontinuity compared to the more positive 'programme of continual strategy renewal'. The consequences are that a focus on execution alone evokes notions of the cessation of strategy as opposed to a combination of short-term outcomes and a dynamic programme of continual, strategically aligned renewal.*

In seeking to improve the success rate of strategy implementation, we need to remind ourselves that in Chapter 2 we described the means to essentially reinvent functionality. Rather than an application for a zero-based strategic plan alone, we saw that its value now lies in its application as the foundation for the roll-out of a programme of continual renewal within a construct that recognises the difference between long and short term strategy. When enacted within this reinvented format, the content of a deliberate strategic plan can be reviewed and renewed on a daily basis, in which case there is no longer any need to go through an annual planning routine (ritual?) at all – it is part of the day-to-day management of the business, and a basis upon which implementation also becomes an ongoing exercise.

The apparatus we proposed as an enabler of continual strategy renewal is a strategy evaluation monitoring mechanism, ideally built into an automated dashboarding technology. As a system- and process-oriented solution, however, we must still consider the all-important *people* component of strategy implementation, which, as we have established, is critical to success. I propose that in order to address this issue, we consider the adoption of a *community of practice* (CoP) as a valid context within which *stakeholder engagement* and a *culture of organisational learning* can be empowered to literally bring strategy to life. Strategically focused stakeholder engagement will facilitate and enable organisational change. Organisational learning is the platform on which strategy and strategic and organisational change, renewal and if necessary reinvention can be informed.

We will explore the application of these people focused elements of strategy after our next instalment of the Cadbury case study. In this chapter we will explore issues of quality of strategy, effectiveness in implementation and overall performance of the Cadbury business.

Transforming the Organisation: From Private to Public and Strategy Implementation at Cadbury

Following its listing in 1962 Cadbury's apparent underperformance had forced its directors to accept the need to look further afield if the company was to increase its share price whilst still maintaining or growing its dividends. In 1964 Cadbury embarked on a programme of acquisition designed to boost growth outside its original market domain. The push resulted in the acquisition of a number of sugar-based confectionery businesses, including Pascall Murray, Trebor Bassett, Barrett, Maynard and Sharps.

In 1965 Paul Cadbury stood down as Cadbury plc Chairman, handing the reins to 35-year-old Adrian Cadbury, who described himself as one of the last Quaker 'Captains of [British] Industry'. Unfortunately, though, whilst there was a change in ownership and change in guard, there was little change in the way the business was run, including the strategy, which retained its underlying focus. We saw in Chapter 4 that the centre of balance in Cadbury's SMI dynamic model of strategic equilibrium (Chapter 1) had changed from inside-out to outside-in to take account of the decline in need for the development of product technology whilst responding to the dramatic changes that were taking place in its markets. The entire consumer packaged goods industry globally had in fact experienced a significant transformation in their traditional sales and supply chain formats that saw a rapid decline in corner store sales and a rapid increase in volume through the new fast and efficient supermarket chains.

Although Cadbury did face increasingly difficult operating results, Adrian Cadbury continued the family theme of working from the company's strengths: its people and other resource-based initiatives. Cadbury was not very well placed to meet this new form of self-serve grocery supply chain business model; psychologically and physically. A need for a dramatic reframing by the upper echelons of the business was required, but a dominant logic was so entrenched at the top that Cadbury found it difficult to walk away from its prevailing business model and loyal customer base – a move that allowed newcomer Mars in particular to make rapid inroads into the supermarket supply chain. It didn't help that Cadbury would – or at least could – have foreseen the emergence of supermarkets some time before their physical arrival into the marketplace.

I previously nominated a dominant logic as a primary cause for Cadbury's slow response to change, Bradley (2008) again provides insight. As we have mentioned previously, the business model adopted by Cadbury was that of a high volume, low cost, limited range provider of chocolate bars. This model emerged during the war years when complexity of just about every feature of the Cadbury product was eliminated through standardisation and simplification of the entire product range. The implication though was that any form of change from this low cost model would require a significant investment in capital. As we all know, investments of that nature take time, and when it is *your* money the decision probably takes a little longer. We previously proposed a dominant logic as an inhibitor to decision making at Cadbury. We can now also see that that logic was enforced with a lack of foresight and strategic thinking that would have prompted a review of the adequacy of Cadbury supply chain infrastructure, well before supermarkets arrived to finally force the issue.

Mars on the other hand, armed with a differentiated product offering that included individually branded chocolate bars (Mars Bars, Snickers, Milky Way) as opposed to a single brand of Cadbury chocolate slabs and gift-boxed creams jumped at the opportunity to leapfrog Cadbury and other competitors into the new self-serve era. Working in alliance with the supermarket chains, Mars emerged with a new strength and presence in the confectionery industry in the UK especially.

Although Adrian Cadbury and his board struggled with the obvious change in the Cadbury channel to market; what they did recognise was a need to respond to the revolution occurring in the end consumer arena. He was aware most of all of the need to respond to the emerging social revolution that occurred in the 1960s and 1970s – a time when 'hippy power' emerged along with an increase in the consciousness of consumer power in general. Adrian Cadbury faced a number of challenges in his role as Chairman, and for the first time in the history of Cadbury there was a need to respond to a level of complexity that required some serious form of *strategic* thinking. Issues he needed to address included clearer lines of responsibility, supply chain redesign but above all else, 'he felt the need to focus on strategy' (Cadbury, 2010).

The corporate strategy adopted by Cadbury had two distinct components (Smith et al., 1990) whose structure, I suggest, we would nowadays treat as being more of a strategic plan. It presents as a short-term solution trying to solve a long-standing problem. Because the difference between strategy and a strategic plan was apparently never recognised by key decision makers at Cadbury, long-standing wicked strategic problems continued to be overlooked. An example of this is Cadbury's two failed attempts to enter the critical US market. What Adrian Cadbury experienced by focusing on short-term planning rather than long-term strategy was an inability to see and feel the end game; put another way, he lacked a systems thinking perspective. Adrian Cadbury did his best to address surface issues, though he was unable to grasp a level of *strategic insight* into the causes of those issues, which ran much deeper in the company history and culture. They potentially included an inability to see a structured future beyond chocolate, an inability to adjust to life as a listed company and an inability to view life from the perspective of its new major customer base (supermarkets).

The first component of the Cadbury (so-called) strategy was a renewed focus on external representation through an imperative to enlarge Cadbury's share of the confectionery market through organic (new product development) and inorganic (acquisition) means. The former focused mostly on confectionery, whilst the newly introduced Foods Division enjoyed an early success with a home-grown product of powdered milk. The majority of growth for the Foods Division was attained through the acquisition of food and drink companies. The second component of the corporate strategy was derived from an internal focus on the rationalisation of the firm's product portfolio. This was delivered through a transformation to more efficient production techniques, a re-focus on core brands, the rationalisation of production facilities, and the acquisition of new manufacturing plant and more concentrated advertising budgets.

It is significant that it is only around this time in the history of both strategy theory and the Cadbury company that publications on strategy began to emerge. Just as external market complexities had a significant impact on Cadbury, so too did a clearer perspective on the need for strategy to unfold in both academic and industrial arena in general. Regrettably (as we can see in Appendix 1), the format of strategy theory was limited to books about strategy and policy (Andrews, 1965), international diversification of the top 25 US corporations (Chandler, 1962) and corporate planning (Ansoff, 1965). Adrian Cadbury would have found the book on diversification useful (into the method of expansion on a national and international scale was firmly on his agenda), but what he really needed to know was how to better understand and articulate long term strategy *and* how to physically *implement* strategy, as opposed to how to diversify, build policy or make a plan.

In the absence of any clear direction on the structure of the discipline of strategy per se, the rationale for Cadbury's acquisition portfolio was based on the logic of leveraging the high-value Cadbury brand into other related (supermarket-focused) areas more than anything else. The push into acquisitions resulted in the purchase of a broad range of food and food-related companies. However, the specifics of the companies acquired by Cadbury seem to be more representative of a householder's supermarket shopping list than a structured acquisition programme for a major corporation with global ambitions. Examples of businesses acquired include a number of sugar-based (as opposed to chocolate-based) confectionery companies, an instant mashed potato company, a meat processing company and other soft drink companies. In later acquisitions and new product releases, product content included wine, soup, biscuits and cakes. The Cadbury acquisition spree peaked in 1969 following the successful merger between Cadbury and soft drink giant Schweppes, the outcome of which was a change in company name to Cadbury Schweppes plc.

The second part of the strategy saw the company embark on a major capital investment programme which included a major restructuring of the entire corporation. This resulted in the relocation of some physical assets, the rationalisation of plant and equipment, and in an uncharacteristic move, potential redundancy of employees. The latter eventuality is not an unusual outcome in many companies, but was considered a radical move by Cadbury at the time as until now its fundamental values had focused on the provision and protection of employee welfare and benefits.

Insight into the size of business that Cadbury plc had become at the time of the Schweppes merger in 1969 is offered by the 2007 annual report: 'a turnover of £262 million, and a trading profit of £21 million'. As a publicly listed company, the financial performance of the business faced unprecedented scrutiny. Prior to its listing, the controlling family's attitude to financial performance was described by Adrian Cadbury as 'very much a point of view that the long term was what mattered and that one shouldn't be too bothered with the fluctuations between one year and the next' (Smith et al., 1990).

In sanctioning Cadbury's defence against takeover by becoming a diversified large conglomerate through the merger with Schweppes, Adrian Cadbury sought to cement the company's position as a major force in the international confectionery and soft drink market. In addition to the merger with Schweppes, Cadbury was successful in penetrating new markets internationally, except North America, through an aggressive international expansion programme that had commenced in the 1960s. Through a protracted process of arbitration and deliberation Cadbury secured a unique foothold in India. It also saw off attempts by Mars to enter the New Zealand market, whilst a clash between Mars and Cadbury in Australia resulted in Cadbury acquiring the leading Australian chocolate firm MacRobertson's in 1967. The result was a market presence that amounted to a 60 per cent share of the Australian market.

The ultimate outcome from this somewhat opportune and loose approach to portfolio management, though, meant that many of the acquisitions and new product launches that had been undertaken to improve performance prior to the Schweppes merger were observed to have actually reduced rather than improved company performance overall. This was a situation that would continue until Cadbury's ultimate takeover. With this observation in mind, two primary attributes of the Schweppes merger justified the move. One was that Schweppes would put the (merged) company beyond the reach of acquisition by predatory corporations such as Kraft and Nestlé. The second was simply, and rather ironically given its track record in implementing strategy that Cadbury was good at implementation but bad at acquisitions, whereas Schweppes was good at acquisitions but not so good at implementation.

Making Strategy Implementation More Successful

In this chapter we will explore the ways and means of delivering the implementation of strategy through the mechanism of strategic plan whilst also ensuring the maintenance of its relevance. We will do this through an examination of a programme of *continual strategy renewal*, including the incorporation of an effective *strategy evaluation dashboard monitoring mechanism* (introduced in Chapters 3 and 4). We will combine this with a different perspective on implementation (through the construct of an automated monitoring mechanism) whilst also introducing the *people component* of strategy evaluation reviewing. This is enacted within the environment of a community of practice, a context of stakeholder engagement and a culture of organisational learning.

It is in the area of stakeholder engagement in particular that the dynamics of a formal learning organisation, becomes an imperative. Even though

I propose that strategy implementation and renewal be enacted through formal or in some cases informal systems and processes, it is always the involvement and leadership of people that makes the difference. Leaders are bound to be more efficient in this strategising activity when their decision making is informed and supported by enabling systems, processes, policy and technology. Their personal skills and collective wisdom are also enhanced when formal learning takes place. Education delivers a higher order of wisdom, and is enhanced further through interaction, open communications, the conduct of strategic conversations (dialogue) and broad-based networking – stakeholder engagement. I propose that the latter be realised through the establishment of a formal community of practice in strategy (discussed later in this chapter), and that the combined knowledge base is as a beneficial way to accomplish the realisation of the firm's overall strategic imperatives.

Strategy Implementation: From a Strategic Plan to a Program of Continual Strategy Renewal

Today it is easy to pass judgement on the validity of the Cadbury rationale that drove its behaviour in the acquisition of Schweppes, as we can see in Appendix 1 (a timeline of the history of strategy). We should not forget though, that only the simplest form of strategy theory was available to Adrian Cadbury during this period. What was emerging in the field of strategy at that time was at least an advancement on the basics of strategic planning; in the form of a representation of portfolio analysis based on an estimate of a firm's market share and potential for growth, although matured versions of this methodology were still a few years away. Although limited in perspective, this would have at least informed Adrian Cadbury's decision making considerably. However, the theory was shown to have limitations because of behavioural failings in practice. It was found to have forced too much attention on the allocation of cash to high-growth, high-market share business units (referred to as stars) with too much being taken away from the more traditional cash-rich business units (referred to as cash cows) – of which Cadbury (the Chocolate Division especially) is a classic example. The regrettable outcome of this was that these traditional cash cows, were starved of base-level financial requirements necessary to keep the cash flowing, meaning that ultimately the highly-prized cash flow would literally dry up.

In this chapter we not only explore the art of strategy implementation that was for a long time the basis of Adrian Cadbury's programme, I ask you also to continue the journey designed to address The Seven Inconvenient Truths of Business Strategy. This requires you to rethink your approach to the way a strategic plan is implemented and to reorient the natural instinct that focuses on the somewhat grandiose and flamboyant terminology of 'flawless execution of strategy' towards the more sustainable terminology of continual delivery, renewal, continual learning or more appropriately, a reinvention of strategic planning. In commencing the discussion, we should consider the reality of *what is*. This begins with the still necessary and better-known *process* (project management) aspects of implementation required to identify, measure, manage and benefit from the realisation of content defined in the strategic plan. This is the programme illustrated in the fully integrated Strategic Management Framework and located within the 'Program of Continual Strategy Renewal' as the process of the strategic change agenda.

Program of Continual Strategy Renewal

We commence our discussion on each of the elements of the programme of continual strategy renewal shown in Figure 5.1 with the strategic objectives identified in the strategic plan and structured within the strategy blueprint. The strategy blueprint is derived from the content contained within the strategic plan and is made up of the specific objectives identified in that plan. We will then review the three elements of implementation, renewal and engagement which include strategy renewal monitoring, a strategic change agenda (referred to above) and stakeholder engagement. The strategy evaluation monitoring mechanism introduced in Chapter 4 is the basis upon which strategy renewal, implementation and engagement is brought about.

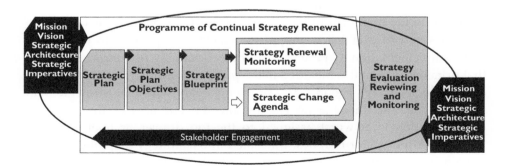

Figure 5.1 **A programme of continual strategy renewal**

Strategy Implementation as a Physical Process: A Programme of Continual Strategy Renewal

The need for a formal process to provide guidance to the effective implementation of strategy is undeniable. In an interview, then CEO of Cadbury, Todd Stitzer described the physical strategic planning process adopted by Cadbury following his appointment 'Every year we have a road map process which seeks to determine the priorities for the next four years. This is a rolling program which is institutionalised within the company, led by the strategy team working closely with Finance and Business units' (O'Regan, 2009). It is my view, however, that rather than a simple rolling programme, a rather more robust and formal programme of 'every day' renewal is applied to the strategic management system consistent with the philosophy of the Strategic Management Framework (see Figure 1.1).

STRATEGY RENEWAL MONITORING

This element of the strategic change agenda is primarily concerned with the monitoring, evaluation and review of the assumptions and guesses that we have discussed previously as being of greatest concern after the strategic plan has been developed. It is important to acknowledge its existence here, it is also discussed in more detail in Chapter 7 as an issue of corporate governance.

STRATEGIC CHANGE AGENDA

The strategic architecture shown in Figure 2.1 demonstrates how a firm's strategic imperatives are represented in its long-term strategy (five to ten years or more). The strategic change agenda then facilitates the roll-out of the shorter-term strategic objectives that are described in the strategic plan and contextualised in the structure of the strategy blueprint. The conventional approach to the treatment of these objectives is to develop a line of sight to outcomes and to establish a project management capability to ensure the plan's implementation. On the surface there is actually nothing wrong with that principle, in fact it is included in the programme illustrated in Figure 5.1 as a strategic change agenda. The problems begin when the strategic plan is signed off and there is no change agenda, but instead the planning documentation is at worst assigned to the top drawer or bookshelf and promptly forgotten, or is at best translated into a strategy mapping/strategy implementation (road map?) programme that ignores future strategy and emerging strategy.

The link between the strategy blueprint and the strategic objectives defined in the strategic plan provides the content for the strategic change agenda, which then becomes the foundation upon which the implementation of the strategic plan is realised – continuously. The alignment of each provides a moderating force and a means to ensure that the content of the strategic plan continues to maintain its relevance, and that updating/continual renewal of strategy is incorporated into this component of the strategy/strategising system.

STRATEGY BLUEPRINT

The strategy blueprint itself is based on the same structure as the strategic architecture, but incorporates shorter-term issues of strategy as defined and articulated in the strategic plan. Instead of addressing the question 'In which markets should we participate?'(a key question when compiling a strategic architecture) for example, the more likely question at the level of a strategy blueprint is 'How will we compete in those markets?' The (prioritised) strategic objectives that are described within the strategy blueprint are treated as independent projects, in a format that justifies the term 'strategic change agenda'. The primary purpose of the strategy blueprint lies in its illustrative capability and its contribution to the make-up of the programme of continual strategy renewal. As you will observe from the Cirque du Soleil case study (Figure 5.3), we have assigned a name to the strategic change agenda which is intended to capture the underlying message of the strategic planning theme of relevance to the period that the strategy blue print is addressing. In this sense, it is quite similar to the application of a Strategic Intent which we defined in Chapter 2.

The illustrative strategy blueprint (Figure 5.3) applicable to Cirque du Soleil follows the now familiar construct of a strategic architecture (Figure 5.2) which appears in the same case. An appreciation of the content of strategy and the strategic plan is highlighted by the content contained in both the architecture and blueprint for Cirque du Soleil, as well as content that isn't there. That is an absence of strategic objectives that are conspicuous as gaps in the strategic architecture and/or strategy blueprint.

CASE STUDY: ILLUSTRATIVE STRATEGIC ARCHITECTURE AT CIRQUE DU SOLEIL

Cirque du Soleil's Strategy

Cirque was founded on a premise that it could compete by offering an innovative entertainment spectacular at a lower cost than other, more traditional circuses. In order to deliver lower costs, its founder, Guy Laliberté, sought to obtain greater value from its asset base through the use of themed shows that allowed variety but consistency in investment in props, lighting and costumes and a simpler venue layout. The trademark blue and yellow tent is used as a brand symbol as well as a low-cost venue, and the show is presented on a stage without a centre ring and with seats distributed around three sides. There are no animals in the Laliberté circus business model. These are difficult to transport around the world, so their high maintenance costs were eliminated. They are also irrelevant to the dancing and acrobatic nature of the show. Cirque's go-to-market service model is to design and launch a new show for the Montreal market, then take it on a tour lasting four or more years to North America, then Europe, Asia and other global destinations.

Focusing on the adult market for live entertainment, Cirque's target audience (and hence its market segments) is reflected in its ticket sales, which include general (public) sales, sponsor sales and concession sales. Sponsorships are offered as a low-key service, but available at a substantially higher price than traditional circuses. Leveraging its creative team and seeking to build on the brand created by the live shows, Cirque has expanded into film and other ventures. These include videos of live performances, behind-the-scenes documentaries and IMAX film formats.

An Analysis of Cirque's Strategy: An Articulation of its Strategic Architecture

Cirque's strategy demonstrates what could be a 'synthesis' between outside-in (market positioning) and inside-out (resource-leveraging) strategies, achieved by continually developing and refining its finely tuned/optimised resource set and delivering each new programme into a highly differentiated (unique) market position. Figure 5.2 depicts an illustrative strategic architecture that reflects Cirque's long-term strategy.

As a true entrepreneur, Cirque's founder, Guy Laliberté, is the sole shareholder of the company; he is renowned for the considerable risks he took to make the venture a success. Cirque is the epitome of a business that has been able to reinvent the industry in which it participates through the delivery of a unique product offering that is much more than a traditional circus. It is an example of an outside-in, 'blue ocean' strategy as proposed by researchers Kim and Mauborgne (2006).

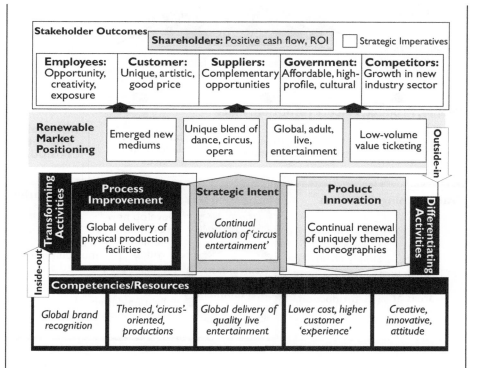

Figure 5.2   Illustrative Cirque du Soleil strategic architecture

The strategy described has remained in place since its inception. It is translated into a strategic plan, which is then implemented on a year-to-year basis. Areas where changes will be reflected the most are likely to be 'activity'-oriented market differentiation and transforming areas. Although the strategic architecture (see above) depicts a suite of activities that will contribute to the transformation of the business, the strategic plan will provide details of ways in which that will be undertaken in the short term. The strategic change agenda of 'reinvention of live entertainment' is realised with each new themed release. The show *Dralion*, for example, is a depiction of the blend of two emblematic creatures: the dragon, symbolising the East, and the lion, symbolising the West. Still running today after its initial release in 1999, the theme represents the four elements that govern the natural order in a human form. Each element is represented by its own evocative colour: air is blue, water is green, fire is red, earth is ochre: 'In the world of *Dralion*, cultures blend, man and nature are one, and balance is achieved.'

In developing *Dralion*, the strategic objective in this instance could have been: 'to conceptualise a multicultural blend of humanity as a theme for our 2002 season'. We have developed an illustrative strategy blueprint (Figure 5.3) that reflects possible content for that year for Cirque.

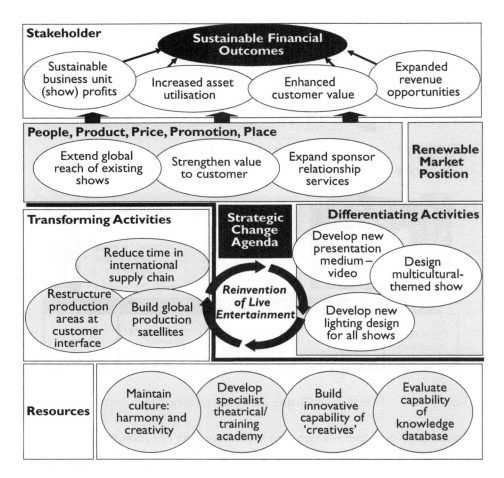

Figure 5.3   Illustrative Cirque du Soleil strategy blueprint

STRATEGY EVALUATION DASHBOARD MONITORING MECHANISM

The strategy evaluation monitoring mechanism shown as an outcome from the element titled Programme of Continual Strategy Renewal in Figure 5.1 incorporates all of the content that is captured as the fundamental control device for each of the programs of strategy renewal monitoring (see Chapter 7), strategy implementation (through the enactment of the strategic change agenda) and in a more conceptual context, the awareness of change that evokes strategic conversations around the need for strategy renewal. Each are enhanced when advanced technology is applied to introduce an automated management reporting capability, ideally through the enabling technology that is provided by an automated dash board reporting mechanism. A dashboard mechanism uses visual displays of charts to depict alerts, trends and graphs of relevance to the foregoing content. The strategy evaluation (dashboard) monitoring mechanism is applied to:

- evoke appropriate responses to the inevitability (risk) of obsolescence of content contained in the strategic plan;

- enable the operation and management of the ongoing strategy evaluation reviewing activity identified in Chapter 3 as an essential component of the continued relevance of strategy content that we identified as the assumptions, guesstimates and leaps of faith that are typical when decisions about the future are made;

- act as the primary monitoring mechanism that facilitates the continual review and renewal of strategy;

- provide a management and control mechanism to the physical implementation of each of the projects that are the physical outcome from the short term strategic plan or its replacement, an interactive strategic planning system.

STAKEHOLDER ENGAGEMENT

As the final component of the programme of continual strategy renewal, stakeholder engagement addresses the human element of implementation. This attribute is the vital lifeblood of the continual renewal of strategy. It consists of the physical activities that are undertaken to ensure strategy is acted upon. Progress of the operation and completion of those activities is monitored through the strategy evaluation dashboard monitoring mechanism, in whatever form and format that takes, as discussed next. Stakeholder engagement is not system- or process-oriented. It is a human activity that thrives on a systems thinking perspective and benefits from individual involvement in the entire vision, mission to implementation landscape.

Bringing Strategy to Life: A Programme of Strategy Measurement, Management, Monitoring, Dashboarding and Stakeholder Engagement

An appropriate strategy evaluation dashboard monitoring mechanism will be tailored to the specifics of the organisation's strategy content, and as an interactive device could reside within an enterprise's intranet facility, taking a key position in the firm's regular management reporting and control mechanism. Its value proposition is to provide the capability for participants to engage in open forums, send and receive emails and provide drill-down capabilities from high-level graphs, charts, and other analytical data and so on. Dashboard monitoring can be developed in manual or electronic formats; the latter drawing on the many different brands of business intelligence (big data) software packages that enable users to develop their own spreadsheet solutions or incorporate them into business intelligence modules available as part of large enterprise wide resource planning systems such as SAP or Oracle.

Once armed with a comprehensive strategy formation system (a combination of strategy creation, implementation and renewal) and access to some form of interactive measurement, management and monitoring system, the reporting of strategy content becomes highly visible. If you include the interactive capabilities of a dashboard mechanism, the notion of Web-enabled strategy is effectively brought to life, with or without the bells and whistles offered by the more advanced, analytically oriented dashboard technology.

The key to success lies in the way this capability is used in practice. Through this process we are seeking to apply individuals' skills in strategy with a blend of meaningful human interaction, strength of leadership, a capacity for open communication, a passion to succeed, a hunger for knowledge and a commitment to tackling the tough issues head-on. It is the combination of all of these characteristics and more that will enable the most savvy business leaders to effectively transform the concept of what was a static, snapshot approach to strategic management in the form of a strategic plan into a truly meaningful, dynamic, continually relevant and professional capability in strategy.

Structured education in contemporary strategy practice and the capture of experience complementing and informing fully documented, explicit knowledge management systems (through manuals and procedure manuals) educates individuals and allows teams to capture, interpret and retain what is known (implicit knowledge) whilst also contributing to what is not known (emerging implicit knowledge) even when individual team members consistently come and go. No matter what combination of people, system and process is applied, therefore, effectiveness will be enhanced considerably when learning takes place and renewal is introduced to both systems and knowledge content. Strategy practices in general, along with the quality of content and by definition organisational performance, will be correspondingly improved each time strategy and planning is enacted and re-enacted.

A well-structured education and engagement programme based on specific company strategy doesn't need to take days to deliver. The extent to which data are captured and reported will occur in direct correlation to the perceived value of each programme. Its inclusion in the reporting capability at any point goes a long way towards improving engagement, understanding and interest, and as a result enhances the effectiveness of strategy implementation and responsiveness to change. It is inevitable that such an education programme will lead to greater strength in strategy practices in general. It will also promote deeper and more meaningful content, greater dialogue in strategic conversations, and ultimately the continual renewal of strategy and the business.

As we will explore in more detail in Chapter 7, this is the very essence of and primary source of benefit from the construct of a learning organisation. Two mechanisms make this happen. One is the establishment of a learning capability that at the least involves the establishment of a formal learning regime (department) within an organisation. Increasingly though, corporations are establishing a formal or informal in-house 'corporate university' (sometimes referred to as an academy) level of capability, a trend that has in fact become a common occurrence among many major global corporations already. A working definition of corporate universities is: 'a unit, approach or concept that supports strategy renewal, implementation and/or optimisation through organisational learning' (Rademakers, 2014). The second is an innovative, less structured and 'agile' approach to executive education, delivered through the establishment of a network of communities of practice in strategy and associated disciplines.

The Role of Strategy in a Learning Organisation

The final component of the successful outcome from strategy is the environment in which the foregoing activities are undertaken, our discussion here continues with the concept of a corporate university. The value of learning in an organisational context has been difficult to appreciate by many and as a result, is often overlooked as a critical management tool.

To illustrate its true value, it is useful to examine the difference between a typical approach to the implementation of a new software system and that of strategy. It is a given that the management of all major projects (especially new information systems) is monitored by a comprehensive evaluation capability and introduced with the support of a change management programme which incorporates broad-based communication forums, information dissemination events and formal education programmes when appropriate. Similarly, when new employees join an organisation there is always some form of induction program offered to them to allow them to get up to speed with the workings, and cultural demands of the business. Managers automatically commit significant resources to the development of an annual strategic plan, but they rarely though provide sufficient support to any other method of change management or education capability associated with that plan, at least not sufficient to facilitate the smooth implementation of the strategic plan. In my experience, the most that is devoted to strategy education and engagement is a communications programme that includes townhall team-building or similar events, and even then the focus is likely to be more on informing staff about the details of a strategic plan whose content has already been locked in than anything else.

In addition to the benefits we have discussed so far on the merits of knowledge accumulation through the mechanism of a learning organisation, we have learned also from Senge (1990) that it provides *the* basis for the development of a *continual and renewable competitive advantage*. This is why firms such as Apple, Mars, Telefónica, Pertamina, Canon, Shell, Kenya Airlines and Ikea all operate their own corporate universities.

It hasn't always been this way. In fact, the notion of a learning organisation was slow to get off the ground. One of the reasons for this is that initially the role of corporate universities was to teach the fundamentals of specific business applications. Banks, for example, established schools to teach aspiring bank tellers how to work in their branches. McDonald's University is famous for its capacity to transfer knowledge that not only focuses on making hamburgers, but also on new product development and various elements of food hygiene. The natural progression from this fundamental necessity has been to develop corporate universities as academies that inform strategy, which in turn facilitates renewal of strategy content, and as a result the continual renewal of the business. As suggested in the approach to strategic planning proposed in this book, it is now more important than ever for strategy practitioners, with or without a corporate university, to adapt and apply the benefits of organisational learning in whatever format as the basis for the realisation of a renewable competitive advantage.

In the absence of a corporate university, it is still very possible to adapt the benefits of organisational learning through the more virtual construct of a network of communities of practice, which we will discuss next.

Enabling Stakeholder Engagement: Operating a Community of Practice

My experience as a strategy practitioner has shown that a formal community of practice (CoP) is a highly effective method in allowing multi-functional teams to manage strategically and also to facilitate effective strategising activity in organisations. Wenger and Snyder (2000) defined a CoP as 'a group of people who share a concern or a passion for something they do and learn how to do it better as they interact regularly'. Notionally supportive of a learning organisation as a way of embedding strategy and strategic thinking, CoPs are important places of negotiation, learning, meaning and identity.

Wenger and Snyder (2000) further distinguish between three modes of belonging to social learning systems. The first is *engagement*, which is achieved through doing things together, talking, engaging in dialogue, producing artefacts and so on. The second is *imagination*, which involves constructing an image of ourselves, our communities and the world. The purpose here is to allow individuals to orient themselves, to reflect on their own situations and to explore possibilities. The third is *alignment*, which involves making sure that local activities are sufficiently aligned with other processes so that they can be effective beyond an individual's own engagement.

CASE STUDY: DUTCH DAIRY FARMING ACADEMY (DFA)

An example of a CoP in practice is the Dutch Dairy Farming Academy (DFA), which seeks to empower Dutch dairy farmers through a membership-based knowledge-sharing system. The DFA acts as a facilitator in a process of inter-firm networking between farmers, and in doing so it acts as a network broker or change agent as a key part of the newly developed knowledge system.

According to Holster et al. (2008), the DFA supports good entrepreneurship by facilitating new ways of learning between farmers who share experiences in formal and informal meetings.

Examples of specific DFA activities include:

- dairy cafés as meeting places for farmers;
- workshops where participants can deepen their knowledge on specific themes together with people from other organisations;
- online forum and webinar sessions on a national and international basis.

The objective in forming CoP networks is to provide individuals with the opportunity to share knowledge and experiences (purpose) in a structured format (organisation) and in a context where they will benefit from learning in a group as a whole (open knowledge sharing). Increasingly, CoPs are being facilitated through Web-enabled/online environments. This provides the means for disparate communities in particular to benefit from networking through various formats, including online forums and core education.

I conclude this chapter with the observation that although I have proposed a fairly dramatic change in the way strategy is conducted, there is nothing new in the components that make up this solution, only the way it is structured. The change merely requires that you adopt a different but not dramatic alteration to your perception of strategy from a process to a system, and an ability to try something new at the standard one would expect of a profession.

Chapter 6

Sharing the Vision:
Creating a Natural Law of Attraction

INCONVENIENT TRUTH NO. 6: AN ORGANISATION'S STRATEGY CONTENT IS OFTEN DISJOINTED AND DISCONNECTED FROM THE EXTERNAL ENVIRONMENT AS WELL AS MANY INTERNAL COMPONENTS OF THE ORGANISATION.

Alignment is often missing between the firm and environment (fit), its mission/vision and realised outcomes, as well as its internal structure across, up and down the organisation, such as innovation and learning.

In addition to the perpetual challenge of aligning an organisation with its external environment, there are also challenges for strategy practitioners in cascading strategy internally; from top to bottom, across the organisation and from bottom to top. From a corporate-wide perspective, a company's performance depends not only on the quality of the performance of the organisation's independent business units, but also 'the quality of integration that exists across Business Units' (Ghoshal and Bartlett, 1999). Another perspective on alignment (or non-alignment) arises from the construct, management, ownership and communication of the strategy itself, from mission, vision and purpose through to the strategic plan and its subsequent implementation – and continual renewal.

In the absence of a formal structure for strategy (prior to the establishment of a strategic architecture or strategy blueprint, for example), lack of alignment could allow gaps to appear in the strategy content as linkages between elements of the strategy are missed.

The Sixth Inconvenient Truth of Strategy

When viewed as the basis for leadership, transformation and renewal of the organisation, I suggest that strength in alignment is critical to the success of a business. It is a case of literally *sharing the vision* – a fundamental component of Senge's (1990) learning organisation to create what I refer to as *a natural law of attraction* that exists between the organisation, its stakeholders (internal and external) and the operating environment within which it must enjoy a sustainable (and *renewable*) 'strategic fit'. Recognising the difficulty in realising any form of attraction/alignment, I refer you to The Sixth Inconvenient Truth of Strategy:

> *An organisation's strategy content is often disjointed and disconnected from the external environment as well as many internal components of the organisation: Alignment is often missing between the firm and environment (fit), its mission/vision and realised outcomes, as well as its internal structure across, up and down the organisation, such as innovation and learning. As a consequence, a lack of fit with the external environment results in poor strategic outcomes. Lack of internal alignment devalues belief in the benefits of the strategic activities and increases levels of risk. It also has a negative impact on a leader's ability to align employees around a common sense of purpose and direction.*

Cadbury demonstrated an extraordinary degree of alignment with its values and the treatment of its stakeholders throughout its history, as exemplified by the wonder of the Bourneville manufacturing facility. Prior to the breakthrough with the success of Dairy Milk Chocolate, though, the company struggled to remain in lock step with its industry environment. It simply couldn't keep up with the changes in chocolate processing technology. Where Cadbury really struggled in its alignment with the external environment was covered in Chapter 5 where it was demonstrated that because Cadbury had enjoyed such a strong relationship with small corner stores and greengrocers prior to the mid-1960s, it found it difficult to adapt to the level of disruption created as a result of the rapid rise of the supermarket. In this chapter we will observe just how difficult it was for Cadbury to make any kind of alignment with proposed partners in the North American market, and the negative impact a lack of alignment of culture and values can have when a bad decision about an acquisition is made.

Cadbury plc: A Lack of Alignment and Failure to Renew – Where Did That Come From?

Of all the international markets in the world in the 1970s, North America remained the most prized, but also the one most resistant to penetration by Cadbury. Hershey, the largest chocolate confectioner in the USA, was identified by the Cadbury Chairman at the time, Adrian Cadbury, to be a natural acquisition. Hershey did not operate in any country other than the USA. Conversely, Cadbury had a presence in many countries other than the USA. Both firms shared a similar culture. Hershey was founded on a religion that held similar values to the Quakers. More than anything else, both wanted to fend off privately owned Mars (Chocolate Division) from entering their respective markets. Adrian Cadbury made a concerted effort to form an alliance with Hershey, but all his approaches were rejected by the Hershey Trust, which was the primary stakeholder in the business following the death of its founder, Milton Snavely Hershey in 1945. The board's temperament was noted by many at that time as being notoriously risk-averse. It seems that Adrian Cadbury was unable to convince Hershey of the benefits of an alliance or any form of alignment between the two businesses.

By the mid-1980s, and despite the merger between Cadbury and Schweppes (to become Cadbury Schweppes plc) in the late 1960s, the company was experiencing further deterioration in its market share. Most of all, the mass production and lean machine that was the Bourneville manufacturing power house had by now become a 'chain around its neck'. Nearly all of Cadbury's competitors were offering a much broader product base, Cadbury was unable to respond physically (as well as a result of a prevailing dominant logic at senior leadership level, as discussed in Chapter 4) because of the inflexibility of Bourneville, and the reputation of its brand. The former was a problem because it was designed for the specific purpose of producing high volumes of chocolate blocks, whereas Mars and other competitors were offering specialist bars or similar (Mars Bars, Snickers, Aero). Secondly, even if they could change, Cadbury would put at risk the one major advantage that was their primary reason for success, that of their brand. If Cadbury were to introduce variations in their product range, surely, it was felt any such variation in brand image would threaten that success.

In a desperate bid to turn the company around, Cadbury once again sought a greater presence in the US market. Another tilt at Hershey was ruled out, its past failure though gave the Cadbury board reason to approve the acquisition of an alternative US chocolate firm, the Peter Paul Candy Company, although it represented only a 10 per cent share of the US confectionery market. Shoring up this operation, Cadbury also proposed to build an independent factory of its own in Hazleton, Pennsylvania, where localised versions of Cadbury products could be produced. In contrast to Hershey, Cadbury Schweppes and the Peter Paul Candy Company shared little in terms of synergy or alignment.

The acquisition proved to be a disaster. The Peter Paul Candy Company was simply too small to provide the leverage required for Cadbury Schweppes to gain economies of scale and national representation in the USA. In fact, the move simply added to the problem of a languishing share price. The situation was compounded by Cadbury's inability to gain any momentum in the US market with its own brand. This resulted in high stock holdings, and thereby a high incidence of inventory write-offs. Ultimately, in 1988, the Cadbury board, admitting that it had a problem in the USA, sold its entire US operations for US$300 million. Ironically, the sale was made to Hershey in a move that allowed it to regain its market lead over Mars, returning it to the number one spot in the market – gallingly, at the expense of Cadbury Schweppes.

In lamenting the poor long-term performance of Cadbury overall, one City of London analyst, David Lang, was prompted to suggest:

> The problem faced by Cadbury really stemmed from the fact that the strategy after the merger with Schweppes in the late 60's was misguided. It was aimed at expansion overseas in a very widespread approach rather than nailing down the profitability and cash generation of the core UK business. Market share was falling away. They were adopting a scattergun approach to marketing. They introduced a vast number of new brands most of which were improperly or unsatisfactorily supported and dwindled away to nothing.
>
> At the same time their strong brands like Cadbury Dairy Milk were not being properly supported. That too was losing market share particularly to Yorkie, which was the tremendously successful introduction by Rowntree-Mackintosh in the middle 1970s. So the company was in a pretty bad way in 1976, compounded by the fact that they had misread the cocoa market that year (meaning that they lost money on commodity trading as well). (Smith et al., 1990)

Significant change was also emerging on the home front in the UK just as the ill-fated attempt to gain a foothold in the USA was under way. In 1988 the Swiss-German firm Jacobs Suchard carried out a dawn raid on Cadbury Schweppes's long-time UK competitor Rowntree, resulting in an instant acquisition of 15 per cent of the firm. However, Jacobs Suchard was apparently not the only one with its sights set on Rowntree, as soon after the raid, global food giant Nestlé made a £2.1 billion hostile bid for outright ownership – which ultimately succeeded. Rowntree at that time was the fourth largest chocolate maker in the world after Cadbury Schweppes and the US firms Mars and Hershey. As with Cadbury Schweppes, Rowntree was well established in traditional markets, and it also exported products to over 130 countries worldwide. In addition to its merger with the UK toffee manufacturer Mackintosh, Rowntree had also merged with the oldest chocolate company in the world, Menier of France.

Nestlé's push for Rowntree was abruptly dismissed by British commentators amid much debate about the ethics of a firm that could move British jobs offshore whilst remaining protected from takeover at home. Swiss law afforded domestic firms virtual immunity from acquisition. The UK press, government and public opinion were all against the acquisition, but a counter-offer proposed by Cadbury never saw the light of day. The UK Government Monopolies Commission had barred it on the grounds that it was not concerned with matters concerning global markets. Following a counter-offer of £2.3 billion from Jacobs Suchard and a further one from Nestlé of £2.5 billion, Rowntree eventually fell into the hands of Nestlé, making it the world's largest food company with over 7 per cent of the global confectionery market.

The only response open to Cadbury Schweppes was to seek further acquisitions along product lines, which resulted in the purchase of Lion Confectionery, the Bassett Group, then the Trebor Group. Consolidation and closer alignment of operations were also pursued by streamlining production processes and rationalising product ranges across the global empire. A focus on the soft drinks market also resulted in the formation of an alliance with Coke (Coca-Cola Schweppes) and the acquisition of the US beverage company Canada Dry, among others. Finally seeing the rational for a more balanced and logical fit in its portfolio, Cadbury elected to divest its interests in food and hygiene, preferring to concentrate on confectionery and soft drinks alone. This represented a significant milestone and realignment back to grassroot core competencies that finally took the company on the path towards becoming a more focused business.

This refocusing counted for little though as in 1989 it was Adrian Cadbury's turn to retire, handing the reins over to his brother Dominic, who elected to continue the same strategy and stance regarding the business strategy deployed by Adrian and Paul Cadbury before him, still with a primary focus on global expansion. As chance would have it, the collapse of the Soviet Union in December 1991 unlocked a vast new market that both Mars and Cadbury sought to cater for. The resources and attention required to do so would hide all of Cadbury's continuing underlying and problematic strategic issues yet again.

By 1995 both Mars and Cadbury had established a presence in Russia as well as Beijing. In the meantime, global acquisitions had included the additional soft drink companies Dr Pepper, 7UP and Snapple.

In 1987 further pressure was placed on the Cadbury Schweppes board as the US firm General Cinema acquired 18 per cent of the company in a move that was widely recognised as an attempt to put Cadbury Schweppes into play as a takeover target. That year also saw the launch of Coca-Cola and Schweppes Beverages (CCSB) as a joint venture. In the early 1990s the phenomenon of globalisation began to have a significant impact on trade in general as competition on a global scale grew significantly, led primarily by consumer-oriented industries in the food sector, particularly confectionery and chocolate. Consolidation of markets, companies, back-office support, procurement, marketing and advertising campaigns moved apace as protection and trade barriers imposed through constraints such as tariffs and import quotas were lowered around the world. Rationalisation of markets, industries and companies led to significant market share consolidation, especially by the operators which were best positioned to benefit from the inherent economies of scale that could be obtained from a global presence.

With the retirement of Dominic Cadbury in 2000, family representation on the Cadbury Schweppes board finally came to an end. At this point, in fact, only 1 per cent of the company was held by members of the Cadbury family (Cadbury, 2010). With the appointment of long-serving non-family member Chief Strategy Officer Todd Stitzer to the position of Chief Executive Officer in 2003, the final chapter of the Cadbury story would soon be written. The real strategic issues that had inhibited performance for years would now be addressed aggressively, and the dominant logic that had engulfed senior management and the board for years now dissipated. The area of greatest concern appeared soon after Stitzer's appointment, when Cadbury Schweppes reported a pre-tax profit fall of almost one-third as the company was hit by restructuring charges and a tough US market for soft drinks. In all, the company posted a 32 per cent decline in pre-tax profit to £564 million, although revenue grew by 22 per cent to £6.44 billion.

In what Stitzer defined as a 'transitional year', Cadbury Schweppes had launched a shake-up of its business since buying the Adams chewing gum division of US pharmaceutical giant Pfizer in March 2003. The result was: 'Underlying earnings per share increased two per cent in constant currency against the background of a major reorganisation, the integration of Adams and difficult trading conditions in many of our key markets.'

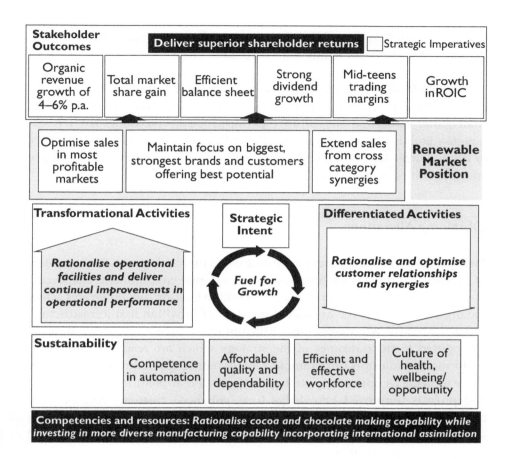

Figure 6.1   Cadbury plc strategic architecture based on strategic plan published in the 2007 annual report

In October 2003 Stitzer moved to improve performance further, announcing plans to slash 10 per cent of Cadbury Schweppes's global workforce of 55,000 and close a fifth of its 133 factories. The measures, dubbed 'Fuel for Growth' by the company, were part of efforts designed to save £400 million a year by 2007. In the 2007 annual report Stitzer observed that the 2003 four-year strategy of 'Fuel for Growth' had come to an end, and that Cadbury plc's new vision was 'to be the world's biggest and best confectionery company'. Describing a strategic change agenda of 'Vision into Action', the new business plan, Stitzer explained, 'encapsulates how we plan to deliver our goals by outlining key priorities – growth, efficiency, capabilities and sustainability – and our financial scorecard shows the financial targets the business plan sets out to deliver'. The actual strategy adopted by Cadbury plc was published in its 2007 annual report and is illustrated in the strategic architecture shown in Figure 6.1. To me, it demonstrates a basis for alignment – corporate-wide.

Stitzer elaborated on the underlying principles of that plan as follows: 'It's meant to portray aspiration – our vision; our governing objectives of delivering shareholder value; and our culture ("performance driven, values led"). It sets targets – both financial and sustainability KPI's – and describes what we have to do to deliver the performance against three priorities – growth, efficiency and capabilities' (O'Regan and Ghobadian, 2009).

Obtaining Alignment

The first question of alignment to be addressed in this chapter is in the context of strategic fit – that of the business and its external environment. The second is an assessment of the issue of alignment within the firm, up, down and across the organisation, and the associated question of fit within that infrastructure. In particular, we will explore the difficulty of cascading content of strategy, as opposed to the outcomes of the strategy which are readily identified as performance indicators (for example, rates of return, cost reduction and market share targets), as opposed to strategic objectives that point to specific actions and projects (improved knowledge base, enhanced customer relationships, building business intelligence capabilities). The third is an assessment of alignment that arises from the construct, management, ownership and communication of strategy.

STRATEGIC ALIGNMENT AS A MATTER OF FIT: INTERNAL COMPETENCIES/ RESOURCES AND THE EXTERNAL ENVIRONMENT AND MARKETS

I recall a situation that arose in a management consulting firm following the onset of the dot.com boom in the early 2000s. It came about as a result of the appointment of a business development manager. Starting afresh in his new role, the executive's highest priority he was told, was to bring about a substantial growth in revenue. Even though he had quite astutely identified an emerging gap in the market that would allow the firm to double its sales in the area of e-business advisory services, the end result was highly disappointing. Although the individual did everything right, including the design and implementation of a highly effective marketing campaign, he had missed the fact that the firm had no consultants sufficiently skilled in the delivery of the new service. As a result, his tenure was short-lived. The moral of this story is that whilst the physical alignment of the firm is important, so is the strategy – as expressed by Chandler (1962), who made the now-famous observation, 'structure follows strategy'.

Lack of alignment between a firm's internal competencies/resources and the external environment and markets in which it chooses to compete can have a significant impact on performance. In lamenting the focus on operational effectiveness rather than strategy in a *Harvard Business Review* article titled 'What is Strategy?'. Porter (1996) made the observation that the importance of strategic fit has been gradually supplanted on the management agenda. Rather than seeing the company as a whole, Porter observed, managers had turned to (the isolated issues) of core competencies, critical resources and key success factors as the basis of competitive advantage. In some way, Porter was lamenting the lack of systems thinking in a firms approach to its realisation of a competitive advantage.

However, the essential theme of the article was that competitive strategy is about doing things differently, not just at a lower cost, or being better (which I agree is a notion of operational effectiveness that is bound to only ever deliver a short-term *comparative* advantage, as opposed to a sustainable *competitive* advantage). As we discussed in some detail in Chapter 2 in order to derive a sustainable competitive advantage, Porter suggests, a firm should deliberately choose a different set of *activities* to deliver a unique mix of value. In stressing his point of view, Porter lamented: 'The most valuable fit is strategy-specific because it enhances a position's uniqueness and amplifies trade-offs. Trade-offs occur when activities are incompatible' (Porter, 1996) – or are lacking alignment.

His reference to activities and his criticism of reliance on one element of strategy alone, suggests a limitation of perspective on strategy *practice*. Porter effectively failed to differentiate between a *market position* as something a firm *has* and a *differentiating activity* as something a firm *does*. The importance of this observation is that the notion of alignment with an emphasis on activities assumes a whole new perspective on strategy, and is embedded with the philosophy that is adopted throughout this book associated with integration between the strategic architecture, strategy blueprint and the construct of the Strategic Management Framework in general (hence the term *fully integrated* Strategic Management Framework); in broad terms, strategy as a system.

This observation further provides validity to the use of the SMI's Dynamic Model of Strategic Equilibrium as a way to identify 'trade-offs' that Porter (1996) describes as being situations where 'more of one thing necessitates less of another'. The SMI Dynamic Model of Strategic Equilibrium was introduced in Chapter 2 (see Figure 2.2) and is illustrated here as Figures 6.1 and 6.2. It explores the degree of balance that does or doesn't exist between the extremes of inside-out, outside-in and the transforming/differentiating activities that link the two within the long-term strategy when expressed in the form of a strategic architecture.

The notion of fit as a central topic of strategy in the context of this book provides insight into the balance that may or may not exist within the elements of the strategic architecture; or the components of the strategy blueprint as an outcome from the strategic plan. Porter suggests that strategic fit among many activities is fundamental not only to competitive advantage, but also to the sustainability of that advantage. It is harder, Porter suggests, for a rival to match an array of interlocked activities than it is merely to imitate a particular process or methodology such as sales force approach, production process or set of product features: 'Positions built on systems of activities are far more renewable than those built on individual activities' (Porter, 1996).

By taking as an example the strategic preferences of restaurants identified in Chapter 2, we can make an assessment of where their strategic positioning within the boundaries defined by the strategic architecture (as shown in Figure 2.2) will be. It is also interesting to compare that proposed position based on the owners' perception of where they are actually located against their customers' perceptions of the same thing. As an example, Figure 6.2 shows a notional assessment of various restaurants' 'possible' perceived position of themselves.

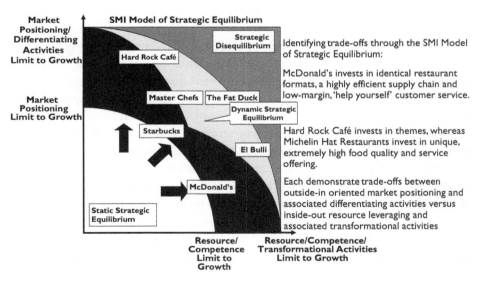

Figure 6.2   SMI Model of Strategic Equilibrium: trade-offs as perceived by restaurateurs

An evaluation of each restaurant's position from an external commentator's perspective proves to be an informative exercise. McDonald's, for example, perceives that it has a core competence in lean operations and a differentiated market offering that relies on customers to serve themselves, in fact McDonald's is at least equally if not more well known (in the business world at least) for its prowess in property acquisition and management. El Bulli, on the other hand, was extraordinarily successful in products and services (market position and differentiating activity), but its investment in transforming activities and core competencies to arrive that level of service was enormous.

El Bulli's owner, Ferran Adrià, describes the ideal customer as someone who 'doesn't go there to eat, but to have an experience'. His approach to the operation of the restaurant was to invest considerable time and resources in the renewal of its competence in food processing. This was applied to the extent where the restaurant closed for half a year in the winter months as the creative team retreated to its 'laboratory of tastes' El Taller ('the workshop') in Barcelona in order to create new combinations of food. As a result of this research retreat, the team produced about 500 new dishes for the season to come.

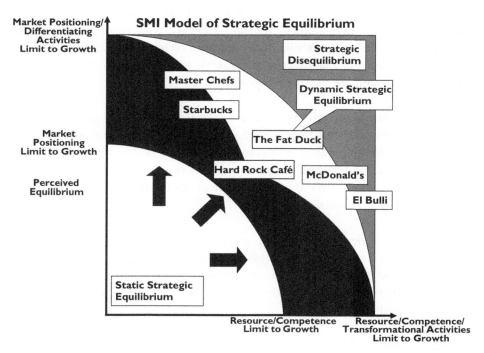

Figure 6.3   SMI Dynamic Model of Strategic Equilibrium as perceived by others

Figure 6.3 shows the location of each restaurant as others could possibly perceive it. My interpretation of El Bulli's location on the SMI Dynamic Model of Strategic Equilibrium is therefore one of extreme, located in the segment identified as the area of 'strategic disequilibrium'. El Bulli regrettably closed its doors in 2011, preferring instead to enter a joint venture with Telefónica in a formal food-based research and development capacity.

Obtaining Strategic Alignment: Exploration, Exploitation and an Ambidextrous Organisation Structure

Strategically, firms are consistently challenged by the need to physically align themselves to the markets in which they choose to participate – and grow. Meyer (2014) highlights the need for continual alignment between the business and environment. He observes that events and forces arising from activities or changes that occur in external environments demand an appropriate response from a business entity. As we saw in Chapter 4, a lack of response is symptomatic of a state of strategic drift, the outcome of which in most cases evokes an involuntary response to change which will prove to be life-saving – or not. The design and management of an appropriate response, though, brings with it an additional set of challenges. Not the least of these are heightened risk and a decline in profits. In particular, a programme of transformation introduces additional elements of risk that are attributable to a number of causes, among which the following are the most important:

1.   Change generally requires a physical investment in tangible assets and an increase in demand for capital. This in turn imposes pressure on operational effectiveness as a result of the need to allocate additional resources to the process of exploration, development and an assessment of new business opportunities – even before an investment is made.

2.   Investment in a change diverts managerial attention and operational resources to new business development, which in turn raises the level of risk. This can have a negative impact on the optimisation of the core business, with no guarantee of an outcome from the new business.

Facing the inevitability of the demand for continued alignment between the firm and its environment is *the* 'strategic challenge', Meyer (2014). 'Even in very stable and conservative environments, change happens where even the mighty must adapt themselves to the unfolding circumstances.' Taking very much a systems view of the operations of a business and market infrastructure, Meyer identifies two primary systems that require alignment in order to maintain an appropriate position of fit between the firm and environment. The first is the market system, whose members are the firm's customers, those to whom a business must offer a sustainable and/or renewable value proposition in order to attract and retain them at an appropriate level of income. A value proposition, Meyer (2014) notes, is 'a bundle of attributes that reinforce each other and together create value for a buyer'. The second is the business system, defined as: 'the way in which an organisation conducts its business; that is, the manner in which a firm creates value for a selected part of the market'.

Meyer adapts the observations made by March (1991) to describe a strategic response to the challenge of alignment and fit, which he suggests is enacted in the form of business development. His solution is to recognise the divide between the two characteristics of business development, he refers to each as being an issue of business *optimisation* and/or business *innovation*. Business optimisation seeks to identify opportunities for business development (and growth) that may be apparent from *exploitation* of the firm's existing business (business model). This, he proposes, is the furthering of 'investments in the existing business systems and resource base in the hope of utilising that base as much as possible'. Business innovation, on the other hand, is about finding new ways to create value outside the existing model. It is about doing things differently, often in ways that are 'new to the industry or even new to the world'. However, the discovery of new opportunities requires significant research and experimentation, in which case 'the mode of business innovation becomes a strategic program of *exploration*' (Meyer, 2014).

The foregoing provides us with an appropriate *strategic response* to the dilemma of maintaining continual alignment. Chakravarthy and Lorange (2008) further propose an organisational structuring solution which addresses this specific dilemma. The writers described the problem they sought to resolve as being: 'How does a business entity resolve the issues of protecting core business, whilst reinventing itself to ensure a sustainable, profitable future?' In arriving at an answer, they undertook extensive research which resulted in the conclusion that one particular organisation structure was more effective than others in facilitating an appropriate programme of innovation, growth and/or renewal as a basis for the delivery of continual alignment between the firm and its environment. In terminology used by Meyer (2014), this meant that the writers sought a way of managing the strategies of both exploitation and exploration at the same time. Their solution was observed to be the introduction or establishment of an organisational structure that looked like an ambidextrous person who is able to use either their left or right hand effectively. They named it the *ambidextrous organisation*.

An ambidextrous organisation is designed to incorporate specific project teams in such a way that they are independent of the mainstream business. Each team is afforded its own operating processes, structures and even culture. They are referred to as 'ambidextrous', however, because although they operate as independent teams, they are integrated into the existing management hierarchy. In other words, organisational ambidextrousness enables an organisation to deploy both explorative and exploitative strategy techniques at the same time, but each is conducted by two independent teams. The superiority of ambidextrous designs became quite apparent from Chakravarthy and Lorange's (2007) research. They found that the performance of those organisations adopting an ambidextrous structure increased substantially, whereas in contrast, the performance of companies that started out with an ambidextrous design then moved to a different one decreased substantially in two out of three cases. Another observation from the research showed that a clear and compelling vision coupled with relentless communication from the company's senior team was crucial in building ambidextrous designs.

As we will see in Chapter 7, the role of organisational learning again comes to the fore when considering change in organisations. The management of an ambidextrous organisation is no exception. As a reasonably complex entity, an ambidextrous organisation can benefit from continual learning as the key objective as the realisation of new business, and new business requires a great deal of knowledge accumulation and dissemination. I impress upon you however our early observations about the purpose of strategy (Chapter 1) where we concluded that a strategic response (responsiveness) is not only proactive and reactive change, it is also a result of an intended design. Designed change is intended to drive a deliberate shift in alignment, not in an adaptive sense (between the firm and its environment), but in a disruptive sense; the design of a new market or industry altogether. Special knowledge that is industry and firm specific is required to do that. Such knowledge is increasingly being developed internally; in the form of learning.

Strategic Alignment: Fit and Fiddle, Aligning Strategy Internally

In addition to the more rigorous and structured issues of alignment, I have identified additional, informative checkpoints that are conducted in practice in the form of a challenge. Once understood, the following questions that make up the challenge of providing useful insight into strategic decision making will help to influence areas of alignment. The first is the commonly quoted interpretation of strategic positioning which was originally formulated by Levitt (1960), who sagely suggested that the key to the future for a company is alignment between current activities and those of its actual market. Levitt enunciated this observation through the question, 'What business are we in?' The reason why railway companies stopped growing, Levitt suggested, was not because the market was filled by others (road, sea and air transport), but rather because it was not filled by the rail companies themselves. Their failing, observed Levitt, was that the railway companies let others take their market away from them because they believed they were in the railway business, not the transport business, which he considered the *actual* business they were in. In making this statement, Levitt was suggesting that the rail companies should have adopted programmes of continual renewal, evolving from railway companies to transport companies, taking advantage of a broader industry perspective and consistently looking to identify product/service substitutes for the declining railway business.

Levitt (1960) is also known to have convinced oil companies to diversify into coal mining in the 1960s because they were in the 'energy business', few of these companies are still involved in coal mining today. An illustration of a *misfit* within the SMI Model of Strategic Equilibrium (Figures 6.2 and 6.3) is I suspect, their acceptance of the fact that that they had little competency in an, albeit related, essentially different skill-based industry of resource extraction (mining) rather than drilling, capping and pumping.

Another perspective on the issue of alignment is associated with an appreciation of customer needs as opposed to definitions of industry in the context proposed by Levitt. It is an answer to the question, 'What problem are we trying to solve for our customer?' An example can be found in the oil industry again. Upon the discovery of oil in the Iranian desert, an antecedent company to British Petroleum (now known as BP plc) formed the Anglo-Iranian Oil Company in order to extract oil deposits from Iran. As a commodity provider of automotive fuel connecting to a supply chain focused primarily on the UK motoring market, the question to be addressed by the Anglo-Iranian Oil leaders would have been: 'How can we provide motorists with a sufficient level of confidence to allow them to venture out in their car and drive wherever they like, whenever they like without a risk of running out of fuel?' The answer could have led to the development of the retail division of BP and the establishment of roadside service stations acting as primary resellers of petrol. Interestingly, the question asked by the same company today, as it has been since the late 1990s, is more likely to be: 'How can we meet the primary needs of the consumers of our oil based products whilst at the same time, incorporate additional (viable) renewable energy solutions into our mix of service offerings?' In fact, this question was asked by BP's Group Chief Executive Lord Browne, who, when addressing a Global Climate Change Conference in 1997, commented that BP's primary challenge was to address the question: 'How can we find a balance between the need for [oil] development and the imperative for environmental protection?'[1]

A reverse perspective of BP's question – 'What problem are we trying to resolve on behalf of our customers?' – prompts further insight into purpose, simply: 'What resources will we have access to or obtain in order for us to resolve those problems better than anyone else?' This question is based on an assessment of value in the sense that value is defined as the set of resources required to address customer needs. To offer a service, a firm must invest in appropriate resources and that investment must deliver a reasonable return. In this case, the final question becomes, 'What value are we providing to our customers?' – or more simply, and possibly more widely recognised, 'What is our value proposition to our customers?'

An example of the application of the question of customer-oriented decision making is smartphones. Consider for a minute the question that BlackBerry's leaders would have asked themselves when challenged by the onset of smart phones. My view is that had they asked the same simple question, 'What customer problem are we trying to solve?' the answer would have informed their decision making to the extent that their go-to-market product offering would have been different to what it eventually was – that is, their true value proposition. Although BlackBerry enjoyed a profitable market presence for a long time, when pitted against more advanced smart phone competitors such as Apple and others using the Android operating system, its future became increasingly uncertain, and an inevitable decline ensued. The reason can be attributed in the main to the fact that BlackBerry failed to renew its product offering within an appropriate timescale, and when it did, it chose to tackle its competitors head-on rather than continuing to focus on its primary point of differentiation, which was their primary appeal to the business market alone. BlackBerry solved the problems of the business executive better than its competitors. Key features that made it successful in the business market

---

1   See www.bp.com/en/global/corporate/about-bp/our-history/history-of-bp/new-millennium.html (accessed 6 May 2014).

included its messaging system, its phones' external keyboard and its strict focus on business-related functionality.

To demonstrate how well the question works in practice, you will observe that many companies have a strategic objective of 'ensuring customer satisfaction'. If a company focuses on this question alone that is as a specific objective, it is bound *not* to be addressing future-oriented issues *as well as* those of today. Car companies, for example, invest enormous efforts in quality and cost-effective production capabilities to ensure their cars meet customer expectations, but as Henry Ford supposedly once quipped: 'If I had asked people what they wanted, they would have said a faster horse.' To make the leap from horses to cars, it was necessary to pre-empt, and indeed lead, customers into newly defined industries and markets whilst at the same time ensuring that existing products always met customer needs and expectations, as opposed to meeting existing expectations alone.

Strategic Alignment: Cascading Strategy Up, Down and Across the Organisation

The second aspect of strategic alignment is the domain of strategy itself, especially the difficulties associated with the cascading of corporate strategy to business units and functional divisions and beyond. In addressing this issue, I noted previously that it is easier to align the *outcomes* from strategy than it is the *objectives*, which I can describe as being the doing components of the strategic plan. Examples include 'implement new customer relationship capability' and 'invest in China'. I would also include vision and mission in this observation. Corporate-level definitions of these topics will be broad-based. Business unit or functional-level applications may need more contextual detail or more specific detail – or more customer focus. At the same time, issues of culture and values will usually remain uniform across the business.

The solution, therefore, is to put the literal content to one side and to cascade the strategy, not the performance measures alone. The differentiation between markets, activities and resources as key components of the structure of strategy (contained within the strategic architecture and strategy blueprint) helps to make this possible. In a sense, this is a continuation of the external assessment of fit discussed above. When setting strategy with the help of the strategic architecture for the first time, it is apparent that markets and differentiating activities are external components of strategy, whereas transforming activities and resources are internal components. As you will observe from the following summary, influential spans of control will be determined by these factors, as will the differences in nature of each component of the strategic architecture. As suggested in Chapter 2, markets and resources are something we *have*; differentiating and transforming activities are things we elect to *do*.

Strategic Architecture as a Basis for Cascading Strategy and Alignment

By way of illustration, I propose that each of the elements of the strategic architecture illustrated in Figure 2.1 are treated as follows when cascading strategy.

RENEWABLE MARKET POSITION

Former CEO of General Electric, Jack Welch famously observed that if the businesses in which GE participated didn't hold the top one or two positions as measured by market share, then they wouldn't remain in the business. Market share, though, is something you have, not something you do. It is not something you can dictate either, although it is certainly something you can influence.

In many instances markets and customer categories will vary by region, locale and in many other ways, or they may be uniform – it all depends. Therefore, cascading strategy in the market space can point to desired outcomes, but more importantly, it can be used as guidance as a means to optimise and tailor different elements of strategy; within appropriate spans of control and in accordance with the specific elements of market share that the specific business or business unit may have access to.

DIFFERENTIATING AND TRANSFORMING ACTIVITIES

The things a firm does differently, uniquely or independently can be compared across business units and can also be taught across business units. When they are inappropriate activities, they can also be stopped across business units. Cascading strategy in this context is afforded greater flexibility and control than the foregoing markets – or the associated resources. Activities are about physical systems and processes and events. Independent business units have control over their activities; corporate offices can watch and judge and provide feedback. But exerting control from the corporate office is difficult.

BUILDING, LEVERAGING COMPETENCIES/RESOURCES

As with market positions, resources are something an organisation *has*, but the differentiation between tangible and intangible is useful. Whereas tangible resources are easy to monitor and compare, intangible resources are subject to change and subjectivity. Competencies in particular may be unique to a small cluster or location. In this context, they may or may not be great contributors to other business units' strategic goals and objectives.

There are differences in strategy at corporate and divisional level. The corporate office generally provides direction on outcomes, support and shared resources, but it is up to the individual business units to respond to their local market and customer requirements as best they can.

Strategic Alignment: Teams Sharing the Vision – Bringing Strategy to Life

As we discussed in Chapter 4, strategy is an individual skill that is conducted and enacted in teams. The extent to which a team will agree to collaborate on strategy is critical to that team's success. This is reason enough for most senior leaders to retain tight control over the creation of strategy, its communication and acceptance across the business is fundamental to some managers' ability to lead.

Physical presentations, town hall meetings and other formal methods of communication are useful ways to explain to everyone what company strategy is. One of the most powerful methods for bringing strategy to life is through the automated dashboarding technology I have referred to earlier as the strategy evaluation dashboard monitoring mechanism, a variation of which includes cascaded strategy and enterprise performance management-based metrics.

So far we have incorporated a number of topics into this system. By the time we have concluded with a final discussion on the use of this instrument in Chapter 7, the format and structure will have become quite substantial. For the purposes of our discussion on alignment here, I suggest that its development will force thinking on content to be included in an aligned and integrated strategy system, as the content on one aspect of a business and its strategy will now be traced and tracked to another. The more interactive and the greater the alignment between strategy and reality of what is actually happening, the greater will be the integrity of the data included in the monitoring system.

We will cover additional components of the proposed strategy evaluation dashboard monitoring mechanism in Chapter 7.

Chapter 7

Strategy as a Profession: Practitioners Working Together, Getting Results

> ## INCONVENIENT TRUTH NO. 7: STRATEGY PRACTICES LACK AN APPROPRIATE PERSPECTIVE OF PROFESSIONALISM.
>
> Strategy is not a natural science, but a socially constructed convention that exists between peers. There is no 'absolute' such as the absolute zero of -273°C. It is a learned capability and a lived experience that professionals *do*, as opposed to systems, processes and capabilities that we *have*.

As the discipline of strategy emerges as robust practice, the number of strategy professionals is growing. In support of this growth there is a groundswell of activity among strategy researchers and academics on an international scale, each supporting the need for transformation in the strategy research agenda. Taking it away from a primary focus of a theory of strategy as one of an economist's perspective of strategic posturing, towards its application as something we *do* – strategy *in* practice. Strategy Professors Whittington and Cailluet observe that: 'As well as something that organisations have, strategy is something that people do. Strategy is a kind of work. In this sense, strategy is a practice like any other, fundamentally equivalent to other practices such as architecture or nursing' (Whittington and Cailluet, 2008).

Jarzabkowski et al. (2009) also stress that strategy in practice is 'something that people do; a lived experience prosecuted by Strategy Practitioners'. The authors describe strategy practices as 'the social, symbolic and material tools through which strategy is done', and a strategy praxis as 'the flow of activity in which strategy is accomplished' (Jarzabkowski et al., 2009). There is a need for all of us to be more strategic in our outlook. To date, our capabilities in undertaking that role – especially in a professional capacity – have been limited.

With the elevation of strategy to the level of a profession, we can expect to instil a standard of thinking that will reduce the expectation that all strategic thinking is done (or heard) by only one person: the CEO. Similarly, we can expect to instil in all managers, leaders and anyone involved in business for that matter, with an appreciation and understanding of strategy, one that will add an extra dimension to the strategic capabilities of decision makers, especially those in the leadership team, and as a result deliver superior performance to that team. There is, however, a need for those individuals to at least understand the fundamentals of strategy in a capacity that is useful in practice and effective in teams.

The Seventh Inconvenient Truth of Strategy

The transformation of theory into practice and the elevation of practice to the level of a profession is the fundamental issue we will address in the final chapter of this book: the manifestation of a professional strategy practitioner whose practice is implemented and renewed by individuals working in teams, within the construct of a learning organisation as an underlying system that facilitates and enables renewal. This is enacted under the guidance and approval of the ultimate owner of strategy: the chief executive officer. So to The Seventh Inconvenient Truth of Strategy:

> *Strategy practices lack an appropriate perspective of professionalism. Strategy is not a natural science, but a socially constructed convention that exists between peers. There is no 'absolute' such as the absolute zero of -273° C. It is a learned capability and a lived experience that professionals do, as opposed to systems, processes, capabilities that we have. As a consequence, over-reliance on science-based academic approaches to strategy practice results in poor outcomes, wrong strategies and sometimes bad strategy. In the absence of a comprehensive method of strategy practice, our understanding is vague, its integration difficult, its application problematic and its implementation all too often sub-standard.*

The last CEO of Cadbury plc, Todd Stitzer, is an example of a strategy professional. Stitzer was an internal appointment to the position of CEO from the role of Chief Strategy Officer (CSO). He therefore represents a success story for all CSOs who aspire to reach the top of a business/corporation. At the same time, his appointment highlights the extremely transient nature of a typical life in a strategy function. Many people are attracted to strategy as a career choice, the role though is just as likely to be a springboard to some other role in a firm, especially when it is a business on the scale of a listed corporation. In many small firms the CEO is also the Chief Strategy Officer by default, in which case skills in strategy are still critical.

The important thing to note about the strategy profession is that even if you do have another role, or are promoted to other positions, the skills and experiences you acquire as a result of a stint in strategy will remain with you for the rest of your life. If you are already a qualified accountant for example, qualifications as a professional strategy practitioner will broaden your perspective and as a result help you to be the best you can be. Experience obtained in the CSO's office in any capacity is a rounding-out process, and one that will assist an individual's elevation to many other career positions.

In continuing the theme of strategy as a profession, I conclude this assessment of The Seven Inconvenient Truths of Business Strategy with the final chapter of the Cadbury story. The discussion will concern its ultimate strategy, its final push forward, and its ultimate demise at the hands of a more aggressive competitor, Kraft Foods Inc.

Emergence of a Reformed, Realigned Cadbury and the Beginning of the End: Welcome to Kraft

In 2008 Stitzer included an updated description of Cadbury Schweppes's corporate plan in its annual report to shareholders. The general thrust of the plan was based on the continuation of a strategic change agenda of 'vision into action', where the vision was 'to be the world's biggest and best confectionery company'. Although Stitzer had been successful in turning around much of the company's poor performance, he emphasised in the annual report the need for more work to be done if it was to fulfil that vision. Stitzer explained that in order to do that, costs would have to be reduced and jobs would have to be lost or transferred overseas. Figure 7.1 (overleaf) illustrates that strategic plan (adapted from Cadbury Schweppes's 2008 annual report).

Although robust actions could be seen to be under way to improve performance at Cadbury Schweppes, a key instigator for reform of the company's financial performance was an American entrepreneur and billionaire, Nelson Peltz, who in 2007 had acquired 3 per cent of Cadbury Schweppes, which was by then valued at around STG £12 billion. Peltz, recognised as an astute investor and adviser, was proposing the company be split in two through the spin-off or sale of the drinks division (the Schweppes business, then estimated to be worth £7–8 billion) as an independent business.

Vision:	Be the world's biggest and best
Governing objective:	To deliver superior shareholder returns

Performance Scorecard:	Organic revenue growth of 4–6%
	Organic total confectionery share gains
	Mid-teens trade margins by end 2011
	Organic strong dividend growth
	Efficient balance sheet
	Growth in ROIC

Priorities:'By 2011 we expect to close around 15% of Cadbury's manufacturing sites around the world and as a result, to also reduce head count.'

1. Growth: fewer, faster, bigger, better
 1.1 Category focus for scale and simplicity
 1.2 Drive advantaged, *consumer*-preferred brands and products
 1.3 Accelerate white space market entry via 'Smart Variety'
 1.4 Create advantaged customer partnerships via total confectionery solutions
 1.5 Expand product platforms, strengthen route to market via partnership/acquisition

2. Efficiency: relentless focus on cost and efficiency
 2.1 Realise price and optimise customer investment
 2.2 Reduce selling, general and administrative cost base
 2.3 Deliver supply chain cost reduction and reconfiguration initiatives
 2.4 Rationalise portfolio
 2.5 Optimise capital management

3. Capabilities: ensure world-class quality
 3.1 Operate *category-led business* enabled through consistent commercial capabilities
 3.2 Invest in *science, technology and innovation* to deliver preferred products at *competitive cost*
 3.3 Drive focused *decision making* and *speed of execution*
 3.4 Sharpen *talent, diversity and inclusiveness agenda*
 3.5 *Leverage partnerships* to streamline processes and reduce costs

Sustainability: | Reduce use of carbon, water, packaging

Promote responsible consumption	Nurture and reward colleagues
Ensure ethical, sustainable sourcing	Prioritise quality and safety

Culture: Creating brands people love	**Purpose:** Performance-driven, value-led returns

Figure 7.1   Cadbury Schweppes's business strategy according to its 2008
annual report

As reported by Deborah Cadbury (2010), the Cadbury Schweppes board had already considered this option, but was concerned at the possibility of the loss of an independent British company to an overseas company. The sheer size of Cadbury Schweppes, it thought, would make it difficult to acquire as a whole. A spin-off would therefore leave the independent business (confectionery) subject to hostile takeover. Prompted by the publicity created by Peltz and in recognition of the need to improve financial performance anyway, Stitzer was moved to take even more action. His first move led him back to the USA and into new discussions with Hershey, again proposing a merger through which Cadbury Schweppes could accommodate a smooth divestment of its drinks division and a corresponding replacement in capital to protect its remaining confectionery business from takeover. This time the Hershey board was more receptive and was inclined to respond positively to the merger proposed by Stitzer. However, when the management of Hershey Foods persuaded the Hershey Trust not to go through with it, the approach was again declined.

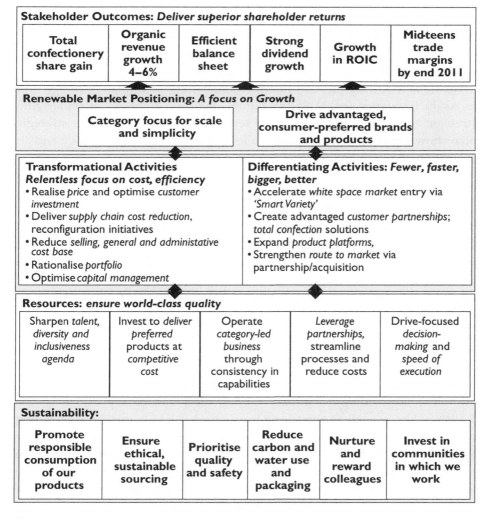

Figure 7.2   Cadbury plc strategic architecture based on the strategic plan published in its 2008 annual report

Ultimately, continued pressure from Peltz along with increased support from institutional shareholders finally swayed the Cadbury Schweppes board to move to offload the drinks division, an exercise which carried with it a £7–8 billion price tag. The first attempt was scuttled by the onset of the Great Recession, however, which immediately eliminated the private equity group that had earlier sought to acquire the business. This development still did not stop Peltz, who continued to lobby other shareholders and the Cadbury Schweppes board to either float or sell the drinks division. In spring 2008 the cost of the proposed demerger soared to an estimated £1 billion – an amount some investors considered to be too high compared to a more intense focus on improving performance within the firm. The board forged ahead anyway, and the demerger came into effect on 2 May 2008. The drinks business was floated independently on Wall Street as the Dr Pepper Snapple Group Inc. In December 2008 it was announced that Cadbury would revert to the name Cadbury plc, and that it would sell its Australian beverage unit to Asahi Breweries for AU$1.185 billion. Figure 7.2 shows an underlying strategic architecture that could have served as a foundation for the strategic plan shown in Figure 7.1, providing a logical structure to the strategy and an indication of alignment.

On 7 September 2009 the inevitable finally happened; Kraft Foods made an unsolicited £10.2 billion (US$16.2 billion) indicative takeover bid for the newly formed Cadbury plc. The offer was rejected immediately, with Cadbury stating that it undervalued the company. Undeterred, on 9 November 2009 Kraft launched a formal hostile bid which valued the company at £9.8 billion. On 19 January 2010, it was announced that Cadbury and Kraft Foods had reached a deal and that Kraft would purchase Cadbury for £8.40 per share, valuing Cadbury at £11.5 billion (US$18.9 billion).

Although Hershey had expressed an interest in buying Cadbury on the grounds that it would broaden its access to faster-growing international markets, on 22 January it announced that it would not counter Kraft's final offer. The acquisition of Cadbury faced widespread disapproval from the British public, as well as opposition from groups and organisations including the trade union Unite, which fought against the acquisition of a company that, according to Prime Minister Gordon Brown, was very important to the British economy. Unite estimated that a takeover by Kraft could put 30,000 jobs at risk. By 2 February Kraft announced it had secured over 71 per cent of Cadbury's shares, thus finalising the deal. Kraft needed to reach 75 per cent share ownership in order to be able to de-list Cadbury from the stock market and fully integrate it as part of Kraft, and this was achieved on 5 February.

The company announced that Cadbury shares would be de-listed on 8 March 2010. On 3 February, Chairman Roger Carr, Chief Executive Officer Todd Stitzer and Chief Financial Officer Andrew Bonfield of Cadbury all announced their resignations. Stitzer had worked at the company for 27 years. Kraft stated that the deal would create a 'global confectionery leader'. In order to fund the acquisition, it had to borrow £7 billion (US$11.5 billion) – the money ironically coming from the UK-based Royal Bank of Scotland.

Making Strategy a Profession

No doubt different readers will offer different views as to the success of Stitzer in his role as Chief Strategy Officer and then Chief Executive Officer. On the one hand he can be applauded for orchestrating a significant rise in the share price that was realised on the sale of Cadbury to Kraft. On the other he may be criticised for losing control of the company, whilst others have already expressed disappointment at the number of jobs lost as a result of the Kraft acquisition. That of course is the challenge of strategy as a discipline, there is rarely one right or wrong answer, but someone has to make the call.

The forgoing and final overview of Cadbury may also highlight the level of influence a CSO really has in a corporation. At the end of the day, Cadbury embarked upon their strategic change agenda (as opposed to strategic intent that we would have expected from a longer term strategy) of 'Vision into Action' following Stitzer's appointment as CEO quite some time after other major corporations (including Mars Inc.) had adopted a similar efficiency drives on the scale described in this chapter, and in Chapter 6. Either Stitzer didn't see the need or didn't have enough authority to move earlier. In the dying era of Cadbury described in this chapter, a continuation of 'vision into action' had, as we saw above, an emphasis on becoming 'the world's biggest and best confectionery company'. Although Cadbury did enjoy a superb representation and presence in the confectionary market, I can't help but wonder how realistic that vision was. More importantly, I wonder how much *better* an alternative vision for Cadbury could have been. As we saw in Chapter 3 (Figure 3.2) a failure to adequately define what the real purpose of restructuring would be, an organisation was bound to be caught in a vicious spiral of value destruction rather than a foundation for a virtuous state value creation through a journey of revitalisation and then continual regeneration.

In assessing the challenge of the journey ahead of us all (as emerging strategy professionals) I will now address some of the primary functions that you will face as you set about raising the standards of strategy practitioners in general, and contribute to its transformation to the standard of a profession. I commence with some thoughts on the concept of strategy as a profession, and go on to explore topics of strategy that professionals should be aware of, including strategic thinking and the mind of the strategist, then on to aspects of strategic governance. I will return to the notion of a learning organisation as a highly complementary role within the office of strategy and the importance of learning as an attribute of the strategy professional at the end of this chapter. This discussion will commence with a review of the concept of a learning organisation through the lens of a corporate university/academy. This will be followed by an assessment of learning as a basis of *renewable* competitiveness. This final chapter – and indeed, the book – concludes with an assessment of the role of the main protagonists in strategy and the work they undertake as consummate strategy professionals: chief strategy officers.

FROM STRATEGY PRACTITIONER TO STRATEGY AS A PROFESSION

The definition of a profession, according to the Australian Council of Professions, is:

> *a disciplined group of individuals who adhere to ethical standards and who hold themselves out as, and are accepted by the public as possessing special knowledge and skills in a widely recognised body of learning derived from research, education and training at a high level, and who are prepared to apply this knowledge and exercise these skills in the interest of others.*
>
> *It is inherent in the definition of a profession that a code of ethics governs the activities of each profession. Such codes require behaviour and practice beyond the personal moral obligations of an individual. They define and demand high standards of behaviour in respect to the services provided to the public and in dealing with professional colleagues. Further, these codes are enforced by the profession and are acknowledged and accepted by the community.*[1]

Strategy as practice is already well placed to meet these criteria. We explored the notion of generally accepted strategising principles at the beginning of this book, these need to be more widely expressed and accepted by individuals in order for a profession in strategy to be nourished, and grow. I do not propose to provide any steadfast definitions of professional strategy principles here.

---

1   See www.professions.com.au/definitionprofession.html (accessed 6 May 2014).

I do aim, though, to lay the foundations for their future development. Internationally, strategy scholars are broadly promoting the concept of strategy as a profession. Whittington et al. (2011), for example, observe that: 'We take strategists as professionals in the unfussy contemporary sense: as people who apply distinct bodies of expertise to problems involving risk and uncertainty'. It is now up to the practitioners in consulting and industry to 'make it happen'.

However, to become a profession (or perhaps as an outcome of recognising strategy as a profession), there needs to be a major change in the way practitioners *do* strategy. Surveys after surveys show the poor state of health of strategy in practice. Research into strategy practices conducted by SMI and RMIT University (Hunter and O'Shannassy, 2007) drew on responses to a questionnaire from 35 of Australia's top corporations in 2004. An analysis of the use of strategic analytical tools from that research consistently showed that most of the effort that goes into strategic planning is committed to the use of tools that add least value and are best suited to static, certain environments as opposed to potentially more relevant, certainly more dynamic, but increasingly uncertain environments. The tools in most widespread use also seem to focus more on exploitation of existing markets rather than exploration of potential future markets. They include competitive analysis (addressing current competitors) at 85 per cent of those surveyed, portfolio analysis (existing products) by 72 per cent and gap analysis (derived from prevailing situational analysis) by 66 per cent. In contrast, in dynamic, uncertain environments where exploitation is representative of new frontiers, actual tool usage was found to be minimal: scenario planning was used by only 37 per cent of those surveyed, game theory 3 per cent and the more complex and most future-oriented tool, chaos theory, was used by no one. Our overall conclusions from the survey ultimately pointed to:

- a lack of use of tools that were more suitable to the reality of modern economies, risk and uncertainty;

- an orientation towards easier-to-use and arguably lower-value tools such as the relatively simplistic Strength, Weakness, Opportunity and Threat (SWOT) matrix.

The latter observation (SWOT analysis) was confirmed by the UK-based Advanced Institute of Management Research (AIM), which, prior to its closure, published results of its research from 2009 that showed that when comparing the tools most used against those most valued: 'Managers do not choose (strategic) tools because of their relevance to the topics they intend to address, but those that are easier to understand and use, as well as those that hold the highest level of legitimacy with their peers i.e. the best known and most frequently used' (Jarzabkowski et al., 2009).

In order to illustrate our preparedness to assume the mantle of professional strategy practitioners, I present in Table 7.1 relevant results from more recent research into strategy practice which illustrates areas where observers and/or participants in strategy would like to not only strengthen their capabilities, but also to spend more time and effort improving various aspects of strategising as a whole. Resolution of these topics is essential, I suggest, if a professional standard is to be realised.

The survey also showed that less than 20 per cent of organisations have a chief strategy officer, although one comment included the observation that the chief executive officer was also the chief strategy officer.

Table 7.1   Responses to SMI/Swinburne University survey on strategy practices, 2013

Changes I would implement to make our strategy more effective would be:	Strongly agree/agree
Enhance our capacity to adapt to change and promote strategic renewal	77%
Spend more time evaluating alternative scenarios of the future	69%
Have the time to experiment more with 'out of the box' thinking	62%
Incorporate deeper analysis and develop more challenging outcomes	58%
Increase the freedom to be far more entrepreneurial with new ideas	58%
Incorporate deeper strategic thinking into our everyday activities	58%
Strengthen our capability in strategy and strategic management	73%
Those who thought their strategy was always relevant and current	31%
Those who thought they could implement strategy more effectively	74%

Primary Functions of the Strategy Professional: Strategic Thinking

Chapter 1 identified the five key elements that give a reason to *do* strategy, which is its purpose:

1.   to articulate what a specific entity's long-term future will look like and to describe the way in which it will realise its long-term goals – its strategy;

2.   to develop a plan that describes strategy and the way it will be implemented and renewed, its strategic plan and the associated programme of continual strategy renewal;

3.   to provide the basis for leadership;

4.   to provide the basis for strategic responsiveness to change;

5.   to provide support for the resolution of 'wicked' strategic problems.

The first two reasons to do strategy have been addressed through the lens of a structured strategic architecture and an associated strategic plan followed by a programme of continual strategy renewal; key components of the fully integrated Strategic Management Framework. We also explored ways in which the framework and associated concepts contribute to a strengthening of individual skills in leadership. In doing so I sought to extend the thinking of Senge (1990) to suggest that individual specialist skills obtained from practical experience, personal mastery and learning together (that is, in teams) contributes to more meaningful strategic decision making overall. An ability to work in, lead and learn as a team that engages in a shared vision for the future, whilst also engaging in ongoing dialogue was shown to elevate the knowledge, confidence, profile and capabilities of teams and their individual members. Similarly, teams that engage in open dialogue and apply a systems perspective to the complex and wicked strategic problems that they must be bold enough to address and resolve also escalates regular methods of decision making to the level of strategy. There are a number of techniques that contribute to more effective strategic thinking (we will discuss these next), I am concerned though that the fourth issue identified as a purpose for strategy – *responsiveness* – demands greater clarity, especially at the level of a profession.

Responsiveness

The issue of responsiveness is associated with leadership and organisational transformation in the sense that leaders who are charged with taking the organisation into an (unknown) future must be able to exhibit an ability to think strategically and a capacity to address levels of complexity as they arise. To think strategically is to apply creativity, insight and foresight to a decision making framework that draws on past experience (wisdom), an appreciation of the present reality coupled with a propensity for disruption and acknowledgement of the variety of possibilities that may require further evaluation as an outcome. Strategic thinking is informed by research, driven by a deep grasp of the issues and a feel for the consequences and potential impact of alternative outcomes. Typical outcomes from strategic thinking exhibit insight and freshness, boldness and credibility. Strategic thinking is not an irregular activity, it is an all-encompassing and everyday activity that captures imagination, evokes inspiration, engenders innovation and ideally instigates new ideas and insight as it paints a picture of new possibilities.

There is no way to describe levels of complexity that may be associated with unplanned, unforeseen events, they must be dealt with as and when they occur. Leaders must always be prepared to respond to those events in ways that either protect the business from harm or allow it to capitalise from the potential of any opportunities that may arise as a result of such events. However, not all events should take organisations completely by surprise. Strategy professionals must remain aware of trends that might become apparent in the internal and external environment at any time. Examples of internally driven, future focused eventualities that may appear as a 'puff of smoke' can be gleaned from data driven by big data, business intelligence/analytics technology, for example, that provide insights into trends, patterns and anomalies that become evident from analysis of the volumes of data that would otherwise have gone unnoticed prior to the ability of computers to 'mine' such information in a meaningful way.

Examples of external future focused events include anomalies in numerous forms of publicly available information that can be obtained from economic reports and other newspaper reports detailing for example changes in consumer pricing and spending patterns, buyer behaviour and levels of fluctuations in stock and commodities where appropriate.

A degree of foresight (enabling a highly proactive response) was afforded to Shell when, in the mid-1970s, the company was found to be far better prepared for the onset of the 1973 Oil Shock than its competitors, as a result of the extensive work it undertook using scenario analysis to evaluate and prepare a range of responses to the impending and significant changes in the oil industry as they were about to unfold. The so-called Oil Shock was a global phenomenon that saw oil prices soar as Egypt and Syria, with the support of other Arab nations, launched a surprise attack on Israel on the holiest day of the Jewish calendar. Israel went on full nuclear alert, loading warheads into planes and long-range missiles. In response, the USA chose to demonstrate its support by re-supplying Israel with arms. This in turn provoked the Organisation of Arab Petroleum Exporting Countries (OAPEC) to retaliate by announcing an embargo on the export of oil. The embargo lasted until March 1974.

As a result of its application of scenario analysis (as explored in Chapter 3), Shell's strategy practitioners were able to not only imagine a range of possible outcomes from the imminent price hike (memories of the future), but also to better prepare their response by getting Shell's leaders to accept that the impending changes were in fact about to occur – a reality that most other sceptical, less well-informed oil company leaders could not accept. Not only did Shell survive this unfortunate episode in the global economic saga, it also went on to achieve far greater things, whereas other oil companies languished for quite a while longer.

Each of these perspectives on the future relies on a view of reality based on known or foreseeable eventualities. Working with the *unknown* is much harder, and is therefore the natural domain of strategy specialists – enter the Certified Strategy Practitioner (CSP). The foundation and justification for a sizeable investment in strategy is based on the observation that 'all our knowledge is about the past, but all our decisions are about the future'. The dilemma for the strategy practitioner is that 'the past is no predictor of the future'. As wise twenty-first-century business executives, though, we have learned to apply specific research methods to our endeavours in strategic thinking, but when conducting our research (reflecting and reviewing) have focused very much on *deductive* research methods whereby a conclusion is reached from general *statements*.

Recognising that this is more of a hard approach to *scientific* research, Rumelt (2010) has proposed we embrace an *inductive* research method more suitable to social science, where conclusions are reached from specific *examples*. The difference is that whilst the conclusion of a deductive argument is generally treated as *certain*, the truth of an inductive argument is generally treated as *probable*. With a probable and uncertain outcome, additional lines of enquiry are encouraged: 'to generate a strategy one must put aside the comfort and security of pure deduction and launch into the murkier waters of induction, analogy, judgment and insight'. Similarly, Gladwell (2006), in his book *The Tipping Point*, explores the term 'thin-slicing' as a reference to the activity of making very rapid decisions with small amounts of information.

Knowledge obtained through this latter component of strategic thinking is informed by a method of judgement that we have identified previously as systemic change (Senge, 1990). Systemic change is driven by systems thinking which encapsulates the need to understand the *cause* of change in certain patterns in behaviour, not just the *potentiality* of change itself. The difference is explained by Senge as being related to a notion of *adaptive* rather than *generative* learning. Adaptive learning is concerned with responsiveness to current or possible events, as well as insightful but fairly predictable unknown futures (as described above). Generative learning is concerned with *creating* change based on an envisioned or desired future as well as *responding to* forced change – but therein lies the challenge.

An ability to create new, unknown futures (especially at the level of Steve Jobs of Apple Inc., for example) requires high ambition, faith, hope and a level of believability in those entrepreneurial types who are proposing ideas for and variations on new or redefined versions of *what could be*. At the same time, the believability of the vision embodied in the redefinition or reinvention of an envisioned future must be grounded in a plausible version of reality as we know it today. A transformation agenda grounded in a credible version of reality then provides the mechanism for and disruption to current expectations that is sufficient to convey and obtain buy-in to ideas and perceptions of new futures and new expectations.

As discussed previously, in this book we have explored the notion of a plausible strategic change agenda which is a component of a programme of continual strategy renewal (Chapter 5) whose progress is monitored through a formal monitoring mechanism. This was in turn confirmed as being a legitimate component of the fully integrated Strategic Management Framework. The propensity to obtain a level of buy-in sufficient to motivate change and to encourage others to make the necessary leap of faith is obtained through a belief in the organisation's foundation skills at a level sufficient to sustain the reinvention/renewal of the organisation. This is then supported by an organisational culture that enables the organisation to continually transform which is in turn fuelled by learning or knowledge accumulation over time.

Chapter 3 identified the Cycle of Organisational Transformation and Renewal through which this level of transformation occurs. The cycle, as demonstrated in Figure 3.2, is made up of the elements of *reframing, restructuring, revitalisation* and *regeneration*. Arguably, organisations enjoying life in a state of regeneration should have no need for restructuring, or revitalisation as they are already doing those things, as a part of their everyday management of the business. For those that may be in strategic drift or have simply found themselves in a position that necessitates the commencement of change, the design, management and selling of reframing is a primary role of the professional strategy practitioner. It requires instilling a different way of thinking, an ability to innovate and dissociate from versions of *what is* whilst not losing the alignment between the existing state of the business and an envisaged future – that is, the *could be* (a precursor to an appreciation of what *will be*, the aspirational articulation derived from content that sits behind a strategic change agenda). However, the dynamics of that envisaged future transcend the known. It is the epitome of a *dare to challenge*. I propose a version of reframing therefore that adopts a level of free thinking that continually exceeds the norm.

Reframing

To demonstrate the difficulty of grasping the depth of the concept of reframing, I refer you to one of the world's most highly regarded chief executive officer's, Jack Welch, who as President of General Electric Inc. (GE) proposed a heroic vision of what *could be*. In GE's 1990 annual report Welch declared: 'Our dream for the 1990s is a boundaryless company … one where we knock down the walls that separate us from each other on the inside and from our key constituencies on the outside.' Welch was describing a vision of a company that would 'remove barriers among traditional functions, recognize no distinctions between domestic and foreign operations, and ignore or erase group labels such as management, salaried, or hourly, which get in the way of people working together' (Hirschhorn and Gilmore, 1992). Although visionary, the depth of change proposed is I think, still limited as it is focused on a perspective on freedom that was more constrained than freed by reinvention. In applying Meyer's (2014) perspective of strategic change discussed earlier for insight, we can see that Welch was pursuing a strategy of exploitation as opposed to one of exploration. Whilst exploitation is commendable, it is more of an element of business as usual than an expression of strategic thinking as I defined previously. I stress that a focus on exploration as well as exploitation (ambidextrous organisation – Chapter 6) is bound to offer a lot more potential for an organisation as it harvests efficiencies and effectiveness from core business whilst nurturing new shoots that will emerge as core businesses in the future.

In response to an appeal to indulge in greater explorative strategic posturing I recommend the strategy professional maintain a visionary and even relentless pursuit of operational excellence. At the same time I urge you to hear the call and adopt the level of reframing expressed by the returning astronauts who experienced first-hand the impact of the overview effect (discussed in Chapter 3) as an example of a truly *systems* focused, boundaryless interpretation of the space ship Earth and as an inspiration to rethink and imagine a new order of today's normal altogether. The overview effect was described by astronauts upon their return to Earth as one that 'enables us (astronauts) to appreciate Earth as a shared home, one without boundaries between nations or species' (White, 1998). In support of their views, they provide a quote from Socrates, the ancient Greek philosopher born *c.* 469 BC who is noted to have proclaimed: 'Humanity must rise above the earth, to the top of the atmosphere and beyond. For only then will we understand the world in which we live.' The astronauts were referring to a view of the world as an integrated system. Welch I suspect, although responding appropriately to the immediacy of the needs of the GE Corporation at that time, was thinking about the world in dimensions of functional silos, managerial hierarchies and business processes; not an integrated, boundaryless system.

The implications of the overview effect on the way astronauts view life and our planet can be readily translated to corporations or business entities. It informs the way the strategy professional can think strategically whilst addressing wicked strategic problems and also the context within which they choose to advise the CEOs of the corporations with whom they collaborate to lead. Although the astronauts' version of the overview effect is focused on the future of the planet Earth, the intensity of their belief is appropriate and inspiring and of direct relevance to corporations: 'the experience of seeing firsthand the reality of the Earth in space, which is immediately understood to be a tiny, fragile ball of life, hanging in the void, shielded and nourished by a paper-thin atmosphere'. From space, the astronauts tell us, 'national boundaries vanish, the conflicts that divide us become less important and the need to create a planetary society with the united will to protect this pale blue dot becomes both obvious and imperative'.

An interpretation of this observation for a professional strategy practitioner in a company of any size could perhaps be:

> the reality of seeing the future of our company in a truly global and boundaryless context as a tiny, fragile entity that, just as a ball of life hangs in the void of customer whims, is shielded and nourished

by a paper-thin support for our ability to continually nourish the key elements of our business that contribute to the continual sustainability of our existence.

For validity, I refer again to Andy Grove's observation mentioned in Chapter 4 that 'only the paranoid survive' (Grove, 1999). For evidence, I refer to the rise and fall, and sometimes ultimate demise, of hundreds of corporations, including IBM, Enron, Kodak, Apple, Pan Am and Ansett Airlines, Nokia (mobile phones), BlackBerry, Arthur Anderson and Lehman Brothers.

Perhaps the most significant contribution is the translation of the overview effect into practice. The realisation of boundarylessness seems even more possible, according to the returning astronauts, 'if only more people could have the experience'. It is my belief that although outer space travel is unachievable for most, experiences that contribute to a motivation and reason to reframe at a certain level are not. We simply need to be thinking differently and acting in the same dynamic way – in the same dimensions as seeing the world from space. Surely, this is at least one role of a corporate university?

An example of an organisation that has realised this height of thinking is an early start-up and philanthropy-driven company called Pollinate Energy. Pollinate set out to solve a wicked health problem prevalent in India's urban slums, caused by the use of kerosene for lighting and cooking which emit toxic fumes when used – especially when these activities are conducted inside the tents and makeshift houses that are typical of slum life. In addressing this problem, Pollinate also faced an unusual logistics challenge whose solution needed to transcend normal supply chain systems and procedures that are used in most developed countries.

Pollinate is a not-for-profit social enterprise which, through the deployment of deferred payment schemes, relationship-based distribution resellers (Pollinators) and the support of volunteers (Australian-sourced university students) to provide access to affordable and clean energy that improves the livelihoods of economic migrants living in urban slums. Pollinate's business model is unique, combining attributes of a learning organisation, innovation in micro-financing, the appeal of spiritual gratification for benefactors as well as a 'beyond borders' experience for advanced economy leaders and future leaders who learn from the opportunity to work among India's urban poor. Those who attend these programmes benefit from the impact of facing the commercial reality of buying, distributing and selling commodity-based products in one of the most transient, challenging and commercially (and physically) difficult environments in the world.

At a commercial level, the company deploys local salespeople (Pollinators) to both create and sell to a disparate, risk-averse customer base in an environment which is destined to grow (exponentially), but politically (from the Indian government's perspective) faces a determination to be transformed from transience and poverty to permanence and wealth. Pollinate's competencies in the supply of renewable energy products to India's poor are supplemented by a fellowship programme that, in addition to providing a unique work experience, facilitates feedback to the company with vital market and competitive intelligence that will allow it to learn, grow and thrive. The Pollinate alumni who are evolving as an outcome from the fellowship programme experience are also proving to be another source of knowledge and a basis for empirical research as well as an incubator for altruistic funding of more dynamic endeavours in the future.

On the surface, Pollinate is not much more than a supplier of a range of products that includes solar-powered lights, phone chargers and fuel-efficient cooking stoves, with the promise of more to come (for example, water and sanitation products, hygiene products and more advanced electronics). Beneath this veneer, Pollinate is evolving a dynamic and relationship-based customer service model that will grow at the same rate as the migration programme allows the movement of people from slums to better accommodation and beyond. Equally, it benefits from knowledge acquired across the board (benefactors, investors, and themselves through very close relationships with their customers) and has the potential to deliver learning and knowledge capabilities in addition to consumer goods, capitalising on the links created by its existing distribution network. In both formats, it represents a promise to transform lives. Pollinate's strategy exists on a knife-edge: high-volume/ low-margin sales to a low-cost, highly transient, education-poor but knowledge- and energy-hungry customer base.

Steve Jobs at Apple Inc. is a corporate-level success story that exemplifies the way systems thinking can be used to transform a company that at the point of his re-appointment as CEO was only days away from bankruptcy. Whilst in the process of turning Apple into the strongest brand in the world, Apple's competitors were preoccupied selling individual products such as computers, notebooks and MP3 players. The difference is that Apple was busy building a fully integrated digital entertainment *ecosystem* – iPods, iPhones and iPads. This form of systems thinking is not all about technology, though. One of the business cases I enjoy working with the most is that of the German automotive tyre company Continental AG. Set in the 1990s, it is the turnaround story of a manufacturer whose ultimate success is attributable to its transformation from a tyre manufacturer alone to that of an automotive braking *systems* manufacturer with wheels and tyres as only part of its customer solution. Ultimately, the system consisted of automotive braking modules, chassis and electronics. It became an illustrative success story for the industry. Air International is an Australian automotive parts manufacturer that has a similar story to tell. This company started out installing air conditioning units into new cars (as an optional extra) and used cars in second-hand car yards, and it grew at a reasonable pace. Following a never-ending search for higher-value products and services, though, Air International ended up as a principal supplier to top-tier automotive companies around the world, providing and assembling ready-made dashboard systems of which air conditioners were only one of the components.

Solving Wicked Strategic Problems

The fifth element of purpose in strategy to be addressed is the provision of support for the resolution of 'wicked' strategic problems, which, along with other cognitive issues, is critical to successful strategic outcomes. Problem resolution is only the front end of a cognition system; decisions made must be articulated and communicated across the business if desired outcomes are to be translated into results. A strength in strategic thinking is also critical as a defining attribute of the would-be professional strategy practitioner charged with continual and strategic decision making. Much of this, I suggest, has implications for the strategic imperatives of the business, and also the dimensions and direction of its future. We have observed that the mavericks associated with likes of Apple and Pollinate most probably rely on intuition as a primary source of strategic thinking. I turn now, though, to one of the world's greatest thinkers on strategy practice, Kenichi Ohmae, to put this form of strategic thinking into perspective.

Strategic Thinking and the Mind of the Strategist

In his book *The Mind of the Strategist* (1983), Ohmae makes the point that despite limited access to resources, money and technology, many Japanese companies are outstanding performers in the marketplace. Ohmae attributes this level of success to the capacity of Japanese CEOs to literally think like strategists: they 'intuitively possess a basic grasp of the fundamental elements of strategy' even though they may have never attended any strategy, or indeed business, courses in their lives.

Ohmae suggests that fundamental to their grasp of strategic intuition is insight, which he defines as consisting of the elements of 'creativity, partial intuition and a propensity to be disruptive of the status quo'. A natural application of intuition results in outcomes from strategic thinking that are often hard to conceive as being credible, but from the strategy professional's perspective, highly desirable. The reason? Unstructured creative thinking leads to innovation and growth. Highly structured inhibited thinking more likely than not will lead to stagnation, strategic inertia and subsequently the onset of strategic drift, as discussed in detail in Chapter 4.

Analysis is a critical aspect of strategic thinking, but analysis per se is not made effective by a systematic approach to analysis alone. Rather, it is often realised through 'a combination of rational analysis, based on the real nature of things and the imaginative reintegration of all different items into a new pattern, using non linear brainpower'. Importantly, Ohmae laments that the need in major corporations to conform to the status quo stifles innovation – a dilemma he attributes to the extent of formality, control, detail and general aversion to risk. Ultimately, he observes: 'As strategic planning processes have burgeoned in companies, strategic thinking has gradually withered away.' The difference between this outcome and the inspirational reframing that arises from the overview effect experienced by astronauts is exactly the point I am trying to make about the importance of the need for reframing as a basis for strategy, strategising and strategic thinking as well as transformation and renewal.

Creativity, is a primary component of strategic thinking according to Ohmae, it is he suggests 'a skill that can't be taught, but can be learned'. It is realised through the nurturing of an individual's sensitivity, strength of will and receptiveness. Significant advances in more effective strategic thinking have been made since Ohmae's observations were published, but they are highly consistent with his observations. They include ways to improve creativity and the introduction of reinvented mental models into the practice of strategising. In recent times, the recognition of the imperative for greater creativity in strategic thinking has led to the application of more advanced techniques in the way we structure our thought processes.

Strategy as design, or more broadly *design thinking*, is an example which, according to a researcher in this specialist field, Liedtka (1998), is a metaphor for *strategy as a process of design*. The principle of design thinking calls for greater rigour in decision making by calling attention to the process of creating a purposeful space, in the sense that design thinking creates:

> *an environment that fuses form and function; builds relationships and capabilities and targets specific outcomes that inspires, at an emotional and aesthetic level, those who work towards a shared purpose. Values also play a pivotal role, as do hypothesis generating and testing and the ability to conjure a vivid picture of a set of possibilities that do not yet exist. (Liedtka, 1998)*

Now, that sounds better.

A second and similarly engaging approach to strategic thinking is described by Martin (2007) as *integrative thinking*. This is a method of problem solving that is enacted through a capacity to hold two opposing ideas in your mind at once. Rather than seeking an either/or (two choices alone) solution to a problem, integrative thinking provides an innovative method of problem solving that incorporates elements of the alternative answers at the same time. The outcome is an improvement to each perspective as a possible solution is developed. Proponents of the integrative thinking methodology propose that strategy practitioners look beyond the obvious solutions and instead embrace ambiguity, messiness and conflicting options to generate a wealth of possible alternatives.

Another still emerging field of research is analysis of the physical structure of the brain and its application to understanding how strategic business decisions are made. Just as Ohmae observed that creative thinking is a form of insight, it has now been demonstrated physically that creativity cannot necessarily be taught, but can be fostered by the application of mental exercises and techniques – *induced* insight, if you like. The physical study of the brain is only in its infancy and, just like strategy theory (until now), has never been synthesised into an integrated framework. The application of the theory of neuroscience to business is making a valuable contribution to strategy as practice, and strategic thinking in particular.

In a recent *Harvard Business Review* article, for example, Waytz and Mason (2013) report evidence that demonstrates how the workings of the brain influence decision making, and in particular *boundaryless* thinking. The brain, according to Waytz and Mason, 'is never at rest and accordingly is occupied in processing internalised existing knowledge that goes beyond the Breaking News or external information about which we are bombarded every day'.

The significance of this observation soon becomes apparent when we learn that this fact allows the brain time to have a little freedom and engage in the activity of transcendence, which is 'an ability to envision what it's like to be in a different place, a different time, and a different person's head, or a different world altogether'.

During transcendence, people's thought processes are able to detach themselves from the external environment. This capability is unique to humans, and it means that having free (unfocused) time (that is, time away from the normal work environment) is beneficial as it allows free thinking. This is an attribute that in turn provides an opportunity to be significantly more creative and innovative as the brain is allowed to become self-absorbed, focused on internal knowledge *sorting* as opposed to the more distractive activity of external knowledge *processing*. This finding offers a level of validity to practices encouraged by Google, for example, which allows its employees up to 20 per cent free time to work on topics of their own choosing. Such a discovery also provides implicit support to the value of a properly designed and managed two-day strategising 'off site', as discussed in Chapter 4.

Strategic Governance

Although strategists and commentators on strategy in general (Ohmae included) lament the over-formalisation and bureaucracy in strategy, the topics of risk management, stakeholder management, strategy evaluation and renewal are of particular relevance to the professional strategy practitioner. As such, the acknowledgment of and adherence to some elements of what I will call *strategic governance* are critical. Topics of particular concern are:

- strategy evaluation reviewing (assumptions);

- strategic risk;

- too much strategy (strategic overstretch);

- stakeholder interests.

STRATEGY EVALUATION REVIEWING (ASSUMPTIONS)

In nearly every chapter of this book I have referred to or explained the notion of strategy evaluation, both shaping and reviewing. I opted to defer the discussion of the invisible component of strategy evaluation reviewing to this final chapter as it is mostly concerned with governance and strategic risk as opposed to planning, growth, strategy and business renewal. The important point here is to remind you that in the preparation, review and renewal of strategy (strategy evaluation shaping), it is necessary to base many decisions on assumptions, estimates and guesstimates – something we would otherwise not do. The inevitably of the necessity to do so is driven by two factors. First are the emotive factors of ambition and aspiration that are critical drivers of the leadership psyche of most business entities. Second is the imperative to make decisions in the here and now about hoped-for outcomes in the future – which, by definition, implies high levels of error and inaccuracy. As emphasised throughout this book, such decision making is fraught with dangers as the future is more than unknown, it does not exist. I therefore propose that as far as possible, the assumptions and guesstimates that are made should be identified, articulated, logged and coupled to the content that makes up the strategy evaluation dashboard monitoring mechanism (as discussed in Chapter 5).

There are numerous examples of areas where a need to undertake some form of assumption about possible future outcomes are evident. When transport infrastructure, tourism resorts and entertainment venues are established for example, the decision to do so is based on assumptions about patronage – amongst many other things. As a specific example though, Sydney's cross-city tunnel has gone bankrupt twice because, contrary to expectations, user patronage targets (the basis for toll income) were never achieved. Other examples include:

- expectations of uptake in technology and other new innovations;

- expectations that third parties will do something in collaboration with you, then don't;

- reliance on financial and economic forecasts on factors such as GDP, inflation and interest rates;

- the passing of legislation at various levels of government and in different countries; at unexpected times.

Resolution and management of this form of strategy evaluation is managed therefore through a program of strategy renewal monitoring as illustrated in Figure 5.1.

ASSESSING AND MANAGING STRATEGIC RISK

In similar vein to the management of assumptions is the monitoring of strategic risk. Risk management in general is a critical component of business, but my focus on strategic risk is concerned with each of the elements of strategy. I propose that the obvious elements at a strategic level are those associated with each of the elements of the Strategic Management Framework, which, as a system, are iterative in nature and interactive in practice. Whereas, for example, a strategic imperative contained within the strategic architecture may be to provide an online education forum for delivery in international markets, the short-term strategic objective contained in the strategy blueprint could be to 'tailor our service offering to English-speaking countries'. The alignment of this objective to the programme of continual strategy renewal would then require a monitoring system that identifies specific trigger points, providing insight into the where, when and how of the physical launch of that service in China, for instance would take place. Inclusion of a Chinese-speaking specialist could be an example of a state of internal readiness. Receipt of enquiries for supply of your products or services from Chinese companies could be a sign of customer acceptance and readiness. Other examples include competitor activity, if any, and uptake of similar products in other non-English-speaking countries.

Both assumptions included as part of the Strategy Renewal Monitoring component of the program of continual strategy renewal (Figure 5.1) and strategic risk are valid components of the monitoring mechanism and alerting mechanisms that we have referred to here. Each are attuned to eventualities, trends and even surprises that may occur in the areas of: competitive intelligence, strategy evaluation reviewing, strategy implementation and the monitoring of the assumptions, guesstimates and estimates that were made as strategy was formulated (strategy evaluation shaping).

AVOIDING STRATEGIC OVERSTRETCH

Whereas strategy in this book has had a strong bias towards strategy as exploration, growth, renewal and reinvention strategy practitioners would do well to consider that strategy is as much about exiting existing businesses or optimising their performance as well as expanding, growing or acquiring new businesses. The results of acquisitions in many instances are remarkable for their lack of success. Schoenberg (2006) estimated that in the UK, the incidence of failure to add value as a result of acquisitions ranged from 40 to 60 per cent. According to other sources, up to 80 per cent of mergers and acquisitions fail to add value.

Whereas acquisitions are driven by a need to make the numbers work as a primary criterion, the thinking behind the strategy driving the acquisition – investment in new business areas or, more simply, continued organic growth – is another matter. Although I would admonish many retail banks for their lack of innovation and strategic thinking on the one hand, their conservative nature and business risk profile (which is very low) combine to suggest that minimal aggression in strategic thinking is required.

To illustrate this, take a look at any of the world's top retail banks. The strategic problem that they were first established to address was *to provide the means to allow money to flow through an economy or economies*, essentially for the purpose of encouraging and then protecting individual savings. Such was the imperative for this that many governments around the world set up their own banks to ensure that the money that did flow was able to do so without encumbrance. At the same time, those governments invited entrepreneurs to establish private banks in order to create competition and encourage innovation in the banking system. In conducting their trade, it was accepted wisdom that banks should carry out their mission in an efficient and effective manner, and at minimum risk in order to protect customer and shareholder interests. Their primary objectives were to present a low-risk money management facility for their customers and to optimise shareholder value for their shareholders. Consciousness of the needs of society was also desirable, but not mandatory. If there were opportunities for a bank to make more money than other banks, and thereby benefit from the delivery of other related services with minimal risk, so be it.

So what are the strategies of the banks? Let's take a look at strategy of the National Australian Bank (NAB) as an example (albeit a public version). Each of the four major Australian banks is protected by law from takeover by another major Australian bank. This is because of Australia's Four Pillar policy, a government-mandated requirement that was designed to reduce the risk of a downside impact on the Australian economy should a bank fail. As the seventeenth largest bank in the world in terms of market capitalisation, NAB's strategy:

> *drives how we do business right across our Group – a set of priorities that informs everything we do. Three years ago, we set ourselves four strategic priorities to:*
>
> - *focus on our strong Australian franchise and manage international businesses for value,*
> - *maintain balance sheet strength,*

- *reduce complexity and cost, and*
- *enhance our reputation.*[2]

On progress against this strategy, NAB reported in the 'Strategic Highlights' section of its 2013 Annual Report (Report of the Directors) that:

> The Group maintained its overall objective to deliver sustainable, satisfactory returns to shareholders. In March 2013 the Group updated its strategy to better align the business to the changing economic landscape and customers' evolving needs. In particular it noted that: Over the past few years we have made significant progress on our key strategic priorities. We have a more balanced and sustainable Australian banking franchise, an enhanced reputation, a stronger balance sheet and increased productivity. We have made solid progress in technology transformation and we have continued to manage our international portfolio for value.[3]

Amid strong criticism from the investment community for its perceived under-performance during the period 2010–13 out of its 123-year history, NAB's current three-year strategic plan is exactly what a bank's should be: ongoing management of the same customer problem that it set out to resolve when it was established, by *being a bank* (or at least, a bank with an Australian franchise).

When we look at what NAB has actually done, though, it is a different story. In the same three-year period, NAB completed the takeover of a sizeable insurance company, MLC, fought tooth-and-nail to resolve chronic under-performance in the operations of its UK acquisition Clydesdale Bank, and suffered significant problems in its information technology systems that had afflicted it for some years. NAB, along with many retail banks, also continues to score low on customer satisfaction. Its acquisition target, Clydesdale also recently took a hit to its bottom line after being caught up in the mis-selling of insurance products. If only NAB had stuck to its strategy of being a bank!

On an international scale, and at a level of detail too deep for our purposes here, commentators have gone so far as to attribute the occurrence of the Great Recession to poor strategies attributable to retail banks and, of course, all other

---

2   See www.nab.com.au/about-us/shareholder-centre/reports-and-presentations/annual-reports-archive/our-strategy (accessed 6 May 2014).

3   See NAB Annual Report 2013, www.nab.com.au/about-us/shareholder-centre/reports-and-presentations (accessed 22 May 2014).

forms of banks whose business models became decidedly confused prior to that extremely unfortunate event.

STAKEHOLDER INTERESTS

There is no denying the importance of the shareholders as the main stakeholders in a business. With a primary focus on financial outcomes, they are in one sense the most important stakeholders, but they are often (for corporations, at least) the least involved in the delivery of those outcomes. As we explored extensively in considering the strategic architecture and strategy blueprint, financial outcomes are just that – outcomes from strategy. All the will and influences in the world won't deliver predetermined financial measures as outcomes unless the firm is able to build a sustainable customer base and conduct the right activities to either differentiate itself in its chosen markets, or continue to both renew and develop its transforming activities and utilise the competencies and resources to which it has access in order to outperform or differentiate itself from competitors.

There is not now, and probably never will be, a hard-and-fast rule determining the right balance between stakeholder and shareholder interests. It is important though for the professional strategy practitioner to be aware of the issues the disparity between each set of interests creates.

Bringing the Learning Organisation to Life; the Notion of a Corporate University (Academy)

As a precursor to a review of the role of the chief strategy officer, it will be useful to highlight the way the learning organisation is evolving over time. If you are in any doubt as to the value of learning, consider Mars presence in China as a superb success story. It starts with the realisation at the time of the Beijing Olympics – 1993 that long term success for Mars Chocolate in that country would require access to well-trained people, at all levels of the business. Up until this time, Mars had no indigenous employees who had sold (and in many cases eaten) chocolate before. To satisfy this need Mars invested in the development of a formal education program, culminating in the formation of the 'Mars Academy in China' in 2003. The results were considered outstanding by both company leaders and those who benefitted from the education program, in particular Mars employees (associates). The program, as told by Allen (2010) resulted in Mars obtaining the number one market position in China (ahead of all world famous chocolate manufacturers that included Cadbury) and now enjoys as much as 40 per cent market share.

Learning in organisations though doesn't have to exist at such a formal level. As we saw with Pollinate Energy, it is in effect building its own *informal* learning capability. Having said that, many major corporations around the world are investing in the development of *formal* corporate university capability (a corporate university is often referred to as an academy). They are doing so in order to encourage a structured, strategically aligned approach to change in a format that we have referred to extensively throughout this book. Pollinate is at the lower, but equally valid, small end of the scale, Rademakers (2014) provides insight into a number of case studies that explain the operations of corporate universities on a global scale.

An example is the now global Mars University, which in 2009 was asked by then President, Paul Michaels, to undertake a review of its internal operations and as an outcome design a corporate university that would 'provide world class programs to unleash the potential of Mars associates [employees] whilst reflecting the global nature of the business and embedding the Mars principles and culture'. The review concluded that Mars University needed to realign itself to the direction in which the corporate strategy was going – way beyond tweaking around the edges of cost management and control. It was recognised that doing so would require the university's wholesale transformation from its traditional role as provider of functional expertise and services designed to assist with improvements in productivity to that of an all-encompassing education facility. Key goals would be to empower and inspire (realising potential and making a difference for individuals, the Mars business, and the planet), and to be a committed ally (making a positive impact as a dedicated partner sharing associates' goals).

The end result is the operation of a corporate university comprised of ten functional colleges (Finance, Sales, Supply, Corporate Affairs and so on) and one cross-functional college (Leadership). Content provided by these colleges is made accessible across the globe, providing a set of resources and learning methods in the form of training courses, e-learning modules, a library and a research facility. At Mars University, the college curricula are created by top Mars associates and supported by external experts.

I use the example of Mars University to demonstrate how a knowledge transfer facility that was once treated as a cost centre has transformed itself into a driver of strategy and leader in the transformation of the business. In fact, Rademakers (2014) points to three different forms of corporate universities in his book:

- **a school** – a facility that teaches fundamental skills that are unique to the business (examples are hamburger making, bank telling and in-flight service delivery);

- **a college** – whose curriculum is applied to transfer knowledge in areas that will assist with the implementation of strategy, or even drive it; skills in the use of Six Sigma process design, the realisation of enhanced customer relationships and increased leadership skills are typical outcomes from initiatives identified as important in the strategic planning activity;

- **an academy** – where (similar to the Mars example), the corporate university is responsible for breaking down barriers to knowledge innovation through the development of leaders; this in effect informs strategy and is a key instigator of the collection and dissemination of knowledge that both informs and extends the capacity for an organisation to exercise proficiency in strategic renewal.

The Role of the Chief Strategy Officer

In this book we have explored many unknowns about strategy, including the not insignificant issue of a fully accepted and understood definition of what strategy is. It will not surprise the reader by now to know that neither is there a clear definition of the role of the ultimate strategy professional: the chief strategy officer. Publicly available research on this topic is limited, but it is developing further as part of the thrust of the academically supported strategy as practice movement we discussed in the beginning of this chapter. Some research into this position has identified certain characteristics. It is my hope that much of the content of this book will make a serious contribution to this effort. Insight into the role of CSO is provided by Powell and Angwin (2012), whose research identified four specific 'archetypes', as opposed to definitions, of the CSO's responsibilities:

1.   **internal consultant** – the type of CSO who adopts a very rational approach to the development of strategy;

2.   **specialist** – a CSO chosen for having highly specialised skills not previously present within the organisation;

3.   **coach** – a facilitator focusing on strategy formulation with the business units;

4.   **change agent** – in contrast to a specialist, acting through the business units as a facilitator to ensure that strategies are enacted with fidelity.

To those who are CSOs as well as those interested in strategy as practice in general, I invite you to join me in making strategy a profession. An interactive dialogue capability has been set up on the Strategic Management Institute's website to facilitate further engagement and dialogue on this topic.[4] There, I hope to perpetuate my intention in writing this book: to make a contribution to the individuals and teams who lead organisations by providing a framework and understanding of ways in which strategy can be effectively put into practice. The individuals who take up this challenge will not all be CSOs. At some point in their careers, though, they will be asked to address wicked strategic issues and later, hand down the franchise of strategically astute knowledge as a form of leadership.

WHO IS A CHIEF STRATEGY OFFICER?

The foregoing explores in some detail the formal role of a chief strategy officer in a major corporation. Cascade that role down to a one-person business, however, and you will observe that the values, philosophies, models, tasks and responsibilities remain the same no matter the size of the organisation. My wife Lyn, for example, runs a two-person interior design business and has already learned a lot about strategies for that business from this book – not so much because it has contributed to new strategy, more because it has contributed to structuring and confirming her existing and intuitive understanding of strategy and ways the discipline can be applied to practice.

When Lyn set out to establish her design business, she knew instinctively there was a market for a designer who would not dictate to clients, was not overly expensive and above all would not be difficult to approach. With a vision of providing interior design solutions to households based on a conscious desire to meet specific customer needs (for example, 'decorate this room around my red motorbike', a vintage Indian model), budgets and idiosyncrasies, the business Lyn built has the following strategic architecture:

---

4   See www.smiknowledge.com.

- **stakeholder outcomes** – return on investment and profitability measures, as well as social and environmental measures;

- **market** – middle- to upper-income-level home owners seeking to make their home a tasteful, professional, warm and welcoming environment at a reasonable price;

- **differentiating activities** – provide an approachable service, an ability to listen to client needs, and offer empathetic solutions;

- **strategic intent:** transform lives through the creation of exciting, aesthetic places in the home;

- **transforming activities** – continual development of the skill base through extended alliance partnering, collaboration and up-to-date knowledge of the latest designs, trends, fashions and providers of hard and soft furnishings;

- **resource base** – excellence in product knowledge, design skills and supply chain management capabilities – in summary, a designer, strategist, leader, manager, controller and shrewd businessperson.

Her business continues to grow year by year.

Conclusion

In concluding this book, I would like to emphasise an observation that most executives make upon completion of our Strategy Master Class accreditation programme: at the end of the day, strategy is a major contributor to a strength in leadership. My own observation that typically follows this comment is: 'Yes, it's very hard to lead an organisation if you don't know which direction you would like to take.' Michael Porter makes a similar observation, adding: 'strategy represents perhaps the most powerful tool available to leaders to get all the individuals in the organisation aligned around a common sense of purpose and direction' (Porter, 2008).

Although strategy is an individual skill, it is conducted most naturally in teams. Winning teams are the backbone of high-performance organisations, and high performance in general. Winning organisations are the best ones to be associated with. Although the challenge is great, the goals high and the effort significant, there is no reason why we can't all enjoy the experience of contributing to the success of a high-performance organisation. We just need to continually refresh the way we look at those organisations, rethink the way they can be optimised and continually reinvent the value proposition they offer to *all* of their stakeholders. However, this is not a trivial pursuit. It is not about form-filling and 'satisficing'. It is about disruption, design, problem solving, inductive reasoning, resolution, resolve – and most of all, meeting the challenge of those inevitable wicked problems head-on. Based on my experience from running strategy accreditation master classes I can attest to the fact that although we can all learn more about better ways to do strategy, it is the way in which that knowledge is applied in practice, at an appropriate level of rigour, vigour and challenge that makes a difference. Whereas I set out to teach better strategy, I am finding that the best graduates emerge as better leaders.

Appendix 1:

The Evolution of Strategy Theory

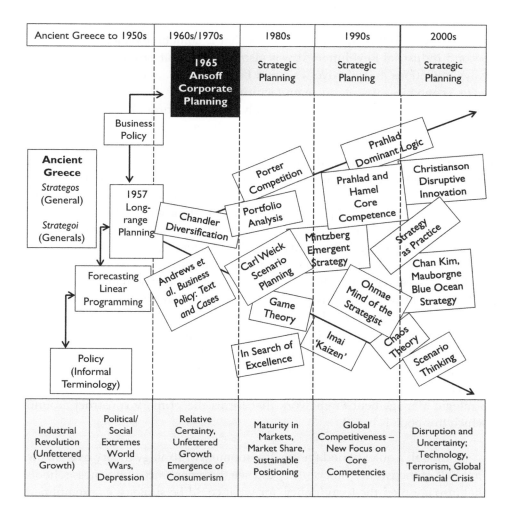

Ancient Greece to 1950s	1960s/1970s	1980s	1990s	2000s

Figure A1.1   A timeline of the history of strategy theory

The ad hoc way strategy theory has evolved over the years can be seen as more of a response to market and business environments than a tool symbolising leadership in strategic thinking (see Figure A1.1). As you will observe from this very brief history, there is a huge gap between the time when the ancient Greeks first coined a reference to strategy (those who prepared a strategy for war were known as *strategoi*) and the arrival of the Industrial Revolution which ultimately led to the state of strategy as we know it in the 2010s.

I include events that occurred in the 1870s in our story of the evolution of strategy theory because this is the time when industry, at least in the form we understand it today, was born – the era that is sometimes referred to as the Second Industrial Revolution. It was also a period that provided insight into ways inventions and discoveries could be duplicated, and most importantly, ways economies of scale in manufacturing could be attained through mass production. Productivity was continually enhanced through the invention of new, powerful machines which in turn could be operated on a mass scale.

An early indication of the logic of the separation between strategy and strategic planning is witnessed by the introduction of a different term for what we now refer to as strategy: *policy*. A good example of the use of the term 'strategy' in the context of policy is offered by one-time CEO of General Motors Alfred Sloan, who in his biography, *My Years with General Motors* (1963), reflects on his views of the capabilities of a past CEO of General Motors, William Durant, when he 'was particularly concerned that [Durant] had expanded General Motors between 1918 and 1920 without an explicit policy of management with which to control the various parts of the organisation'. In this case, it seems Sloan was more concerned with the way strategy was being implemented rather than the strategy itself. But Sloan appears to be expressing an opinion that he would have preferred to have seen what we now understand as a strategic plan – a control device guiding strategy implementation, as opposed to an articulation of a long-term strategy for the business as encapsulated in the Strategic Management Framework that forms the primary construct around which this book is based.

Although a quiet period for the development of strategy theory overall, the first half of the twenty-first century did see the emergence of business schools that also adopted the term 'policy' for what could be strategy, as exemplified by the Capstone MBA course, which also adopted the 'policy' theme, in which the subject was simply named 'Business Policy'. In its early years, business policy was taught through extensive review and analysis of case studies. The significance of the term 'policy' is the fact that the course was designed to give students insight into difficult problems that affected the firm as a whole, not just one function. Although closely aligned, evidence of the academic use of the term 'business policy' has never attempted to distinguish between strategy and strategic planning per se, even though the tension that emerges from the differentiation is never far from the surface.

The earliest book to be used in support of the Business Policy course was also one of the first three books that considered strategy as a discipline. Published in 1965 and authored by Learned et al., its title was *Business Policy: Text and Cases*. The launch of this book symbolised the world's return to normality in some way, in the sense that the extended periods of Depression and world wars were now over and serious policy making and management could once again be researched and applied to a business context.

The mix of strategy practices that has evolved since the mid-1960s has done so in a somewhat random and ad hoc manner, as demonstrated in Figure A1.1. As the notion of the strategy 'guru' has begun to fade and the concept of strategy as practice, and more importantly strategy as a profession, starts to emerge and indeed consolidate, it is becoming increasingly apparent to academics and practitioners alike that a reliance on strategic planning alone as a management method for the future is insufficient. As we have observed from the proposed integrated Strategic Management Framework that also provided the structure of this book, there is much more to strategy than what is proposed by any one guru, including the 'Father of Strategy' himself, Igor Ansoff. Consistent with the dilemma faced by Alfred Sloan described above, Ansoff acknowledges that he only wrote his book *Corporate Strategy* (1965) because he had observed that at that time there was 'an absence of a practical method of strategic decision making within a firm'.

Appendix 2:

Fully Integrated Strategic Management Framework

Figure A2.1 Fully integrated Strategic Management Framework

Bibliography

Allen, L.L. (2010), *Chocolate Fortunes: The Battle for the Hearts, Minds, and Wallets of China's Consumers*, New York: American Management Association.

Ambrosini, V. and Bowman, C. (2009), 'What Are Dynamic Capabilities and Are They a Useful Construct in Strategic Management?', *International Journal of Management Reviews*, 11(1), 29–49.

Amit, R. and Schoemaker, P.J. (1993), 'Strategic Assets and Organizational Rent', *Strategic Management Journal*, 14(1), 33–46.

Andrews, K. R. (1965), *The Concept of Corporate Strategy*, Homewood, IL: Dow Jones-Irwin.

Ansoff, H.I. (1957), 'Strategies for Diversification', *Harvard Business Review*, 35(5), 113–24.

Ansoff, H.I. (1965), *Corporate Strategy*, New York: McGraw-Hill.

Argyris, C. and Schon, D. (1978), *Organizational Learning: A Theory of Action Perspective*, Reading MA: Addison-Wesley.

Australian Public Service Commission (2007), *Tackling Wicked Problems: A Public Policy Perspective*, www.apsc.gov.au/__data/assets/pdf_file/0005/6386/wickedproblems.pdf (accessed 6 May 2014).

Baghai, M., Coley, S. and White, D. (1999), *The Alchemy of Growth: Practical Insights for Building the Enduring Enterprise*, Reading, MA: Perseus Books.

Baghai, M., Coley, S.C., White, D., Conn, C. and McLean, R.J. (1996), 'Staircases to Growth', *McKinsey Quarterly*, 4, 38–61.

Bradley, J. (2011), *Cadbury's Purple Reign: The Story Behind Chocolate's Best-Loved Brand*, West Sussex, John Wiley & Sons.

Cadbury, D. (2010), *Chocolate Wars: From Cadbury to Kraft – 200 Years of Sweet Success and Bitter Rivalry*, London: Harper Press.

Chakravarthy, B. and Lorange, P. (2008), *Profit or Growth? Why You Don't Have to Choose*, Harlow: Pearson Education.

Chandler, A.D. (1962), *Strategy and Structure: Chapters in the History of the Industrial Enterprise*, Cambridge, MA: MIT Press.

Chandler, A.D. (1977), *The Visible Hand: The Managerial Revolution in American Business*, Cambridge, MA: Harvard University Press.

Clark, C. (2005), *Predictors of Success of Strategic Retreats: The Impact of Organisational Approaches to Strategic Planning, Event Design, and Demographic

Factors – a Study in Micro-strategy, Sydney: Macquarie Graduate School of Management, Macquarie University.

Collins, J. (2009), *How the Mighty Fall: And Why Some Companies Never Give In*. New York: HarperCollins.

Collins, J.C. and Porras, J.I. (1994), *Built to Last: Successful Habits of Visionary Companies*, New York: HarperCollins.

Courtney, H., Kirkland, J. and Viguerie, P. (1997), 'Strategy Under Uncertainty', *Harvard Business Review*, 75(6), 67–79.

Coutu, D. (2009), 'Why Teams Don't Work: An Interview with J. Richard Hackman', *Harvard Business Review*, 87(5), 98.

de Geus, A. (1997), *The Living Company*, Boston, MA: Harvard Business School Press.

De Wit, B. and Meyer, R. (2010), *Strategy: Process, Content, Context – an International Perspective*, 4th edn, Boston, MA: Cengage Learning.

Doz, Y.L. and Kosonen, M. (2008), *Fast Strategy: How Strategic Agility Will Help You Stay Ahead of the Game*, Harlow: Pearson Education.

Drucker, P. (1954), *The Practice of Management*, New York: Harper & Row.

Flood, R.L. (1999), *Rethinking the Fifth Discipline: Learning Within the Unknowable*, New York: Routledge.

Forster, J. ([1874] 2011), *The Life of Charles Dickens*, vol. 3, Cambridge: Cambridge University Press.

Fox, C. (2008), 'The Strategy Fad is Dead, Long Live Thinking', *Australian Financial Review* (Abstracts), 30 December.

Ghoshal, S. and Bartlett, C. (1999), *The Individualised Corporation: A Fundamentally New Approach to Management*, London: William Heinemann.

Gladwell, M. (2006), *The Tipping Point: How Little Things Can Make a Big Difference*, New York: Hachette Digital.

Gottliebsen, R. (2001), 'Ansett Airlines, the Best and Worst of Times', *The Australian*, 9 September.

Gouillart, F. and Kelly, J. (1996), *Transforming the Organization*, New York: McGraw-Hill.

Grove, A. (1999), *Only the Paranoid Survive: How to Exploit the Crisis Points that Challenge Every Company*, New York: Doubleday.

Hackman, J.R. (2009), 'Why Teams Don't Work: Interview by Diane Coutu', *Harvard Business Review*, 87(5), 98–105.

Hamel, G. and Prahalad, C.K. (1989), 'Strategic Intent', *Harvard Business Review*, 67(3), 63–76.

Hamel, G. and Prahalad, C.K. (1994), *Competing for the Future*, Boston, MA: Harvard Business School Press.

Henderson, B.D. (1979), 'The Product Portfolio: Growth Share Matrix of The Boston Consulting Group', in H. Mintzberg and J.B. Quinn (eds), *The Strategy Process: Concepts, Contexts, Cases*, 678–80.

Hickman, M. (2013), 'Heston Blumenthal: For My Next Trick, a Toast Sandwich', *The Independent*, 13 August.

Hirschhorn, L. and Gilmore, T. (1992), 'The New Boundaries of the Boundaryless Company', *Harvard Business Review*, 70(3), 104–15.

Hjørland, B. and Christensen, F.S. (2002), 'Work Tasks and Socio-cognitive Relevance: A Specific Example', *Journal of the American Society for Information Science and Technology*, 53(11), 960–65.

Hodgkinson, P., Whittington, R., Johnson, G. and Schwarz, M. (2006), 'The Role of Strategy Workshops in Strategy Development Processes: Formality, Communication, Co-ordination and Inclusion', *Long Range Planning*, 39(5), 479–96.

Holster, H., Klerkx, L. and Elzen, B. (2008), 'Stimulating Entrepreneurship: The Impact of a New Way of Organizing Dairy Farmers', paper presented to 8th European International Farming Systems Association Symposium, 6–10 July, Clermont-Ferrand, France.

Hubbard, G., Samuel, D., Cocks, G. and Heap, S. (2007), *The First X1: Winning Organisations in Australia*, 2nd edn. Milton Queensland: John Wiley and Sons.

Hunter, P. (2000), 'Strategic Revitalisation: A Strategic Business Model of Innovation and Growth', unpublished doctoral thesis, *Royal Melbourne Institute of Technology*.

Hunter, P. and O'Shannassy, T. (2007), 'Contemporary Strategic Management Practice in Australia: "Back To the Future" in the 2000s', *Singapore Management Review*, 29(2), 21–36.

Jarzabkowski, P. and Spee, A.P. (2009), 'Strategy-as-Practice: A Review and Future Directions for the Field', *International Journal of Management Reviews*, 11(1), 69–95.

Jarzabkowski, P., Giulietti, M. and Oliveira, B. (2009), *Building a Strategy Toolkit: Lessons from Business*, London: Aston Business School and Advanced Institute of Management Research.

Johnson, G., Whittington, R., Scholes, K. and Pyle, S. (2011), *Exploring Strategy: Text and Cases*, Harlow: Financial Times/Prentice Hall.

Kharif, O., Lachapelle, T. and Nazareth, R. (2011), 'Nokia Breakup Worth 52% Gain to Battered Shareholders: Real M&A', *Bloomberg News*, 3 June.

Kim, C.W. and Mauborgne, R. (2004), 'Blue Ocean Strategy', *Harvard Business Review*, 82(10), 76–84.

Kim, C.W. and Mauborgne, R., (2006), *Blue Ocean Strategy: How To Create Uncontested Market Space And Make Competition Irrelevant*. Boston, MA: Harvard Business Press.

Learned, E.P., Christensen, C.R., Andrews, K.R. and Guth, W.D. (1965), *Business Policy: Text and Cases*. Homewood, IL: R.D. Irwin.

Levitt, T. (1960), 'Marketing Myopia', *Harvard Business Review*, 38(4), 45–56.

Liedtka, J.M. (1998), 'Strategic Thinking: Can It Be Taught?', *Long Range Planning*, 31(1), 120–29.

Mankins, M.C. and Steele, R. (2005), 'Turning Great Strategy into Great Performance', *Harvard Business Review*, 83(7), 65–72.

Mankins, M.C. and Steele, R. (2006), 'Stop Making Plans; Start Making Decisions', *Harvard Business Review*, 84(1), 76.

March, J.G. (1991), 'Exploration and Exploitation in Organisational Learning', *Organisation Science*, 2(1), 71–87.

Martin, R. (2007), 'How Successful Leaders Think', *Harvard Business Review*, 85(6), 60–67.

Martin, R.L. (2010), 'The Execution Trap', *Harvard Business Review*, 88(7–8), 64–71.

McDermott, R., Snyder, W. and Wenger, E. (2002), *Cultivating Communities of Practice: A Guide to Managing Knowledge*. Boston, MA: Harvard Business School Publishing.

McGrath, R.G. (2013), *The End of Competitive Advantage: How to Keep Your Strategy Moving as Fast as Your Business*, Boston, MA: Harvard Business Review Press.

Meyer, R.J.H. (2007), *Mapping the Mind of the Strategist: A Quantitative Methodology for Measuring the Strategic Beliefs of Executives*, Rotterdam: Erasmus Research Institute of Management.

Meyer, R.J.H. (2014), 'Strategy Development for Continuous Learning', in M. Rademakers, *Corporate Universities: Drivers of the Learning Organization*, Abingdon: Routledge.

Mintzberg, H. (1987), 'Crafting Strategy', *Harvard Business Review*, 65(4), 66–75.

Mintzberg, H. (1990), 'The Design School: Reconsidering the Basic Premises of Strategic Management', *Strategic Management Journal*, 11(3), 171–95.

Mintzberg, H. (1991), 'Learning 1, Planning 0: A Reply to Igor Ansoff', *Strategic Management Journal*, 12, 463–6.

Mintzberg, H. (1994), *Rise and Fall of Strategic Planning*, London: Simon and Schuster.

Ohmae, K. (1983), *The Mind of the Strategist: The Art of Japanese Business*, Harmondsworth: Penguin.

O'Regan, N. and Ghobadian, A. (2009), 'Successful Strategic Re-orientation: Lessons from Cadbury's Experience: An Interview with Todd Stitzer, Chief Executive of Cadbury', *Journal of Strategy and Management*, 2(4), 405–12.

Pine, J. and Gilmore, J. (1998), 'Welcome to the Experience Economy', *Harvard Business Review*, 74(4), 97–105.

Porter, M. (1980), *Competitive Strategy: Techniques for Analysing Industries and Competitors*, New York: The Free Press.

Porter, M. (1985), *Competitive Advantage: Creating and Sustaining Superior Performance*, New York: The Free Press.

Porter, M. (ed.) (1986), *Competition in Global Industries*. Boston, MA: Harvard Business School Press.

Porter, M. (1996), 'What is Strategy?', *Harvard Business Review*, 74(6), 61–78.

Porter, M. (2008), *On Competition*, updated and expanded edn, Boston, MA: Harvard Business School Press.

Powell, T.H. and Angwin, D.N. (2012), 'The Role of the Chief Strategy Officer', *MIT Sloan Management Review*, 54(1), 15.

Prahalad, C.K. (2010), 'Why Is It So Hard to Tackle the Obvious?', *Harvard Business Review*, 88(6), 36.

Prahalad, C.K. and Bettis, R.A. (1986), 'The Dominant Logic: A New Linkage between Diversity and Performance', *Strategic Management Journal*, 7(6), 485–501.

Prahalad, C.K. and Hamel, G. (1990), 'The Core Competence of the Corporation', *Harvard Business Review*, 68(3), 79–91.

Rademakers, M. (2014), *Corporate Universities as Drivers of Organizational Learning*, London: Routledge.

Rigby, D. and Bilodeau, B. (2009), *Management Tools and Trends 2009*, London: Bain & Company.

Rittel, H. (1972), 'On the Planning Crisis: Systems Analysis of the "First and Second Generations"', *Bedriftsøkonomen*, 8, 390–96.

Roos, J., Victor, B. and Statler, M. (2004), 'Playing Seriously with Strategy', *Long Range Planning*, 37, 549–68.

Rumelt, R. (1991) 'Evaluating Business Strategy' in H. Mintzberg, J. Quinn. *The Strategy Process, Concepts, Contexts, Cases*, 3rd edn, New Jersey: Prentice Hall.

Rumelt, R. (2010), *Good Strategy, Bad Strategy*, New York: Crown Publishing Group.

Schoenberg, R. (2006), 'Measuring the Performance of Corporate Acquisitions: An Empirical Comparison of Alternative Metrics', *British Journal of Management*, 17(4), 361–70.

Schwarz, M. (2009), 'Strategy Workshops: Facilitating and Constraining Strategy Making', *Journal of Strategy and Management*, 2(3), 277–87.

Senge, P.M. (1990), *The Fifth Discipline: The Art And Practice of the Learning Organisation*, New York: Doubleday/Currency.

Shapiro, C. (1989), 'The Theory of Business Strategy', *Rand Journal of Economics*, 20(1), 125–37.

Sloan, A. (1963), *My Years with General Motors*, Harmondsworth: Penguin.

Smith, C., Child, J. and Rowlinson, M. (1990), *Reshaping Work: The Cadbury Experience*, Cambridge: Cambridge University Press.

Snyder, C.R. (2000), 'The Hope Mandala: Coping With the Loss of a Loved One', in J.E. Gillham (ed.), *The Science of Optimism and Hope*, Philadelphia, PA: Templeton Foundation Press, 129–42.

Teece, D. (2010), 'Business Models, Business Strategy and Innovation', *Long Range Planning*, 43(2), 172–94.

Teece, D., Pisano, G. and Shuen, A. (1997), 'Dynamic Capabilities and Strategic Management', *Strategic Management Journal*, 18(7), 509–33.

Vaara, E. and Whittington, R. (2012), 'Strategy-as-practice: Taking Social Practices Seriously', *The Academy of Management Annals*, 6(1), 285–336.

Waytz, A. and Mason, M. (2013), 'Your Brain at Work', *Harvard Business Review*, 91(7), 102–11.

Wenger, E.C. and Snyder, W.M. (2000), 'Communities of Practice: The Organizational Frontier', *Harvard Business Review*, 78(1), 139–46.

White, F. (1998), *The Overview Effect: Space Exploration and Human Evolution*. Reston, VA: American Institute of Aeronautics and Astronautics.

Whittington, R. and Cailluet, L. (2008), 'The Crafts of Strategy', *Long Range Planning* (special issue), 41(3), 241–7.

Whittington, R., Cailluet, L. and Yakis-Douglas, B. (2011), 'Opening Strategy: Evolution of a Precarious Profession', *British Journal of Management*, 22, 531–44.

Index